Discrimination in Latin America

Discrimination in Latin America

AN ECONOMIC PERSPECTIVE

Edited by
Hugo Ñopo
Alberto Chong
Andrea Moro

A COPUBLICATION OF THE INTER-AMERICAN
DEVELOPMENT BANK AND THE WORLD BANK

ISBN: 978-0-8213-7835-9
eISBN: 978-0-8213-8082-6
DOI: 10.1596/978-0-8213-7835-9

Library of Congress Cataloging-in-Publication Data
Discrimination in Latin America : an economic perspective / Hugo Ñopo, Alberto Chong, and Andrea Moro, editors.

    p. cm.—(Latin American development forum series)
Includes bibliographical references and index.
ISBN 978-0-8213-7835-9—ISBN 978-0-8213-8082-6 (electronic)

    1. Minorities—Latin America—Economic conditions. 2. Minorities—Latin America—Social conditions. 3. Discrimination—Economic aspects—Latin America. 4. Sex discrimination against women—Economic aspects—Latin America. 5. Race discrimination—Economic aspects—Latin America. I. Ñopo, Hugo. II. Chong, Alberto. III. Moro, Andrea, 1967-

    F1419.A1D57 2009
    305.80098—dc22

    2009035875

Cover design by Ultra Designs.

Latin American Development Forum Series

This series was created in 2003 to promote debate, disseminate information and analysis, and convey the excitement and complexity of the most topical issues in economic and social development in Latin America and the Caribbean. It is sponsored by the Inter-American Development Bank, the United Nations Economic Commission for Latin America and the Caribbean, and the World Bank. The manuscripts chosen for publication represent the highest quality in each institution's research and activity output and have been selected for their relevance to the academic community, policy makers, researchers, and interested readers.

Advisory Committee Members

Alicia Bárcena Ibarra, Executive Secretary, Economic Commission for Latin America and the Caribbean, United Nations

Inés Bustillo, Director, Washington Office, Economic Commission for Latin America and the Caribbean, United Nations

José Luis Guasch, Senior Adviser, Latin America and the Caribbean Region, World Bank; and Professor of Economics, University of California, San Diego

Santiago Levy, Vice President for Sectors and Knowledge, Inter-American Development Bank

Eduardo Lora, Principal Adviser, Research Department, Inter-American Development Bank

Luis Servén, Research Manager, Development Economics Vice Presidency, World Bank

Augusto de la Torre, Chief Economist, Latin America and the Caribbean Region, World Bank

Titles in the Latin American Development Forum Series

Discrimination in Latin America: An Economic Perspective (2010) by Hugo Ñopo, Alberto Chong, and Andrea Moro, editors

The Promise of Early Childhood Development in Latin America and the Caribbean (2010) by Emiliana Vegas and Lucrecia Santibáñez

Job Creation in Latin America and the Caribbean: Trends and Policy Challenges (2009) by Carmen Pagés, Gaëlle Pierre, and Stefano Scarpetta

China's and India's Challenge to Latin America: Opportunity or Threat? (2009) by Daniel Lederman, Marcelo Olarreaga, and Guillermo E. Perry, editors

Does the Investment Climate Matter? Microeconomic Foundations of Growth in Latin America (2009) by Pablo Fajnzylber, Jose Luis Guasch, and J. Humberto López, editors

Measuring Inequality of Opportunities in Latin America and the Caribbean (2009) by Ricardo de Paes Barros, Francisco H. G. Ferreira, José R. Molinas Vega, and Jaime Saavedra Chanduvi

The Impact of Private Sector Participation in Infrastructure: Lights, Shadows, and the Road Ahead (2008) by Luis Andres, Jose Luis Guasch, Thomas Haven, and Vivien Foster

Remittances and Development: Lessons from Latin America (2008) by Pablo Fajnzylber and J. Humberto López, editors

Fiscal Policy, Stabilization, and Growth: Prudence or Abstinence? (2007) by Guillermo Perry, Luis Servén, and Rodrigo Suescún, editors

About the Editors

Hugo Ñopo, a Senior Research Economist on Education at the Inter-American Development Bank (IDB), is based in Bogota, Colombia. He received his PhD in Economics at Northwestern University. Before joining the IDB, he was an Assistant Professor at Middlebury College and a Research Fellow at GRADE. He has also been professor at different universities in Peru. He is a Research Affiliate at the Institute for the Study of Labor (IZA), in Bonn, Germany. He has served on the editorial boards of various journals, and his research has been published in such journals as the *Review of Economics and Statistics, Economics Letters* and *Economic Development and Cultural Change*, among others.

Alberto Chong is a Principal Research Economist at the IDB. Before he joined IDB, he taught at Georgetown University, and worked at the World Bank, the IRIS Center at the University of Maryland at College Park, and the Ministry of Finance of Peru. His research interests cover very broad areas in development economics. His most recent interests include issues related to post-privatization, corporate governance, institutions, trust, and income inequality. He has published extensively in such academic journals as the *Review of Economics and Statistics*, the *Journal of Public Economics*, the *Journal of International Economics, Economics and Politics*, and several others. His recent books include *Costs and Benefits of Privatization in Latin America* and *Investor Protection in Latin America,* both co-edited with López-de-Silanes.

Andrea Moro is an Associate Professor of Economics at Vanderbilt University. He received his PhD in Economics at the University of Pennsylvania. He taught at the University of Minnesota and was Senior Economist at the Federal Reserve Bank of New York. He has written widely on race and gender labor market inequality in the presence of asymmetric information. His research has been published in such journals as the *American Economic Review*, the *Journal of Economic Theory*, and the *Journal of Public Economics*.

About the Contributors

David Bravo is with the Centro de Microdatos, Departamento de Economía Universidad de Chile.

Natalia Candelo is with the University of Texas at Dallas, Department of Economics. CBEES – Center for Behavioral and Experimental Economic Science.

Juan-Camilo Cárdenas is with the Universidad de los Andes in Bogotá.

Marco Castillo is with the Georgia Institute of Technology.

Julio Elías is with the Banco Central de la República Argentina and the Universidad del CEMA.

Víctor Elías is with the Universidad Nacional de Tucumán.

Eduardo Gandelman is with the Universidad ORT Uruguay.

Néstor Gandelman is with the Universidad ORT Uruguay.

Alejandro Gaviria is with the Universidad de los Andes in Bogotá.

Ragan Petrie is with Georgia State University.

Giorgina Piani is with the Departamento de Economía, Universidad de la República Oriental del Uruguay.

Sandra Polanía is with the Università degli Studi di Siena.

Lucas Ronconi is with the Universidad Torcuato Di Tella.

Máximo Rossi is with the Departamento de Economía, Universidad de la República Oriental del Uruguay.

Julie Rothschild is with the Universidad ORT Uruguay.

Claudia Sanhueza is with the Instituto Latinoamericano de Doctrina y Estudios Sociales (ILADES), Universidad Alberto Hurtado.

Rajiv Sethi is with Barnard College, Columbia University.

Ximena Soruco is with the Fundación Sur (Cuenca, Ecuador).

Máximo Torero is with the International Food Policy Research Institute.

Sergio Urzúa is with the Department of Economics and the Institute for Policy Research, Northwestern University.

Contents

Foreword

Social Inclusion: Let's Give Social Capital a Chance

In addition to posing a profound moral problem, social exclusion produces a tremendous inefficiency that is detrimental to the economy, democracy, and the whole of society. Discrimination leads to a very unequal distribution of opportunities, which in turn prevents society from benefiting from a greater human capital, independent of race, that could contribute to higher rates of production, productivity, and competitiveness. Therefore, discrimination impedes economic growth and poverty reduction.

I was born into a country where discrimination has recently been estimated to explain nearly 60% of the labor-earnings gap between indigenous and non-indigenous men. Across Latin American countries, indigenous peoples—as well as other marginalized groups—receive lower rates of income return for each year of schooling. It is exceedingly difficult to quantify the damage to a nation's GDP from the deprivation of quality education and the distortion of incentives that arise from social exclusion. I can, however, imagine the waste of my own human potential that could have so easily occurred had I not been able to escape from extreme poverty.

I was born in a small, remote village in the Peruvian Andes at 12,000 feet above sea level. As one of sixteen siblings, I had to work in the street from the age of six, shining shoes and selling lottery tickets to supplement the family income. Through the result of a statistical error, I have had the chance to study and teach at some of the world's most prestigious universities, to work as an economist in a number of multilateral institutions, and to become the first South American President of indigenous descent to be democratically elected in 500 years. Despite my good fortune, I can never forget the millions of my brothers and sisters in Latin America who remain trapped in extreme poverty. As the cruel sisters of social exclusion, poverty and inequality rob them of their freedom, steal their human dignity, and deny them the right to provide their children with a better future.

My own escape from poverty arose from an accidental opportunity to access education. In order to help others make this same journey to freedom, I decided to pursue graduate degrees in education and economics, and to work as a professor during a large part of my career.

Thus, it is a great honor for me to preface this collection of new research that seeks to educate us on the current state of discrimination in Latin America. I congratulate and express my gratitude—which I think would also express the gratitude of millions of excluded people—to all of the authors for their innovative use of new methodologies and data sources applied to the study of discrimination. These researchers have studied a wide range of groups, defined by gender, ethnic origin, socio-economic status, occupation, stature, parental education, nationality, and migration status, among other traits.

I consider it prudent of the researchers to have taken a cautious approach to the interpretation of their data, since many challenges confront research on social prejudice. For example, discrimination and its victims can sometimes exist in a vicious cycle where causality is not entirely clear. Specifically, some parts of society might discriminate against a particular group, thereby contributing to this group's educational and economic disadvantage; on the other hand, although other elements of society do *not* discriminate against the defining trait of this group, the group's members might nevertheless find themselves marginalized as the result of their lower level of education and consequent poverty.

It is revealing, then, that questionnaire respondents in all of the 18 Latin American countries surveyed reported that they believe poverty—more than any other group characteristic—is the root cause of discrimination. It is worth noting, though, that in the Andean region poverty is highly correlated with ethnicity.

In addition to the difficulty of knowing how and when poverty is the cause or the effect of discrimination, respondents can easily feel ashamed or embarrassed to reveal stigmatized views. For example, in one nation covered in this book (Ecuador), more than six times as many people reported the existence of racism in their country, compared with those who actually admitted to having racist attitudes themselves. Although discrimination has become better disguised, the depth of discrimination has perhaps not been significantly reduced.

To complicate the problem further, our political perspectives can color the lens through which we understand the problem of discrimination, the extent to which we perceive the multiple causes of marginalization, our value judgment regarding the distribution of resources across society, and the accessibility of opportunities for attaining these limited resources. There are many politicians who manipulate the prejudicial forces between groups for their personal benefit or for that of their group; a true leader, however, strives to unite people for the common good of all groups and individuals.

Whatever the origin of traditional prejudices, our increasingly globalizing world demands that we reflect, as objectively and dispassionately as possible, on the enormous costs of social exclusion. Although some pay this price more directly than others, there can be no doubt that all of society suffers from systematic failures to engage the full human potential of all groups. After all, a country that neglects half of its renewable natural resources would be acting irrationally, and it would be at a disadvantage with respect to an equivalent country that makes full use of these resources.

Today, as our economies move away from a dependence on exporting raw materials, it is becoming more and more crucial to invest in our full human capital. There is no better economic investment that a community or a nation can make than investing in the minds of its people.

As for the political soul of a nation, democracy and freedom cannot be defined by the single day of an election; they are living values at the core of a culture of equal opportunity and meritocracy. Can the poor afford democracy? Or perhaps we should ask whether *democracy* can withstand the existing high levels of poverty and social exclusion.

A truly healthy democracy requires more from us than merely doing business with other groups in the virtual marketplace of the Internet; rather, we must look into each other's eyes and recognize our common humanity. The strength of a globalized world lies in direct human contact, and in a mutual knowledge and a mutual respect for our cultural diversities. This book testifies that there is indeed a close connection between knowledge and respect; experiments show that providing information on an individual's performance is a powerful antidote to irrational discrimination.

It is the responsibility of society's leaders—and indeed, of all of us—to provide equal levels of healthcare, nutrition, and education to the millions of socially excluded and impoverished people in our countries; thus, we will ensure that their ability to maximize their human potential, and that society's ability to recognize their worth and contribution, does not depend on a statistical error.

Alejandro Toledo, PhD
President of Peru (2001–2006)

President, Global Center for Development and Democracy Consulting
Professor, Freeman Spogli Institute for International Studies; Stanford
University Distinguished Fellow, Center for Advanced Studies in the
Behavioral Sciences/Stanford University

Acknowledgments

This book was written with the support of the Latin American Research Network at the Inter-American Development Bank (IDB). Created in 1991, this network aims to leverage the capabilities of the IDB's Research Department, improve the quality of research performed in the region, and contribute to the policy agenda in Latin America and the Caribbean. Through a competitive bidding process, the network provides grant funding to leading Latin American research centers to conduct studies on the economic and social issues of greatest concern to the region today. The network currently comprises nearly 300 research institutes in the region and has proven to be an effective vehicle for financing quality research to enrich the policy debate in Latin America and the Caribbean.

Many individuals provided comments and suggestions: Eduardo Lora, Gustavo Marquez, Jacqueline Mazza, Claudia Piras, and Laura Ripani. The editors also want to thank the Bank and colleagues who participated in formal and informal discussions and workshops on background papers, and who provided comments during the revisions. Bruno Chong, Marco Chong, Miski Ñopo, Maria Ñopo, Anna Serrichio, Irma Ugaz, and Luisa Zanforlin provided inspiration and guidance. Valuable input was also provided in the production of this book by Patricia Arauz, Sebastian Calonico, Rita Funaro, Raquel Gomez, Lucas Higuera, Alejandro Hoyos, and John Dunn Smith at the Inter-American Development Bank. Book design, editing, and print production were coordinated by Susan Graham and Denise Bergeron in the World Bank's Office of the Publisher.

The views and opinions expressed in this book are those of the authors and do not necessarily reflect the official position of the IDB, its Board of Directors, or the Advisory Committee.

Abbreviations

3PP	third-party punishment game
Col$	Colombian peso
CV	curriculum vita
DDG	distributive dictator game
DG	dictator game
ECV	Encuesta de Calidad de Vida
ENAHO	Encuesta Nacional de Hogares
MCMC	Markov chain Monte Carlo methods
NGO	nongovernmental organization
OLS	ordinary least squares
SISBEN	A composite welfare index used to target groups for social programs in Colombia
SPS02	Chilean Social Protection Survey 2002
TG	trust game
UG	ultimatum game

1

What Do We Know about Discrimination in Latin America? Very Little!

Hugo Ñopo, Alberto Chong,
and Andrea Moro

There is a strong belief that Latin American societies are highly discriminatory. According to the conventional wisdom, the more diverse the society, the more discrimination there is. This is considered to be particularly true in the case of race. According to this long-held perception, it is believed that the fairer the skin of the individual, the higher the social status. In turn, social status is typically highly correlated with the economic power of the individual. In fact, Latin America has often been regarded as a region with deep ethnic and class conflicts. Although there is plenty of anecdotal evidence that Latin American societies do indeed behave in a highly discriminatory fashion, social sciences have crafted almost no scientific evidence to back up this perception. Behind this problem is the lack of solid, unbiased, and systematic data necessary to provide convincing empirical evidence on this issue as well as the lack of empirical methods that can help to identify any specific discriminatory behavior as opposed to related behavior that appears to be discriminatory but might not be. For example, the fact that Afro descendants and peoples of indigenous descent have, on average, lower earnings than mestizos or whites in Latin American cities may well be the result of differences in endowments of human capital and not necessarily due solely to discrimination, as the collective tends to think.

Recently, social scientists have begun using innovative techniques and new data sources to explore the extent to which ethnicity and class constructions may have an impact on socioeconomic outcomes. For instance,

Latinobarómetro is a relatively new survey that helps to shed light on discrimination from previously hard-to-tackle angles. This 18-country opinion survey of the region explores perceptions about broad political and socioeconomic aspects of Latin America, including discrimination. A simple question from this regional survey—Which groups do you think are the most discriminated against, or do you think that there is no discrimination?—yields a remarkable response, not only for what the question explicitly says, but, more important, for what the responses actually imply. For instance, in the survey of 2001, when asked to indicate the group most discriminated against, 27 percent of the respondents indicated the poor, only 16 percent indicated the indigenous population, and 9 percent indicated blacks. About 4 percent indicated that there is no discrimination. All of the 18 Latin American countries surveyed indicated that poverty is the main driver of discrimination. Other socioeconomic factors, such as education or social networks, were also indicated as explaining unequal treatment. Only 5 percent of the respondents indicated that demographic factors, such as race and gender, are a cause of discrimination. Taken at face value, this finding is truly remarkable: the factors typically believed to be crucial in explaining discrimination in the region appear to be of little or no relevance to individuals' perceptions.

Furthermore, academic economic research has explored the roots of discrimination in developed countries on the basis of both race and gender; the Latinobarómetro survey indicates that race and gender are not particularly relevant for Latin America. According to this evidence, societies in Latin America may not discriminate on the basis of observable phenotypic traits. However, respondents may confuse factors that lead to socioeconomic inequality with discrimination. In other words, poverty and education can well be regarded as the effect of discrimination rather than the cause, and individuals tend to tangle causes and effects. For example, in countries that are relatively homogeneous in terms of race, the perception of poverty as a key factor in discrimination is relatively low. This is the case in Uruguay, where only about 20 percent of Latinobarómetro respondents linked discrimination with poverty. By the same token, in countries that have more racial diversity, Latinobarómetro respondents indicated that poverty is a crucial issue with regard to discrimination. This is the case in Peru, for example, where nearly 41 percent of Latinobarómetro respondents cited poverty as the most important reason for unequal treatment. Moreover, the perception of discrimination appears to be stronger in poorer countries. All in all, the perception of poverty as a driver of discrimination is stronger in the Dominican Republic and Nicaragua. It is lower in Costa Rica, Mexico, and Uruguay.

Ad hoc surveys measuring perceptions of discrimination reveal a complex picture. For instance, 88 percent of a representative sample of Peruvians reported having experienced at least one instance of discrimination (Demus 2005). The results of the First National Survey on Discrimination in Mexico (Sedesol 2005) show that 9 out of every 10 individuals who have a disability, an indigenous background, or homosexual orientation or who are elderly or members of a religious minority think that discrimination exists in their country. The Survey of Perceptions of Racism and Discrimination in Ecuador (Secretaría Técnica del Frente Social 2004) reveals that 62 percent of Ecuadorians accept that there is racial discrimination in their country, but only 10 percent admit to being openly racist. Afro descendants are perceived to suffer the greatest discrimination in Ecuador.

Perception surveys, besides providing an avenue for prima facie explorations, have serious limitations for analytical work, as the measurement error with which these variables are captured is correlated with an individual's characteristics and behaviors (Bertrand and Mullainathan 2004b). An additional concern arises from the result that most people believe that the "poor" are an object of discrimination. Wage or employment discrimination, in general, makes the targeted groups poorer than they would be without the racial animus held against them. To what extent are people poorer because of discriminatory practices or because of a smaller endowment of skills? If the interviewees are not capable of making such a distinction, their perception might be biased. In other words, only with additional evidence can the researcher conclude that the lower economic condition of the poor is due to discrimination as opposed to lower human capital endowment.

The Economic Literature on Discrimination

In order to analyze the sources, behaviors, and effects of discrimination, the economic literature has developed tools to improve our understanding of the mechanisms beyond the answers provided by opinion surveys. While those approaches may suffer from different types of biases and limitations, they inform more transparently the conditions under which differential outcomes may be interpreted as originating from discriminatory behavior.

Discrimination is a process that may take place under different circumstances or markets and be based on different discriminatory characteristics such as race, ethnicity, or gender. Altonji and Blank (1999) define discrimination as "a situation in which persons who provide labor market services and who are equally productive in a physical or material sense are treated unequally in a way that is related to an observable characteristic such as race, ethnicity, or gender. By 'unequal' we mean [that] these persons receive different wages or face different demands for their services at a given wage." This is the *unequal treatment for the same productivity* definition, which outside of labor markets would indicate unequal treatment for the same characteristics. Additionally, it is useful to distinguish between preference-based discrimination (people treating members of certain groups differently simply because they do not like them) and statistical discrimination (people using group membership as a proxy measure for unobserved characteristics). The latter corresponds to the popularly held notions of stigmatization or stereotyping.

In an attempt to classify the methodological tools, we briefly summarize next the advancements of the profession using regression analysis, market tests, experiments, audit studies, and structural methods.

Regression Analysis

The most important and widely used tool in investigating group-based inequality remains regression analysis (see, for example, the surveys by Donohue and Heckman 1991 or by Altonji and Blank 1999). This is typically performed by regressing the variable measuring the discriminatory outcome (wage, job acceptance, mortgage acceptance) on a set of explanatory variables, including a group (gender, race) dummy. A significant coefficient on the group dummy is usually interpreted as evidence of discrimination. Some researchers prefer to adopt a different specification by regressing separately each demographic group on a set of explanatory variables. Then, the estimated coefficients can be used to decompose the average group differential into a component that measures group inequality due to differences in the average value of the explanatory variables and a residual component that is interpreted as discrimination (the so-called Blinder-Oaxaca decomposition; see Oaxaca 1973 and Blinder 1973). While the decomposition is not unique, it can suggest how much inequality there would be if groups were identical, on average, in their observable characteristics.

There are two principal concerns regarding regression analysis. The first is omitted-variable bias. For example, if, in trying to measure wage discrimination, the explanatory variables do not include all the factors that determine the wage, then the residual cannot be an adequate measure of discrimination. The second problem is that, even if the procedure fails to find evidence of discrimination, group differences in the explanatory variables may still be the outcome of discriminatory practices that the econometric model is trying to take into account.

Market Tests

A second approach tries to detect evidence of discrimination by looking at market outcomes implied by a theory of discrimination that the researcher implicitly or explicitly posits. This approach has been advocated by Gary Becker in a *Business Week* article (Becker 1993) criticizing the "Boston-Fed" study of mortgage discrimination (Munnell and others 1996). Becker views discrimination as motivated by racial animus: "An employer discriminates when he refuses to hire applicants from a group even though they would produce more profit than those who are hired. Employees discriminate if they refuse to work alongside members of a group even though they can earn more by doing that. The corollary here is that if a company chooses not to hire members of a group, its decisions may not be discriminatory if hiring others who are cheaper or more productive results in more profits."

The suggestion, therefore, is that discriminatory firms should be less profitable. Hence, if wage discrimination exists against minorities, firms employing minorities should be more profitable. Similarly, if banks discriminate in lending against minorities because they adopt stricter standards in granting loans to minorities, minorities should have lower default rates.

Other market test studies of discrimination include Smart and Waldfogel (1996), which studies discrimination against articles written by minorities by comparing citation rates by race; Ayres and Waldfogel (1994), which studies discrimination against black defendants by judges in setting bond by looking at flight probabilities; and Knowles, Persico, and Todd (2001), which studies discrimination against minorities in motor vehicle searches.

Experiments

Another possibility is to use experiments, either in laboratories or in the field. Holt, Anderson, and Fryer (2006) use this methodology to test for the presence of racial stereotypes. Some lab experiments use dictator games, or "investment games," in which subjects only know each other's last name. The idea is to see, for example, whether a subject will behave differently if he or she knows that his or her opponent belongs to a given demographic group.[1] The main criticism of this approach is that the special environment in which experiments are conducted may cast doubts on the generalizability of the results. Experimental games are, by their nature, very special, and their monetary rewards sometimes are of limited importance compared with marketplace incentives.

Audit studies try to place comparable members of different demographic groups into the same socioeconomic setting in an attempt to measure differences in their economic outcomes. For example, a male and a female of similar characteristics and ability may be sent for a job interview to detect whether the male is more likely to get the job. Early examples of this methodology are Newman (1978) and McIntyre, Moberg, and Posner (1980). One advantage of audit studies is that the investigator can, to the extent that the appropriate pair of individuals can be chosen, control for more characteristics than what can be achieved using survey data. In addition, audit studies allow the researcher to investigate discriminatory behavior that does not directly affect market outcomes. For example, they allow for a direct examination of the hiring process, while survey data can only detect employment segregation and wage inequality. Field experiments such as the one in Bertrand and Mullainathan (2004a) use a similar methodology. In order to exert additional control on the pair characteristics, they avoid using human subjects. Instead, they send fictitious résumés to help-wanted ads found in newspapers.

Heckman and Siegelman (1993) and Heckman (1998) criticize these studies because it is hard and expensive to find partners who are good matches. In addition, they claim that audit studies undersample the main avenues through which people get jobs, since only job openings advertised in newspapers are audited and not jobs obtained through social networking. They also point out that such methodology is not exempt from omitted-variable bias. When employing audits to analyze discrimination, the implicit assumption is that analysts know which characteristics are relevant to employers and when such characteristics are sufficiently close to make them indistinguishable to the employer. If an omitted characteristic is relevant to the employer, the audit method works only if the mean of the unobserved variable is the same for the two groups. If the included and omitted characteristics are correlated, then making the included characteristics as identical as possible may accentuate differences in the omitted characteristics, increasing the bias. Field studies are not immune to such criticism.

Structural Methods

Another set of studies tries to model explicitly the decision process that generates discriminatory outcomes. The model's prediction is then matched with the data in order to provide estimates of the fundamental parameters of the model, including those that determine preferences or technologies that are gender or race biased. Bowlus and Eckstein (2002) and Flabbi (2009), for example, estimate a search model of the labor market where employers have gender animus. The distribution of wages and unemployment duration of females and males identifies the bias that employers may have against female workers. Moro (2003) estimates a model of statistical discrimination in order to detect whether racial wage inequality is partly an effect of the labor market adopting a "bad," more discriminatory equilibrium. Structural methods of equilibrium models are capable of performing meaningful counterfactual policy analysis that cannot normally be done using standard reduced-form coefficients obtained from standard regressions (the reduced-form coefficients being sensitive to the policy that is under study). However, they are sometimes criticized for sensitivity to the model chosen by the investigator and, in some circumstances, for reliance of the econometric identification on the assumptions of functional forms.

This Volume

The chapters presented in this volume adopt a variety of these methodological tools in order to explore the extent to which discrimination against women and demographic minorities is pervasive in Latin America. For instance, in chapter 2, Castillo, Petrie, and Torero present a series of experiments to understand the nature of discrimination in urban Lima, Peru. They design and apply experiments that exploit degrees of information on performance as a way to assess how personal characteristics affect how people sort into groups. Their results show that behavior is not correlated with personal socioeconomic and racial characteristics. That is, if discrimination exists in urban Lima, this cannot be explained by rational expectations theories of statistical discrimination. However, their results show that people do use personal characteristics to sort themselves into groups. Height is a robust predictor of being desirable, as is being a woman. Looking indigenous makes one less desirable, and looking white makes one more desirable. The experiments also show that, once information on performance is provided, almost all evidence of discrimination (or preferential treatment) vanishes. This leads Castillo and his co-authors to conclude that there is evidence of stereotyping or preference-based discrimination, but that clear information trumps discrimination.

Along similar lines, in chapter 3, Cárdenas and his research team use an experimental field approach in Colombia to better understand pro-social preferences and behavior of both individuals involved in the provision of social services (public servants) and potential beneficiaries of those services (the poor). They conducted field experiments using dictator, ultimatum, trust, and third-party punishment games, as well as a newly designed distributive dictator game, in order to understand the traits and mechanisms that guide pro-sociality, including altruism, reciprocal altruism, reciprocity, trust, fairness, aversion to inequity, and altruistic (social) punishment. To do this, they recruited more than 500 public servants and beneficiaries of welfare programs associated with health, education, child care, and nutrition in Bogotá, Colombia. The overall results replicate the patterns of previous studies using these experimental designs: that is, individuals show a preference for fair outcomes, positive levels of trust and reciprocity, and willingness to punish, at a personal cost, unfair outcomes against either themselves or third parties. By using more information about the participants, these researchers are able to explain the observed variations in these behaviors. The results provide evidence that the poor trigger more pro-social behavior from all citizens, including public servants, but public servants show more strategic generosity by controlling their pro-social behavior toward the poor, depending on attributes of the beneficiaries or the recipients of offers in these games. They show favorable treatment toward women and households with more dependents, but discriminatory behavior against particularly stigmatized groups in society, such as ex-combatants from the political conflict and street recyclers.

Similarly, in chapter 4, Elías, Elías, and Ronconi try to understand social status and race during adolescence in Argentina. They asked high school students to select and rank 10 classmates with whom they would like to form a team and use this information to construct a measure of popularity.

They then explore how students' characteristics affect their popularity, finding that physically attractive students are highly ranked by their peers. The effect is only significant in co-ed (boys and girls) schools, suggesting that the result may be driven by mating. Other traits such as skin color, nationality, and parental socioeconomic background do not affect popularity among peers, although ethnic origin and parental education are statistically significant in some specifications. Their findings are informative about discrimination in the school system. In particular, it appears that the unequal treatment based on race and nationality found in other social environments in Argentina is not present among adolescents attending school.

In chapters 5 and 6, Bravo, Sanhueza, and Urzúa present two studies covering different aspects of the labor market using different methodological tools. Based on an audit study by mail, their first study attempts to detect gender, social class, and neighborhood-of-residence discrimination in hiring practices by Chilean firms. They sent fictitious curriculum vitae (CVs) for real job vacancies published weekly in the newspaper *El Mercurio* of Santiago. Strictly equivalent CVs in terms of the applicant's qualifications and employment experience were sent out, only varying in gender, name and surname, and place of residence. The study allows differences in call response rates to be measured for the various demographic groups. Their results, obtained for more than 11,000 CVs sent, show no significant differences in callback rates across groups, in contrast with what is found in other international studies using the same tool.

In a second study, they use a structural model to analyze gender differences in the Chilean labor market. They formally deal with the selection of the individuals into level of schooling and its consequences for gender gaps by allowing for the presence of heterogeneity in both observables and unobservables, where the latter are linked to unobserved scholastic ability. They show that statistically significant gender differences exist in several dimensions of the Chilean labor market. They also show that these gaps depend on the level of schooling of the individuals considered in the analysis. For example, their results indicate that there are no gender differences in labor market variables among college graduates (except in the case of hourly wages). They interpret their results with prudence. Instead of interpreting their findings as decisive evidence of the existence of discrimination in the Chilean labor market, they argue that future research based on better information might indeed explain some of the unexplained labor market gaps. Their results represent a new and important attempt to provide a full understanding of the structural causes of gender gaps in the Chilean labor market, but they are not conclusive.

In chapter 7, Soruco, Piani, and Rossi measure and analyze possible discriminatory behaviors against international emigrants and their families remaining in southern Ecuador (the city of Cuenca and the rural canton of San Fernando). Through a combined methodological approach (ethnographic, in-depth interviews, media analysis, and two surveys), they seek new insights into this, up to now, hidden type of discrimination in the country. Their findings suggest some channels through which discrimination against these families may take place, as emigrant families are seen as "economically irrational" (they do not invest the remittances they receive in productive and sustainable activities and, therefore, do not contribute to the national economy) and as "irresponsible" (they abandon their families in search of better living conditions); their children are perceived as poor performers in school. The general perception is that the children of emigrants do not have a future in the country and that they will most probably (try to) leave the country as their parents did. These discriminatory perceptions and attitudes toward emigrants and their families are the first step in the development of discriminatory behavior. The discriminatory attitudes follow a cultural pattern: the closer a person is to the dominant culture (urban, adult, married, well educated, with high income, fully employed), the more probable he or she is to discriminate against emigrants and their families. Women show more discriminatory attitudes than men, which could be related to the "family sin" charged to emigrants when they abandon their children, family, and home country.

In chapter 8, Gandelman, Gandelman, and Rothschild use micro data on judicial proceedings in Uruguay and present evidence that female defendants receive a more favorable treatment in courts than male defendants. This happens in the form of longer foreclosure proceedings and higher probabilities of being granted an extension in evictions and dispossessions. This form of positive discrimination may have general equilibrium effects, the authors speculate, that adversely affect female access to mortgage credit and, in turn, homeownership.

The chapters in this volume present a variety of attempts to detect and measure discrimination and to identify some of the mechanisms through which discrimination occurs. In sum, the panorama of evidence presented here is mixed. While many results seem to agree with popular beliefs and perceptions of the average Latin American, others challenge these views and suggest different avenues through which discrimination may occur. The extent to which some of this scientifically crafted evidence challenges popular perceptions creates an opportunity for a fruitful discussion of discrimination and its mechanisms in Latin America. We hope that this volume will contribute to such a discussion.

Note

1. See, for example, the study by Gneezy and Rustichini (2004) on differences in competitiveness by gender or an experimental study by Hoff and Pandey (2004) on India's caste social structure. There is also a psychology literature using experiments (see, for example, Siegel and Steele 1979).

References

Altonji, Joseph, and Rebecca Blank. 1999. "Race and Gender in the Labor Markets." In *Handbook of Labor Economics,* vol. 3C, ed. Orley Ashenfelter and David Card. Amsterdam: North-Holland.

Ayres, Ian, and Joel Waldfogel. 1994. "A Market Test for Race Discrimination in Bail Setting." *Stanford Law Review* 46 (May): 987–1047.

Becker, Gary. 1993. "The Evidence against Banks Doesn't Prove Bias." *Business Week,* April 19.

Bertrand, Marianne, and Sendhil Mullainathan. 2004a. "Are Emily and Greg More Employable Than Lakisha and Jamal? A Field Experiment on Labor Market Discrimination." *American Economic Review* 94 (4, September): 991–1013.

———. 2004b. "Do People Mean What They Say? Implications for Subjective Survey Data." *American Economic Review* 91 (2, May): 67–72.

Blinder, Alan S. 1973. "Wage Discrimination: Reduced Form and Structural Estimates." *Journal of Human Resources* 8 (fall): 436–55.

Bowlus, Audra, and Zvi Eckstein. 2002. "Discrimination and Skill Differences in an Equilibrium Search Model." *International Economic Review* 43 (4): 1309–45.

Demus (Estudio para la Defensa de los Derechos de la Mujer). 2005. *National Survey on Exclusion and Social Discrimination.* Lima: Demus.

Donohue, John, and James Heckman. 1991. "Continuous vs. Episodic Change: The Impact of Affirmative Action and Civil Rights Policy on the Economic Status of Blacks." *Journal of Economic Literature* 29 (4, December): 1603–43.

Flabbi, Luca. 2009. "Gender Discrimination Estimation in a Search Model with Matching and Bargaining." *International Economic Review* (forthcoming).

Gneezy, Uri, and Aldo Rustichini. 2004. "Gender and Competition at a Young Age." *American Economic Review Papers and Proceedings* 94 (2, May): 377–81.

Heckman, James J. 1998. "Detecting Discrimination." *Journal of Economic Perspectives* 12 (2): 101–16.

Heckman, James J., and Peter Siegelman. 1993. "The Urban Institute Audit Studies: Their Methods and Findings." In *Clear and Convincing Evidence: Measurement of Discrimination in America,* ed. Michael Fix and Raymond Struyk. Washington, DC: Urban Institute Press.

Hoff, Karla, and Priyank Pandey. 2004. "Belief Systems and Durable Inequalities: An Experimental Investigation of Indian Caste." Policy Research Working Paper 3351 (June 25), World Bank, Washington, DC. http://ssrn.com/abstract=610395.

Holt, Charles, Lisa Anderson, and Roland Fryer. 2006. "Discrimination: Experimental Evidence from Psychology and Economics." In *Handbook on Economics of Discrimination,* ed. William Rogers. Cheltenham, U.K.; Northampton, MA: Edward Elgar Publishing.

Knowles, John, Nicola Persico, and Petra Todd. 2001. "Racial Bias in Motor Vehicle Searches: Theory and Evidence." *Journal of Political Economy* 109 (1): 203–29.

McIntyre, Shelby J., Dennis J. Moberg, and Barry Z. Posner. 1980. "Discrimination in Recruitment: An Empirical Analysis; Comment." *Industrial and Labor Relations Review* 33 (4, July): 543–47.

Moro, Andrea. 2003. "The Effect of Statistical Discrimination on Black-White Wage Inequality: Estimating a Model with Multiple Equilibria." *International Economic Review* 44 (2, May): 457–500.

Munnell, Alicia, Geoffrey Tootell, Lynn Browne, and James McEneaney. 1996. "Mortgage Lending in Boston: Interpreting HMDA Data." *American Economic Review* 86 (1, March): 25–53.

Newman, Jerry M. 1978. "Discrimination in Recruitment: An Empirical Analysis." *Industrial and Labor Relations Review* 32 (1, October): 15–23.

Oaxaca, Ronald L. 1973. "Male-Female Wage Differentials in Urban Labor Markets." *International Economic Review* 14 (October): 673–709.

Secretaría Técnica del Frente Social. 2004. *Survey of Perceptions of Racism and Discrimination in Ecuador.* Quito: Secretaría Técnica del Frente Social.

Sedesol (Secretaría de Desarrollo Social). 2005. *First National Survey on Discrimination in Mexico.* Mexico City: Sedesol.

Siegel, Judith M., and Claude M. Steele. 1979. "Noise Level and Social Discrimination." *Personality and Social Psychology Bulletin* 5 (1): 95–100.

Smart, Scott, and Joel Waldfogel. 1996. "A Citation-Based Test for Discrimination at Economics and Finance Journals." NBER Working Paper 5460, National Bureau of Economic Research, Cambridge, MA.

2

Ethnic and Social Barriers to Cooperation: Experiments Studying the Extent and Nature of Discrimination in Urban Peru

Marco Castillo, Ragan Petrie, and Máximo Torero

Trust plays an important role in our choice of personal interactions. Trust is reflected in where we choose to live, whom we choose to befriend, and the groups to which we belong. While many choices are made with information on the qualities or reputations of others, some choices may be made with little more information than the impressions we form by driving through a neighborhood or viewing the clientele of a store. Lack of information can therefore hinder economic exchange if people misperceive the trustworthiness of others. People may withdraw from or never enter into interactions with certain segments of the population because of superficial perceptions, and initial perceptions might persist even in the face of evidence contradicting them. In the long run, society may suffer persistent losses due to exclusion if enough sorting takes place.

Marco Castillo is with the Georgia Institute of Technology, Ragan Petrie is with Georgia State University, and Máximo Torero is with the International Food Policy Research Institute. This paper was undertaken as part of the Latin American and Caribbean Research Network Project "Discrimination and Economic Outcomes." The authors would like to thank the Inter-American Development Bank for funding as well as Kevin Ackaramongkolrotn, Jorge de la Roca, David Solis, and Néstor Valdivia.

How important are these types of misperceptions in determining group composition and therefore economic outcomes? In this chapter, we explore the salience of both performance and observable characteristics in how people sort into groups. We conjecture that people use observable characteristics, such as gender or race, to choose group members because they lack better information on future performance. However, even if people use personal characteristics only as a way to gauge information, if performance and characteristics are highly correlated, then we cannot tease apart which of the two is most salient in group membership. We use a series of experiments that break this correlation and allow us to assess which of the two criteria—personal characteristics or performance—is more salient. Furthermore, we use a cross section of the population as a way to reach a more diverse population of subjects than is normally found in standard laboratory experiments with college students.

Discrimination and social exclusion in the form of racial or ethnic discrimination seem to be critical in a multiracial and multilingual country such as Peru, where indigenous groups and ethnic minorities are more likely to be poor than other groups. Previous work has shown that social exclusion in access to different markets—labor, credit, education—is a crucial issue in Peru. Discrimination and exclusion related to ethnicity, culture, physical appearance, and religion take place in ways both obvious and subtle. Moreover, as shown by Castillo and Petrie (2007), using data collected from the Peruvian Truth and Reconciliation Commission, some patterns of human rights violations are difficult to reconcile with theories of statistical discrimination. If exclusion in Peru combines statistical and preference-based discrimination, it is important to identify the extent of each and to devise institutions that diminish both.

Group membership may have important economic benefits, such as the benefits from belonging to a trade association or investment group. If the composition of the group dictates the benefits, then we may need to be careful about whom we choose to be in our group or to which group we choose to belong; such sorting could have important consequences for which groups do well economically and which groups do not. If certain groups are unfortunate enough to have, for example, weak social networks and are perceived as having an untrustworthy appearance, they may be excluded from high-performing groups and only be able to find membership in low-performing groups. Also, people conscious of discrimination might exclude themselves from groups as a way to avoid being discriminated against.

In this chapter, we use the results of repeated linear public goods game experiments to explore these issues. Repeated public goods experiments are a natural environment in which to study trust, as they offer participants an opportunity to engage in reciprocal behavior. Level of cooperation, or reciprocity, has been found to depend on the initial propensities that people in the group have to cooperate (Andreoni and Petrie 2006). People will therefore sort themselves into groups of high performers. If people are not altruistic, then trust becomes important in this environment. Without trust in others' willingness to contribute to the public good, social benefits will not be achieved.

Since identification of discrimination for other than statistical reasons requires breaking the correlation between actions and appearances, we conducted several experimental treatments that manipulate the correlation between behavior and appearances. Subjects were shown digital photographs of others in the experiment and information on past performance and then were asked to choose whom they would like to have in their group. Our approach is novel in that it manipulates the equilibrium at the experiment level to identify sources of discrimination. A policy implication of this study is therefore to identify the changes in incentives necessary to reduce the prevalence of discrimination.

Our results show that people discriminate based on appearance and socioeconomic characteristics despite the fact that there is no correlation between those characteristics and performance. That is, discrimination in urban Lima cannot be reconciled with theories of statistical discrimination. While the evidence is consistent with the presence of stereotyping or taste-based discrimination, we also show that providing information on previous performance makes evidence of discrimination disappear almost completely. While this is encouraging, there also is evidence of preference-based discrimination since stereotyping is no longer a reasonable explanation once information on performance is revealed.

Appearance and Information

Why might we think that appearance and information will interact to affect decisions? Previous research supports the notion that the social context of decisions can affect outcomes. Research in experimental economics has shown that being able to identify one's partner increases levels of altruism in dictator games (Bohnet and Frey 1999; Burnham 2003) and that combining identification and information on past actions increases cooperation in public goods games (Andreoni and Petrie 2006). Also, people may have mistaken perceptions of behavior, expecting women to be more trusting than they actually are (Petrie 2004).

Identification alone can increase cooperation, but specific characteristics of a partner, such as gender and beauty, can affect decisions. People are more cooperative and trusting with attractive people (Andreoni and Petrie 2006; Eckel and Wilson 2002; Petrie 2004), and attractive people make more money (Hammermesh and Biddle 1994; Mobius and Rosenblatt 2005). Decisions are also affected by the ethnic composition (Cummings and Ferraro 2003) and the gender and age composition of the experimental group (Carter and Castillo 2003).

Sorting, or preference for individuals with certain observable characteristics, may reflect preference-based or statistical discrimination. Previous
research using audit studies and field experiments has shown that there
is evidence of both. Audit studies suggest findings consistent with preference-based discrimination (Riach and Rich 2002), but List (2004) suggests
that audit studies cannot distinguish this from statistical discrimination.
List uses a sequence of field experiments at a sports card market to show
that differentiated behavior is more likely due to statistical discrimination
than to pure discrimination.

To our knowledge, our work is the first to present evidence consistent with taste-based discrimination in the experimental literature. The
research shows the advantage of experimental methods in tackling difficult identification issues. It also shows the importance of measurement
of personal characteristics and sampling in the study of race and height
in experiments.

Theoretical Motivation

Standard economic reasoning implies that the way people sort into groups
reveals their incentive to form coalitions. People sort into the groups
that maximize expected future gains, and observable characteristics of
participants are important insofar as they reveal information on likely
strategies to be played. In equilibrium, people play their best responses
to their expectations of others' behavior and others' expectations of their
behavior. This means that people will adjust their behavior according to
their beliefs of what others are likely to do.

Observable characteristics are likely to be more salient and to affect
play in games in the absence of information on the likely play of others.
This is the basis of statistical discrimination. Also, behavior toward others might be due to preferences for or against certain others, regardless of
beliefs. If people have preferences for the composition of the group, how
people sort into groups no longer reflects solely the incentive to maximize
expected future gain.

Since one's quality as a partner is private information, there might be
incentives to signal quality or to obtain information on the quality of others, and people would have an incentive to form reputations. In order to
avoid any reputation effects, we need to eliminate the incentive to form a
reputation in early rounds of the game.

This suggests a natural test of theories explaining sorting into groups.
Theories of statistical discrimination suggest that appearance affects sorting only because it provides information on expected behavior. Once
information on behavior is provided, the role of appearance must be
muted. But what if behavior is correlated with appearance? For example,

what if Caucasians are indeed more cooperative? If this is the case, then we cannot determine whether sorting along social characteristics in the presence of information on past behavior is evidence of pure discrimination or statistical discrimination. This identification problem can be resolved if this correlation can be broken, so that any subsequent sorting along social characteristics is due to pure discrimination. Our experimental design allows us to observe whether people engage in statistical discrimination or pure discrimination when choosing groups.

The Sample

The site for our experiments is urban metropolitan Lima in Peru. This site lends itself to Internet-based experiments that draw from a larger population because Internet cabins are common in Lima and a high proportion of the population has expertise in using the Internet. According to a survey conducted in 2003, there were 476 Internet cabins distributed across all districts of Lima. This amounts to around 1 computer per hour per 10 people (assuming 10 computers per cabin, 12 hours of service, and an urban population of 5,681,941, according to the census of 1993). This characteristic allowed us to conduct Internet-based experiments with non-college student populations—an important distinction, given that students belong to a potentially highly unrepresentative segment of the population, thus reducing the external validity of the results and preventing us from drawing clear policy implications. By drawing on this broader population, we are able to look more accurately at the extent of discrimination.

Our sampling strategy was twofold. First, we wanted to create an environment in which people of various social distances who might not normally interact with one another could. Second, we wanted to have a sample that was representative of the young working population in metropolitan Lima. To this end, eligible subjects were 20–35 years of age, lived in metropolitan Lima, had labor market experience, were currently working, knew how to use the Internet, and had an e-mail account. In addition, we sought to keep a gender and income balance so that subjects would be distributed homogeneously across gender and income levels. To ensure a diverse population in our sample, we worked with two companies that specialize in conducting surveys and recruiting subjects.[1] We also drew samples from clusters of owners of small, medium, and microenterprises.[2]

The protocol used for the experiments was simple enough to include large segments of the population. The interface was graphical and required simply that the subjects knew how to use a computer mouse. However, because our experiments relied on Internet protocols and the ability to use a computer, we likely excluded some segments of the population that might

suffer more marked patterns of discrimination. Therefore, our results give
a lower-bound estimate to the extent of discrimination.

According to the population census of 1993, our sample covers most
of the districts in metropolitan Lima and is highly correlated with the distribution of the population with complete or incomplete higher education
(see figure 2.1).[3] To investigate the comparability of our sample to the
population in other dimensions, we compared our experimental subjects
to a subsample from the Encuesta Nacional de Hogares (ENAHO) 2004.
The subsample complies with the eligibility criteria for all of our subjects.
The advantage of using the ENAHO as a comparison group is that it is
representative of metropolitan Lima and therefore useful in helping us to
identify any selection bias in our sample. Our experimental subjects and
the ENAHO comparison group have a similar distribution among almost
all the variables (age, gender, monthly income, average education, and
language), but our experimental subjects are slightly more educated. This
comparison gives us confidence that the subjects in our experiment are a
good representation of the larger population in metropolitan Lima.

As noted, because our experiments relied on Internet protocols and
the ability to use a computer, we likely excluded some segments of the

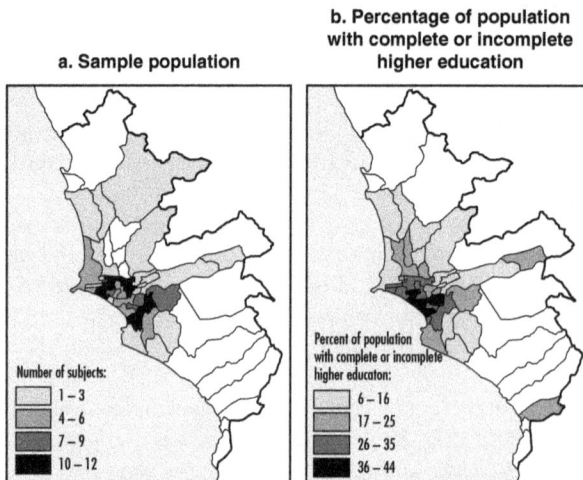

Figure 2.1 Distribution of the Sample in Comparison with
Population with Complete or Incomplete Higher Education,
Lima, Peru

Source: Population Census 1993.

population that might suffer more marked patterns of discrimination. Previous experience by the researchers in rural areas in South Africa and Central America shows that illiterate subjects are able to understand experimental procedures presented in a graphical manner. The experiments in this research required simply that the subjects knew how to use a computer mouse.

Experimental Design

We used a linear public goods game to explore discrimination in group formation, a design first developed and used by Castillo and Petrie (2006). Each subject was given a 25-token endowment and told to decide how to divide the endowment between a private investment and a public investment. Each token placed in the private investment yielded a return of 4 céntimos to the subject.[4] Each token placed in the public investment yielded a return of α_i to the subject and every other member of the group. The return to the public investment, α_i, was 2 céntimos in three of the four treatments. There were 20 subjects in each experimental session. Subjects were randomly assigned to a five-person group and played 10 rounds with that same group. At the end of each round, subjects learned their payoff, π_i, and the total number of tokens contributed to the public investment by the group, G. Subjects made decisions privately on a computer and did not talk to one another. They did not interact with other subjects in any way other than through decisions on the computer.

In total, subjects played three 10-round sequences, and each 10-round sequence was with an assigned group. At the end of the first 10-round sequence, subjects were again randomly assigned to a new five-person group, and at the end of the second 10-round sequence, subjects were asked to choose their group for the final 10 investment decisions. Subjects did not know that they would be asked to choose their group before this point in the experiment. This was a surprise. This design element was important to avoid biasing subject behavior. No personal or individual contribution information was revealed in the first 20 rounds of the game.

In order to create an incentive for people to reveal whom they would prefer to have in their group, we created the following procedure. Subjects ranked all of the other 19 subjects in the session from 1 (most preferred) to 19 (least preferred). We provided subjects with some information on the other subjects in the room to use for ranking. The information was either the average amount contributed to the public investment during the second 10-round sequence, the subject's photo, or both. Subjects used that information to create a list from most preferred to least preferred. Digital photographs of subjects were taken at the beginning of the experiment, and photographs were head shots, similar to a passport or identification photo.

Once all subjects had submitted their lists, groups were formed in four steps. First, one person was chosen at random. A group was formed that included the randomly chosen person and the top four people on his or her list. Second, one person from the remaining 15 people who had not been assigned to a group was randomly chosen. A group was formed with that person and the first four people on that person's list from the remaining people who had not previously been assigned to a group. Third, one person from the remaining 10 people who had not previously been assigned to a group was randomly chosen. The first four people on that person's list among the remaining people were put in a group with that person. Fourth, anyone not already assigned to a group was put in a group together. Once groups were formed by this procedure, subjects then saw a screen with information corresponding to the subjects in their new group. Subjects played the last 10 rounds with that group. During these last 10 rounds, at the end of each round, they saw the same information they saw during the previous 20 rounds: their payoff, π_i, and the total number of tokens contributed to the public investment by the group, G. No other information was revealed either when making decisions or at the end of each round.

This sorting mechanism is similar to the one suggested in Bogomolnaia and Jackson (2002). The mechanism is incentive compatible if preferences over groups are additive in the preferences over its members. Additivity in this context means that if Pablo prefers María's company to Gabriela's company, then Pablo always prefers a group that exchanges Gabriela for María, regardless of who the other members of the group are. Under these conditions, revealing the ordering of others is a weakly dominant strategy for Pablo. If Pablo is not chosen, he is indifferent in the ranking he reveals, but if he is chosen, he is better off by revealing his true rankings. Since preferences over others' company is additive, it does not matter whether he is chosen first or last.

Some may argue that additivity of preferences over others' company may be a strong assumption. Some combinations of people might be less successful than others. For instance, women might be very cooperative with other women, but less cooperative with men. Therefore, a woman might be chosen to be part of a group when other women are available, but not when mostly men are available.

There is another mechanism that is incentive compatible, regardless of preferences over groups. If people are able to rank all possible groups that one could be paired with, we would not need to be concerned with the additivity assumption. Unfortunately, this option would be impractical since the number of groups to be ranked would be exceedingly large.[5] For this reason, we opted for the mechanism described above, which is easy to explain to subjects and can be implemented quickly once subjects have submitted their list of rankings.

There were four experimental treatments: contribution only, photo only, contribution and photo, and two types. Treatments differed in the α_i

assigned to each person and the information that was shown to subjects when they were asked to rank the other subjects.

In the contribution-only, photo-only, and contribution-and-photo treatments, all subjects were assigned $\alpha_i = 2$ céntimos, so the price of contributing to the public good was 2. It is in the group's interest for everyone to contribute their full endowment to the public investment, but each individual in the group maximizes his own payoffs by putting all of his tokens in the individual investment. In the contribution-only treatment, when subjects were asked to rank others, they saw the average amount contributed to the public good in the second 10-round sequence by all other subjects in the room. Because groups were randomly assigned in the first and second sequences, all subjects had an equal probability of being assigned to any given group. Therefore, while contributions in a public goods game are a function of preferences, learning, and group behavior, no subject is any more likely to be in a "good" or "bad" group. Average contribution behavior in the second sequence should reflect average performance in a public goods game and minimize the effects of learning.

In the photo-only treatment, when subjects were asked to rank others, they saw the photos of all other subjects. And in the contribution-and-photo treatment, subjects saw the photo and the average amount contributed to the public good in the second 10-round sequence. The average was listed below each subject's photo.

In the two-types treatment, as in the contribution-and-photo treatment, when subjects were asked to rank others, they saw the photo and average contribution to the public good in the second 10-round sequence. In the two-types treatment, however, $\alpha_i \in \{0.5, 5.0\}$ céntimos. Half of the subjects were randomly assigned a value of 0.5, and half were randomly assigned a value of 5.0. Subjects kept the same value for all 30 rounds of play. All subjects knew this information before making decisions. A subject with $\alpha_i = 5.0$ has a price of contributing to the public good of 0.8. If he is selfish or altruistic, he should invest his entire endowment in the public good. If he is not altruistic or is inequality averse, however, he might not contribute his full endowment, despite the low price of giving.[6] A subject with $\alpha_i = 0.5$ has a price of contributing to the public good of 8, so investing in the public good is very expensive. We would expect subjects assigned the low α_i to invest little to nothing in the public good. In all cases, we expect there to be a clear separation in the contribution behavior between those assigned a low and those assigned a high price of giving. Complete separation is not necessarily expected due to the asymmetry faced by subjects within a group. Because subjects were randomly assigned incentives, however, performance and appearance should not be correlated. The two-types treatment is important to our ability to identify whether appearance or performance affects sorting.

Each treatment was run twice, and each experimental session had 20 subjects. An experimental session lasted at least two hours. In total, 160 subjects participated in the four treatments. Each session ended with an extensive questionnaire. The experiments were conducted on computers in two computer labs at Pacific University in Lima. Two treatments were run at the same time, so subjects were randomly assigned to treatments. Since most subjects worked full time, the experiments were conducted on weekend afternoons.

In the contribution-only, photo-only, and contribution-and-photo treatments, average payoffs were $19.65 (standard deviation $1.36). In the two-types treatment, average payoffs were $33.75 (standard deviation $6.87).[7]

Race and Height Classifications

We were interested in knowing whether people sort into groups based on physical characteristics. While a person's sex is easy to determine, a person's race is not. We wanted to develop an independent measure of the race of a person that reflects the general perception of that person. Therefore, we used raters—people who did not participate in the public goods experiment but who were drawn from the same cohort as subjects in the experiment—to rate the photos of the subjects in terms of race as well as height. A rater only rated the photo in terms of one characteristic—race or height—not both.

For race ratings, because the most popular self-classification of race in Peru is mestizo (mixed race), it was important for us to have a measure of race that could adequately capture this mixing. For this reason, we used the race classification method developed by Torero and others (2004) and Ñopo, Saavedra, and Torero (2004). Instead of classifying a subject along one dimension of "white" or "mestizo," we evaluated subjects on their racial intensity in four categories: white, indigenous, black, and Asian, which are readily recognized as distinct racial groups. This gave a more nuanced measure of race and more accurately captured racial mixing in Peru.

To obtain these ratings, we had 20 persons not involved in the public goods experiment (10 women and 10 men) rate each subject along each of these four dimensions. Each dimension was rated from 0 to 10, with 0 being complete absence of the dimension and 10 being the most intense. Raters were instructed to choose whichever number between 1 and 10 best described the person for each of the four racial dimensions. The four numbers did not need to add up to 10. The raters were told that if they thought that a person belonged to only one racial group, they should give that person a 10 for that racial dimension and a 0 for all other dimensions. Raters were shown the photos one by one on a computer screen and asked to choose the intensity of each dimension by clicking a button. Raters could easily move back and forth between the photos to check or change their answers. Ratings took about one hour, and each rater was paid $9.67 for his or her time.

For estimated height, we followed the same procedure as with race. The only difference is that the 10 men and 10 women were asked to guess the height, in centimeters, of each person in the photo. Raters were free to choose any number for the height.

In terms of agreement among raters, there was usually a high degree of agreement regarding race. Along the white dimension, pairwise correlations among raters range from 0.31 to 0.76, with an average of 0.57. For the indigenous dimension, correlations range from 0.02 to 0.64, with an average of 0.41. For the black dimension, correlations range from 0.19 to 0.82, with an average of 0.50, and for the Asian dimension, correlations range from –0.02 to 0.81, with an average of 0.37.[8]

While the rating scale ranged from 0 to 10 for race, some raters did not use the full range of the scale. For example, for race, some used intensities up to 10 and some only up to 6. To be able to make comparisons across raters, we standardized each rater's rating by his or her own mean and standard deviation. This allowed us to take an average across all 20 raters' standardized ratings for race or height to obtain the final ratings we use to analyze the data.

For race, the most likely intensities in the subject population are white and indigenous. While some subjects displayed intensities in the dimensions of black and Asian, the majority of subjects displayed the greatest intensities in the dimensions of white and indigenous. This is in line with the general population in Peru, where blacks make up 2 percent of the population and Asians make up 3 percent. Average intensity is 2.83 for white, 3.91 for indigenous, 1.89 for black, and 1.31 for Asian.

Because the majority of our subjects identified themselves primarily as a mix of white and indigenous, in the next section we concentrate on these two dimensions in our analysis of contributions and ranking. A person is considered white if her average racial intensity rating in the white dimension is above the median and her average racial intensity rating in the indigenous dimension is below the median. A person is considered indigenous if her average racial intensity in the indigenous dimension is above the median and her average racial intensity in the white dimension is below the median.

Results and Discussion

Table 2.1 presents descriptive statistics of the experimental subjects.[9] Three out of five subjects are men, and the average age is 26 years. As mentioned, our sample is slightly more educated than the population at

Table 2.1 Descriptive Statistics

Variable	Number	Mean	Standard deviation	Minimum	Maximum
1 = male	160	0.61	0.49	0	1
Age (years)	160	26.28	4.23	20	35
Education (years)	160	15.07	1.72	10	19
1 = college degree	160	0.29	0.46	0	1
1 = incomplete college degree	160	0.32	0.47	0	1
European grandparents (number)	157[a]	0.17	0.60	0	4
Indigenous grandparents (number)	157[a]	0.31	0.89	0	4
Height (meters)	160	1.69	0.08	1.52	1.94
Family size	156[a]	4.95	2.24	1	13
1 = religious high school	160	0.44	0.50	0	1

Source: Authors' calculations.
a. Self reporting by individuals.

large. On average, participants have three or more years of postsecondary education, and 29 percent have a college degree. The sample also reflects the ethnic and cultural makeup of Lima's population. Among the sample, 17 percent has at least one grandparent whose mother tongue is neither Spanish nor any other Peruvian indigenous language. In addition, 31 percent of the sample has at least one grandparent whose mother tongue is indigenous to Peru. While stature is a self-reported variable, we find great variation in height. On average, a male subject reported being 1.73 meters tall and a female subject reported being 1.63 meters tall. Finally, experimental subjects live in households with an average of five persons.

What Did People Do in the Experiment?

Figures 2.2 and 2.3 show the aggregate behavior in all experimental sessions. Across all rounds of the first sequence of the experiment, contributions to the public good range from 23 percent of subjects'

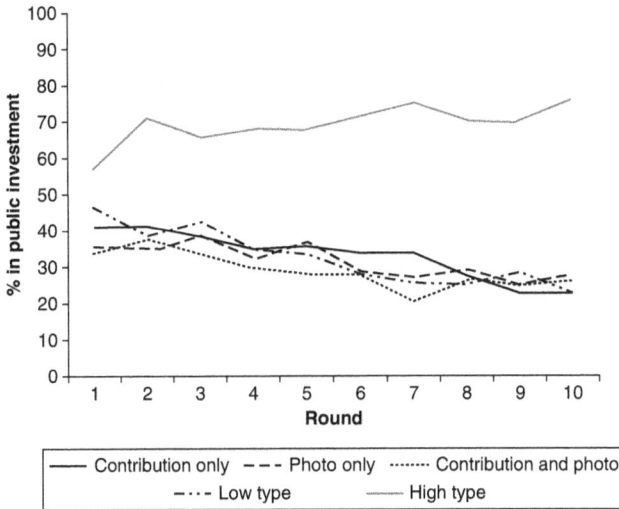

Figure 2.2 Contributions to the Public Good, First Sequence, by Type of Treatment

Legend: Contribution only — — — Photo only ········ Contribution and photo — ·· — Low type ———— High type

X-axis: Round (1–10), Y-axis: % in public investment (0–100)

Source: Authors' calculations.

endowments for low type in the two-types treatment to 46 percent of subjects' endowments in the contribution-only treatment. As commonly observed (see Kagel and Roth 1995), contributions tend to decline with time. Contributions decline to 22 percent for low type in the two-types treatment and to 22 percent in the contribution-only treatment. A similar pattern is observed in the second sequence of the experiment, shown in figure 2.3. Contributions in the first round of the second sequence of the experiment range from 23 percent in the photo-only treatment to 75 percent for high type in the two-types treatment. Contributions in the last round of the second sequence decrease to 14 percent in the photo-only treatment and to 23 percent for low type in the two-types treatment.

Moreover, the incentives of the two-types treatment successfully induce a separation in behavior between high and low types. High type contributes 50 percentage points more to the public good than low type. The figures also show convergence toward the play of dominant strategies by high type.

Figure 2.3 Contributions to the Public Good, Second Sequence, by Type of Treatment

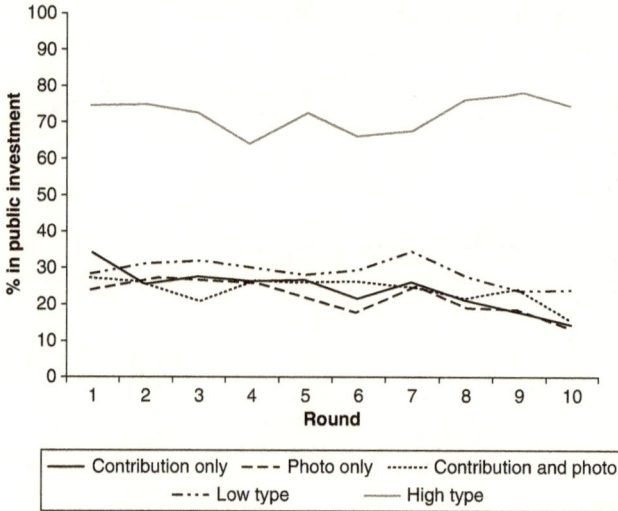

Source: Authors' calculations.

A basic premise in theories of statistical discrimination is that people of different backgrounds might behave differently; therefore, in the absence of better information, ethnic or cultural background can be used as a proxy of behavior. For instance, migrants might experience unfavorable market conditions, causing them to behave selfishly. Conversely, more-affluent subjects can afford to be more altruistic or to take more risks. Table 2.2 shows a series of regressions aimed at determining whether different people do behave differently. All regressions include group-level fixed effects in order to control for the fact that different levels of contributions might be due to social interactions within a particular group. The regressions also include random effects at the individual level to control for the fact that the same person's decisions are correlated.[10]

The regressions in table 2.2 show that behavior is not correlated with personal characteristics. On average, contributions decrease by 10 percent from round 1 to round 10. There is a slight effect of taller people giving more in the two-types treatment. It is further instructive to compare the column showing results from the combination of the contribution-only, photo-only, and contribution-and-photo treatments with the column showing the results for all treatments.

Table 2.2 Percent of Endowment Contributed to the Public
Good (Sequence 2), by Type of Treatment

Variable	Contribution only, photo only, and contribution and photo	Two types	All treatments
1 = male	4.62	–3.03	3.19
	(0.21)	(0.75)	(0.37)
Age (years)	0.10	–0.81	–0.13
	(0.78)	(0.40)	(0.70)
Education (years)	0.55	–2.74	–0.57
	(0.56)	(0.14)	(0.51)
Height (meters)	–1.56	117.36	27.78
	(0.95)	(0.03)	(0.21)
1 = white > median; indigenous ≤ median	–0.16	–2.90	–0.96
	(0.96)	(0.74)	(0.77)
1 = white ≤ median; indigenous > median	–1.55	4.09	–0.30
	(0.68)	(0.70)	(0.94)
1 = religious high school	–1.72	5.99	1.16
	(0.58)	(0.48)	(0.70)
1 = low type	n.a.	n.a.	–13.44
			(0.72)
1 = high type	n.a.	48.01	30.37
		(0.00)	(0.42)
Round	–1.19	–0.12	–0.93
	(0.00)	(0.73)	(0.00)
Constant	26.49	–113.41	n.a.
	(0.51)	(0.19)	
Individual random effects	Yes	Yes	Yes
Group fixed effects	Yes	Yes	Yes
Within R^2	0.0360	0.0003	0.0209
Number of observations	1,200	400	1,600

Source: Authors' calculations.
Note: Numbers in parentheses are *p* values. n.a. = not applicable.

Table 2.2 shows that personal characteristics are of little help in pre-
dicting the behavior of others. This result is useful in interpreting the
results presented in the following section. Ethnic background, measured as
intensity of a racial characteristic, is not correlated with behavior at all.

How Were People Ranked?

The previous section shows that there is little evidence supporting the hypothesis that personal characteristics correlate with behavior. This section investigates whether personal characteristics are used when choosing groups. The regression is based on a few covariates due to the fact that results are not altered significantly by the inclusion of additional ones. Ethnicity is measured by the average standardized intensity variable of white and indigenous described in the section on racial classification. We use these aggregated racial intensities to create a discrete variable determining whether a person is white or indigenous.

Table 2.3 reports the ordinary least squares (OLS) regression for rankings separately for each treatment.[11] The dependent variable is the rank that a person is given. That is, a person with a rank of 1 is ranked highest, and a person with a rank of 19 is ranked lowest. Given how rank is defined, the interpretation of the sign of coefficients must be adjusted

Table 2.3 OLS Regression on Individual Ranking, by Type of Treatment

Variable	Photo only	Contribution and photo	Two types
Age (years)	0.06	0.03	–0.02
	(0.28)	(0.32)	(0.67)
1 = male	2.89	0.09	–0.00
	(0.00)	(0.81)	(0.99)
Height (meters)	–10.37	–0.85	–1.10
	(0.00)	(0.65)	(0.66)
Expected rank	n.a.	0.83	0.64
		(0.00)	(0.00)
1 = white > median; indigenous ≤ median	0.19	–0.06	–0.71
	(0.73)	(0.86)	(0.14)
1 = white ≤ median; indigenous > median	1.47	–0.34	–0.19
	(0.00)	(0.28)	(0.68)
Constant	23.48	2.30	6.17
	(0.00)	(0.46)	(0.13)
R^2	0.05	0.70	0.43
Number of observations	760	760	760

Source: Authors' calculations.

Note: Highest = 1; lowest = 19. Numbers in parentheses are *p* values. n.a. = not applicable.

accordingly. If a coefficient is positive, then the variable associated with it tends to lower the person's rank. If a coefficient is negative, the presence of the covariate tends to improve the person's rank.

Two covariates require extra explanation. Expected rank is a variable indicating the rank that a person should have if only contributions to the public good are used to rank others. The expected coefficient on this variable should be 1 if information on others' behavior is the only relevant information in creating ranks.

Participants seem to have understood that having high contributors in the group is the best strategy. For instance, expected rank alone explains 67 percent of the variance of ranks in the contribution-only treatment (not shown in table 2.3). Expected rank remains a strong predictor of rank in all treatments where information on previous contribution was provided.

Despite the fact that personal characteristics have no bearing on what people did in the experiment, they tend to predict how people are ranked. In the photo-only treatment, men are ranked, on average, 2.89 ranks lower than women. Height also has a strong effect on how people are ranked: 10 extra centimeters of height increases rank by 1. Tall women are therefore ranked rather high. Due to the fact that people only saw the picture of other participants, the result for height is puzzling. Height might be correlated with other characteristics captured in a photo and therefore might not measure the impact of height per se. However, as mentioned, we collected data from independent people to see whether people are able to guess the height of others correctly by looking at head-shot pictures. Indeed, the average estimated height reported by independent raters is highly correlated with real height even after controlling for sex and ethnicity. That is, we cannot discard the hypothesis that height itself explains how people are ranked.

Relevant for the question of racial discrimination, the regression on rankings made in the photo-only treatment also shows that people who look indigenous are ranked 1.47 ranks lower. Table 2.3, however, shows that discrimination based on race is present only when no information on past performance is available. Rankings made in the treatment with both contributions and photos show that race indicators are no longer significant. That is, the regressions are consistent with stereotyping, but not with preference-based discrimination.

Who is doing the discriminating? Table 2.4 shows how men and women rank others. In the photo-only treatment, both men and women rank tall women higher, but men rank people who look indigenous lower. Women react more strongly to tall women than do men. In the contribution-and-photo treatment, women rank people who look indigenous lower. Men do not react to racial characteristics.

Table 2.5 shows how white and indigenous people rank others. Both groups rate tall women higher, but only whites rate indigenous-looking

Table 2.4 OLS Regression on Individual Ranking, by Type of Treatment and Gender

Variable	Photo only		Contribution and photo		Two types	
	Men	*Women*	*Men*	*Women*	*Men*	*Women*
Age (years)	0.06	0.04	0.01	0.08	0.07	-0.10
	(0.31)	(0.63)	(0.68)	(0.22)	(0.21)	(0.03)
1 = male	2.76	3.12	0.05	0.07	0.26	-0.25
	(0.00)	(0.00)	(0.89)	(0.93)	(0.69)	(0.62)
Height (meters)	-9.17	-12.56	-1.08	0.41	-2.95	0.79
	(0.03)	(0.03)	(0.75)	(0.92)	(0.46)	(0.80)
Expected rank	n.a.	n.a.	0.86	0.73	0.55	0.73
			(0.00)	(0.00)	(0.00)	(0.00)
1 = white > median; indigenous ≤ median	0.39	-0.23	-0.11	0.12	-1.09	-0.41
	(0.58)	(0.81)	(0.75)	(0.86)	(0.16)	(0.49)
1 = white ≤ median; indigenous > median	1.84	0.74	0.01	1.34	-0.42	-0.03
	(0.00)	(0.42)	(0.97)	(0.06)	(0.56)	(0.96)
Constant	21.06	27.85	2.93	-0.53	7.96	4.27
	(0.00)	(0.00)	(0.39)	(0.94)	(0.22)	(0.66)
R^2	0.05	0.04	0.74	0.61	0.32	0.55
Number of observations	494	266	551	209	361	399

Source: Authors' calculations.
Note: Highest = 1; lowest = 19. Numbers in parentheses are *p* values. n.a. = not applicable.

Table 2.5 OLS Regression on Individual Ranking, by Type of Treatment and Race or Ethnicity

Variable	Photo only		Contribution and photo		Two types	
	White	Indigenous	White	Indigenous	White	Indigenous
Age (years)	0.03	0.13	0.02	-0.01	0.10	-0.09
	(0.71)	(0.13)	(0.55)	(0.87)	(0.04)	(0.12)
1 = male	4.08	2.58	0.73	-0.01	-0.12	0.40
	(0.00)	(0.00)	(0.07)	(0.99)	(0.82)	(0.56)
Height (meters)	-10.89	-11.99	-2.07	-0.32	-2.60	1.71
	(0.07)	(0.03)	(0.31)	(0.93)	(0.45)	(0.67)
Expected rank	n.a.	n.a.	0.92	0.73	0.80	0.69
			(0.00)	(0.00)	(0.00)	(0.00)
1 = white > median; indigenous ≤ median	-0.63	1.20	-0.35	0.25	-0.42	-1.39
	(0.51)	(0.18)	(0.27)	(0.70)	(0.52)	(0.07)
1 = white ≤ median; indigenous > median	1.97	0.91	0.21	0.83	-0.09	-0.53
	(0.03)	(0.28)	(0.56)	(0.19)	(0.88)	(0.48)
Constant	24.21	24.43	3.28	3.16	3.73	3.33
	(0.00)	(0.00)	(0.33)	(0.62)	(0.50)	(0.66)
R^2	0.12	0.03	0.90	0.54	0.68	0.48
Number of observations	247	304	228	266	228	266

Source: Authors' calculations.
Note: Highest = 1; lowest = 19. Numbers in parentheses are p values. n.a. = not applicable.

people lower. When information on contributions is known, this is a
strong predictor of rank. Whites do rank men lower in the contribution-
and-photo treatment, and they also rank older people lower in the two-
types treatment. But this effect is rather small.

Tables 2.6 and 2.7 show OLS regressions that further investigate the
presence of discrimination across treatments.[12] Table 2.6 shows a linear
probability model of the likelihood of being in the top four of any list. As
mentioned, being a man decreases the probability of being among the top
four, and height increases the probability of being among the top four.
Table 2.7 shows the likelihood of being in the bottom four of any list. Both
of these tables confirm previous results.

Finally, the results for the two-types treatment are interesting because
subjects were induced to behave quite differently regardless of their looks
or background. Despite this, we find that looking white increases the
likelihood of being named among the top four. Also, looking indigenous
increases the likelihood of being named among the bottom four.

Table 2.6 Probability of Being in the Top Four, by Type
of Treatment

Variable	Photo only	Contribution and photo	Two types
Age (years)	−0.01	−0.00	0.00
	(0.14)	(0.39)	(0.21)
1 = male	−0.17	−0.02	0.05
	(0.00)	(0.57)	(0.18)
Height (meters)	0.60	−0.19	−0.19
	(0.02)	(0.27)	(0.32)
Expected to be in group	n.a.	0.68	0.52
		(0.00)	(0.00)
1 = white > median; indigenous ≤ median	−0.00	0.00	0.15
	(0.92)	(0.97)	(0.00)
1 = white ≤ median; indigenous > median	−0.11	0.02	0.04
	(0.00)	(0.61)	(0.27)
Constant	−0.49	0.43	0.20
	(0.22)	(0.14)	(0.50)
R^2	0.04	0.52	0.34
Number of observations	760	760	760

Source: Authors' calculations.
Note: Highest = 1; lowest = 19. Numbers in parentheses are *p* values. n.a. = not
applicable.

Table 2.7 Probability of Being in the Bottom Four, by Type of Treatment

Variable	Photo only	Contribution and photo	Two types
Age (years)	–0.00	0.01	–0.01
	(0.72)	(0.01)	(0.01)
1 = male	0.14	–0.04	0.02
	(0.00)	(0.24)	(0.58)
Height (meters)	–0.62	–0.03	–0.34
	(0.02)	(0.86)	(0.12)
Expected to be in group	n.a.	0.74	0.48
		(0.00)	(0.00)
1 = white > median; indigenous ≤ median	0.13	0.09	0.01
	(0.00)	(0.00)	(0.72)
1 = white ≤ median; indigenous > median	0.15	0.12	0.08
	(0.00)	(0.00)	(0.05)
Constant	1.10	–0.14	0.82
	(0.01)	(0.59)	(0.01)
R^2	0.03	0.63	0.28
Number of observations	760	760	760

Source: Authors' calculations.

Note: Highest = 1; lowest = 19. Numbers in parentheses are *p* values. n.a. = not applicable.

Conclusions and Policy Implications

We have presented a series of experiments aimed at determining the nature of discrimination in urban Lima, Peru. Subjects played a linear public goods game and were allowed to sort into groups. Our experiments systematically manipulated the information available about others when sorting into groups. This allowed us to examine what is more relevant to group formation: information on past performance or physical characteristics. We recruited a diverse sample of individuals currently working in the labor market to participate in the experiments.

Our experiments show that subject behavior is not correlated with personal characteristics, including ethnicity and socioeconomic standing. That is, there is little room for statistical theories of discrimination. However, our experiments also show that people do use the personal characteristics of others when given the opportunity to choose partners. Our research finds evidence of preference-based discrimination or stereotyping. Moreover, evidence of discrimination or stereotyping vanishes almost completely once information on others' behavior is provided.

Nonetheless, subjects tend to prefer groups of tall people, women, and white-looking people. While evidence of discrimination is almost completely eliminated by revealing information on others' behavior, there is still evidence that race is an important factor even when information is revealed. Intriguingly, while tall women are preferred in the absence of information, they are less likely to be selected for the top ranks when information is revealed. The effect of race, however, is constant. This effect even survives when subjects are given incentives that make their behavior orthogonal to their personal characteristics.

The fact that not everyone uses others' characteristics in ranking in the same way provides further evidence of stereotyping or taste-based discrimination. While there is agreement across genders and ethnicities that taller people and women are more desirable partners, the effect of race on rankings is basically explained by the behavior of men and white participants. Since our experiments show that discrimination can be erased when information on performance is available, we conclude that these results are an expression of prejudice.

Our research has important policy implications. People seem to have preconceptions of the behavior of others that create a barrier to access. That is, if people are excluded based on their appearance, those being excluded are denied the opportunity of showing what they are capable of doing. Given that once information is revealed most discrimination goes away, creating opportunities for people to interact with one another is advisable. While our experiments show that information on others' performance is quite useful in solving initial stereotypes, it is clear that, in practical terms, it is difficult to provide precise and reliable measures of a person's performance. That is, it is not clear that policy makers have the tools to make signals clearer or to make measurement of performance in the workplace better. It is also entirely possible that, while discrimination in the workplace is diminished through public intervention, other avenues such as marriage or neighborhood sorting survive.

Overall, our research shows that carefully designed experiments are useful for identifying the nature of discrimination.

Notes

1. This mechanism ensured that the opportunity to participate in the experiment was distributed equally across the population. From these databases, we sampled all of the potential subjects that complied with all of our criteria. From the resulting subsample, we performed a random lottery and selected the individuals to be part of the experiment.
2. We also recruited from Gamarra (an industrial area in metropolitan Lima). We drew on a pre-census of all the establishments in Gamarra, and this allowed us

to randomly select buildings from which to invite subjects. This area is one of the largest clusters of small- to medium-size enterprises in metropolitan Lima and represents a rich mix of population with regard to place of origin and socioeconomic background.

3. This includes the following categories: incomplete non-university tertiary, complete non-university tertiary, incomplete university tertiary, and complete university tertiary.

4. There are 100 céntimos in 1 nuevo sol (the Peruvian currency). At the time of the study, US$1 = S/.3.2.

5. With 20 subjects, each subject would need to rank 3,876 groups.

6. Palfrey and Prisbey (1997) show evidence consistent with subjects not contributing their full endowment, even when it is payoff dominant to do so.

7. The minimum wage in Peru is about US$1 per hour.

8. The Cronback alpha for inter-rater reliability is another measure of agreement among raters. The coefficient is 0.9565 for the white dimension, 0.9285 for the indigenous dimension, 0.9451 for the black dimension, and 0.9113 for the Asian dimension.

9. Three post-experiment surveys are missing from the sample.

10. Results are robust to different specifications.

11. The results in tables 2.3 and 2.4 are similar if using rank-ordered logit or robust standard errors. The reported results do not use robust standard errors. The results are also similar if using racial intensities of trained raters.

12. The results in tables 2.5 through 2.7 are similar if using probit or robust standard errors.

References

Andreoni, James, and Ragan Petrie. 2006. "Beauty, Gender, and Stereotypes: Evidence from Laboratory Experiments." Experimental Economics Working Paper 2006-2002, Georgia State University, Atlanta.

Bogomolnaia, Anna, and Matthew O. Jackson. 2002. "The Stability of Hedonic Coalition Structures." *Games and Economic Behavior* 38 (2): 201–30.

Bohnet, Iris, and Bruno Frey. 1999. "The Sound of Silence in Prisoner's Dilemma and Dictator Games." *Journal of Economic Behavior and Organization* 38 (1): 43–57.

Burnham, Terence C. 2003. "Engineering Altruism: A Theoretical and Experimental Investigation of Anonymity and Gift Giving." *Journal of Economic Behavior and Organization* 50 (1): 133–44.

Carter, Michael, and Marco Castillo. 2003. "An Experimental Approach to Social Capital in South Africa." Agricultural and Applied Economics Staff Paper 448, University of Wisconsin-Madison.

Castillo, Marco, and Ragan Petrie. 2006. "Discrimination in the Lab: Experiments Exploring the Impact of Performance and Appearance on Sorting." Andrew Young School of Policy Studies Research Paper 07-17, Georgia State University, Atlanta.

———. 2007. "Discrimination in the Warplace: Evidence from a Civil War in Peru." Andrew Young School of Policy Studies Research Paper 07-37, Georgia State University, Atlanta.

Cummings, Ronald, and Paul Ferraro. 2003. "Inter-Cultural Discrimination in the Ultimatum Game: Ethnic Bias and Statistical Discrimination." Environmental

Policy and Experimental Laboratory Working Paper 2003-02, Georgia State University, Atlanta.

Eckel, Catherine, and Rick Wilson. 2002. "Conditional Trust: Sex, Race, and Facial Expressions in a Trust Game." Working Paper, Rice University, Houston. http://www.ruf.rice.edu/~rkw/RKW_FOLDER/PC_2002_RKW.pdf.

Hammermesh, Daniel, and Jeff Biddle. 1994. "Beauty and the Labor Market." *American Economic Review* 84 (5): 1174–94.

Kagel, John, and Alvin Roth. 1995. *Handbook of Experimental Economics*. Princeton, NJ: Princeton University Press.

List, John. 2004. "The Nature and Extent of Discrimination in the Marketplace: Evidence from the Field." *Quarterly Journal of Economics* 119 (1): 49–89.

Mobius, Markus, and Tanya Rosenblatt. 2005. "Why Beauty Matters." *American Economic Review* 96 (1): 222–35.

Ñopo, Hugo, Jaime Saavedra, and Maximo Torero. 2004. "Ethnicity and Earnings in Urban Peru." IZA Discussion Paper 980, Institute for the Study of Labor (IZA), Bonn, Germany.

Palfrey, Thomas R., and Jeffrey E. Prisbey. 1997. "Anomalous Behavior in Public Goods Experiments: How Much and Why?" *American Economic Review* 87 (5): 829–46.

Petrie, Ragan. 2004. "Trusting Appearances and Reciprocating Looks: Experimental Evidence on Gender and Race Preferences." Unpublished mss., Georgia State University, Atlanta.

Riach, Peter A., and Judith Rich. 2002. "Field Experiments of Discrimination in the Market Place." *Economic Journal* 112 (483): F480–518.

Torero, Maximo, Jaime Saavedra, Hugo Ñopo, and Javíer Escobal. 2004. "An Invisible Wall? The Economics of Social Exclusion in Peru." In *Social Inclusion and Economic Development in Latin America,* ed. Mayra Buvinic, Jacqueline Mazza, and Ruthanne Deutsch. Washington, DC: Inter-American Development Bank.

3

Discrimination in the Provision of Social Services to the Poor: A Field Experimental Study

Juan-Camilo Cárdenas, Natalia Candelo, Alejandro Gaviria, Sandra Polanía, and Rajiv Sethi

State provision of social services to the poor takes place within an exchange relationship in which a local officer, representing the state's social welfare function, delivers services to the poor, based on limited resources that need to be allocated according to criteria compatible with the state's priorities. In turn, the state's priorities are supposed to reflect the social choice preferences of citizen-voters with respect to redistribution and assistance to the poor.

Because of the nature of this relationship, where private information and coordination failures can emerge, the quality and distribution of those services are subject to potential problems of efficiency and equity when local officers deliver services that are not compatible with the social welfare function. For instance, providers may include particular groups that should not receive services or may exclude others that should be covered. Further, there is room for corruption and misallocation of resources for private interests. In general, there is a principal-agent problem, and observation of the provider's actions can be costly.

Juan-Camilo Cárdenas and Alejandro Gaviria are with the Universidad de los Andes in Bogotá; Natalia Candelo is with the University of Texas at Dallas; Sandra Polanía is with the Università degli Studi di Siena; and Rajiv Sethi is with Barnard College, Columbia University. This paper was undertaken as part of the Latin American and Caribbean Research Network Project "Discrimination and Economic Outcomes." Many people contributed to the execution of this project.

We therefore rely to some extent on the moral, normative, and self-regulatory systems reflected in the individual preferences of the local officer. The (private) decisions of the local officer are mediated by his or her individual social preferences with respect to altruism, reciprocity, trust, and distributive justice toward the beneficiaries of social programs. These traits and mechanisms, we believe, capture most of the important aspects of pro-social behavior that provide the basis of the social contract and public policies aimed at helping the most vulnerable groups in society.

If the social preferences of the local officers are well aligned with the social welfare function of the policy being implemented, the outcomes will be socially desirable with regard to efficiency and equity. Otherwise, scarce resources targeted at the poor may be misallocated, reducing the effectiveness of the policy.

The study presented in this chapter is aimed precisely at understanding the micro foundations of the interactions involved in the provision of social services to the poor. In particular, it uses an experimental approach to understand the preferences and behavior of both the individuals who are involved in the provision of social services and the individuals who are potential beneficiaries, the poor. The study draws subjects from the general population of public officials and citizens in the city and not from college students, as usually done in experimental studies.

Pro-social preferences are essential for understanding behavior in social exchanges where there is room for strategic use of private information, which may lead to losses in social efficiency and equity. Such is the case when agents (public officials) have to deliver services to the poor on behalf of the principal (policy makers and citizen-voters). We implemented a battery of canonical experiments used for measuring social preferences (Bowles 2004; Camerer and Fehr 2004) in order to capture a series of components of pro-sociality—namely, distributive justice, altruism, reciprocity, reciprocal altruism, fairness, trust, and social sanctioning. These elements are essential within a social contract that, as in Colombia, expects to deliver social services to the more vulnerable groups of society.

In this study, we explore the foundations of pro-social behavior by public officials as well as the poor in the delivery of social services (education, health services, and nutrition). Dimensions such as altruism, reciprocity, aversion to inequity, trust, distributive justice, and social sanction are all important in understanding the reasons why, as a society, we target resources toward the poor. However, these dimensions might be influenced by factors that should—and others that should not—guide the allocation of resources (for example, level of education or number of dependents as opposed to race or marital status). Discretion on the part of public officials might lead to discrimination against certain groups, creating social losses related to equity and efficiency in the allocation of scarce public resources. In addition, the poor who are actual or potential beneficiaries of social programs might also self-discriminate if their expectations about the processes of discrimination affect their expectations of or application for such services.

Our experimental strategy emerges from the hypothesis that the allocation of resources to the poor is mediated by (a) the social preferences and behavior of the local officials in charge of the provision and (b) the preferences and behavior of the potential beneficiaries that could affect self-selection and self-discrimination. The overall null hypothesis is that public officials will allocate resources according to the constitutional mandate and the objectives of the specific public policy, based on the attributes of the recipients. The null hypothesis also implies that, according to the constitutional mandate, there should be no discrimination against certain groups based on their race, ethnicity, occupation, marital status, or other conditions (such as being displaced—*desplazado*—by violence from their previous residence to the city).

Using the experimental designs and the collection of data on recruited subjects, we were able to capture a significant portion of public officials' motivations when allocating resources, as well as the motivations of the poor when expressing their expectations and observing their realized outcomes both outside our lab and during our experiments.

We designed a battery of five two-person games where players 1 represent public officials who allocate resources to provide social assistance or aid to players 2 (the poor) based on the sociodemographic characteristics of the latter. The games designed for the study are a dictator game (DG), a strategy method ultimatum game (UG), a trust game (TG), a third-party punishment game (3PP) and a distributive dictator game (DDG).[1]

As far as we know, there are no previous experimental studies on other-regarding or pro-social behavior in which both senders and receivers have the characteristics of our sample (actual public officials and actual beneficiaries of these programs), except partially the studies by Fong, Bowles, and Gintis (2005) and a new study by Fong and Luttmer (2008) with Katrina victims, both being conducted with U.S. samples.

Each of our participants took part in a session with all five games, but interacted with different people in each game, repeating the interaction with the same player on only a few occasions. All games were played as one-shot interactions, with no communication or pre-play interaction among players. In all cases, players had partial information about the sociodemographic characteristics of each other.

We recruited both *target* subjects (actual public officials and actual beneficiaries of social programs) and *control* subjects (students and employees in the public and private sectors). By target players, we mean people who, in their daily life, face the type of choices the study wants to address. Target participants were recruited in public social service organizations and in welfare programs' waiting lines, on the streets, and in various lower-income neighborhoods. Controls were recruited among students and employees. In a fifth game, a third player judged and allocated resources to punish behavior considered antisocial. These third players were recruited from the overall population.

The target sample participating in the study came from public officials working for different government organizations and from beneficiaries of education, health, nutrition, and child care programs in different locations in Bogotá. The set of experimental and survey data contains information on a total sample of 513 subjects who participated in all of the experimental activities. Although we recruited 568 people, for various reasons 55 of them did not show up for the games stage. All recruits were given Col$2,000[2] as part of their show-up fee in order to induce credibility and to subsidize the cost of transportation from their home or workplace to the campus site we assigned for the experiments stage. Once they agreed to participate and attended their sessions, they were paid the rest of their earnings based on the decisions in the experiments. An additional Col$2,000 was paid to each participant to cover his or her cost of transportation back home. On average, each participant in the roles of players 1 and 2 received Col$16,400 and Col$9,300, respectively.

Overall, our results replicate the pattern of similar experiments regarding pro-social behavior such as altruism, reciprocity, fairness, altruistic punishment, and social norms across the world (Cárdenas and Carpenter 2008; Fehr and Gachter 2002; Gintis and others 2005; Henrich and others 2004, 2006). However, we explore a particular context of social exchange in which states undertake to help the poor through the decisions of local officials and the individual preferences of those officials may affect outcomes. The data show that vulnerable groups do trigger more pro-sociality on the part of service providers, although some unexpected results, such as less pro-sociality on the part of actual public officials and some variation due to the characteristics of the recipients, should give rise to interesting debates about the distributive justice arising from the discretionary power of public servants.

Discretion and Discrimination in the Provision of Social Services

Discrimination and social exclusion in various domains of economic life can create losses in efficiency and equity. Particular characteristics of individuals—many of which they do not choose during their lives but which they have acquired for genetic or other reasons—cause them to be excluded from receiving the benefits of certain social exchanges regarding the market, the state, or life in the community. Such exclusion creates efficiency losses in many cases, and equity problems in general, as credit, land, and labor markets are subject to discrimination and exclusion. The political arena can also exclude people from expressing their preferences and affecting outcomes in their favor.

Much of the theoretical and empirical literature can be classified into two major approaches—statistical discrimination (Arrow 1973; Phelps 1972) and the taste for discrimination (Becker 1971)—that focus on imperfect markets where room for discrimination can affect economic outcomes.[3] The housing and labor markets are among the most frequently studied domains in the discrimination literature. Experiments, audit studies, surveys, and other methods have been used to explore how workers can be discriminated against in labor contracts and job application processes. Race and gender have been systematically tested as characteristics where discrimination can occur and create equity and efficiency losses. Housing and credit markets have also been subject to inquiries regarding discrimination.

Less studied, however, are issues of discrimination in the provision of social services, particularly to the poor. Social programs aimed at improving access to education, health, and child care for the poor are good examples of these settings. As in imperfect markets, the provision of public goods and social services by the state can also be subject to discrimination, with certain individuals treated in a less favorable way than others with equivalent constitutional rights or under the same provider and location. Unfortunately, being poor often coincides with having some of the characteristics for which individuals are discriminated against and excluded. Indigenous and Afro descendants frequently appear among the poorest and most excluded in the Latin American region and therefore are especially vulnerable. Migrants (*campesinos*) from rural areas additionally suffer various kinds of discrimination when seeking access to the same services that others have received.

Latin America, as one of the world's most unequal regions but also one of the most diverse in terms of race, ethnicity, and social background, imposes special challenges with respect to discrimination and social exclusion. Furthermore, the region is undergoing a dramatic transformation of urban-rural dynamics that is creating particular problems we have yet to understand in depth. Persistent rural poverty and inequality, economic changes in the agriculture sector, cultural change, political conflicts, and civil wars have created a migration to the cities that is challenging the state's provision of public goods and social services, particularly to the poorest citizens, who are expanding the metropolitan populations of the region. Meanwhile, decentralization and devolution of the state are creating greater challenges to local governments, which are charged with providing these services to the poor in cities that are evolving into worlds within worlds, with both wealthy neighborhoods and slums with severe social needs. Thus political tensions in the developing and developed world emerge when the excluded can observe that others have access to public goods and social services that they do not.

Governments have responded with systems targeting the very poor, creating survey procedures and algorithms to rank poor households for the distribution of such social services. Many of these targeted programs, labeled as SISBEN[4] (Irarrázaval 2004), are in place in the region. These programs target the most vulnerable in an attempt to discriminate in a positive way that achieves redistributive goals. Yet negative discrimination and exclusion remain. Irarrázaval (2004) recognizes that some individuals remain excluded as a result of the manipulation of information. His estimations suggest that these problems may exist in Chile and Colombia. Some of these could occur because of discrimination, but the evidence does not support this contention. Núñez and Espinosa (2005) also find statistical support from the Encuesta de Calidad de Vida 2004 in Colombia for the existence of errors of inclusion (households that should not be but are receiving subsidies) and errors of exclusion (households that are in need but are excluded), discriminating against households with elderly persons, persons displaced by violence, and household heads with low levels of education.

Gaviria and Ortiz (2005) provide statistical evidence for Colombia suggesting that minorities may be asymmetrically assisted, for instance, in the subsidized health program. Using self-reported data for ethnicity, they find that the indigenous have higher likelihoods of being included in the state-subsidized health program[5] than Afro descendants, controlling for factors such as location, education, age, consumption, and employment. The causalities, however, are still undefined. One plausible reason is that greater amounts of national government transfers flow to areas with larger fractions of indigenous groups than to areas with Afro descendants. Also, the indigenous have a longer tradition of social cohesion and organization for asserting their rights before the government than Afro descendants, who only recently, during the new constitutional process, have engaged in social organization and collective action. Discrimination may explain why Afro descendants are less likely than others to enter the social protection program given the steps involved in targeting, enrollment, and service delivery.

Further, there is documented evidence in sentences from the constitutional court in Colombia[6] using the mechanism of the *tutela*,[7] where individuals who have been classified erroneously argue that their rights and the principle of equality have been violated in their classification into the SISBEN indexing system.

In general, behavioral issues are at the core of the problem. For instance, if there is a "taste for discrimination," those who generate discrimination (employers) will have to show it in their other-regarding preferences, which could be validated empirically or experimentally.

Bertrand and Mullainathan (2004) have devised a clever experiment in the field, randomly sending constructed résumés in response to newspaper ads for job postings and observing the probability of being called for an interview, to test for discrimination in the labor market based on prejudices emerging from the names used and without photos or ethnic background. The results are astonishing: not only did being identified as black decrease the probability of getting an interview, but the marginal gains from other characteristics such as education and home location mattered more strongly for résumés with a "white" name. Those results, however, only explain the thoughts and behaviors of those deciding to call applicants for an interview.

As for government programs that provide social protection to the poor, rather little has been said about the behavioral aspects of local officials' decision making. We can agree that programs and policies aimed at helping the poor are based on pro-social preferences of the majority who vote and thus elect and appoint the officials who will run those programs. Still, the contract between officials and the electorate is incomplete and subject to asymmetries of information. In addition, the individual preferences of those in government and executing the programs are often unobservable.

Yet if we recognize that we are in a world of imperfect markets and public goods problems, the role of the state, as evidenced by the behavior and preferences of its representatives, is crucial. As eloquently stated by Bowles and Gintis (2000, 1425), "Many are now convinced that John Stuart Mill's injunction that we must devise rules such that the 'duties and the interests' of government officials would coincide should be shelved, along with the assumptions of the Fundamental Theorem of Welfare Economics, in the museum of utopian designs."

Motivations from the Field

Before conducting the experimental sessions, we reviewed at least two important sources of data regarding violations of constitutional rights based on discrimination. One is the constitutional court, and the other is the Defensoría del Pueblo (public ombudsman). Both of these gave us an idea of how to construct our protocols and how to design the recruitment strategy across public agencies and geographic locations of the city.[8] These data showed an increase in the number of cases that allege discriminatory actions from the state and provided some clues regarding the kind of characteristics to include in the treatment and control variables for our experiments.

In regard to the purpose of this study and based on the results, we introduced into the random sample demographic features that are subject to discrimination. In addition, we included the category of *reinsertados,*[9] because in the process of this inquiry we found numerous cases in which these individuals experienced social exclusion when they applied for a social service.

The experimental strategy for this project emerged from the hypothesis that discrimination in the provision of social services to the poor is mediated by (a) the social preferences and behavior of the local officials in charge of the provision and (b) the preferences and behavior of the potential beneficiaries that could affect self-selection and self-discrimination. Therefore, we designed an experiment in which these two players (service providers and beneficiaries) interact and are informed by the characteristics that might affect the strategic behavior in the interaction. Some of those characteristics are supposed to guide the decisions of the providers in the correct direction—that is, aligned with a social welfare function that reflects their society's preferences—but other characteristics may bias behavior toward discriminatory outcomes and against the constitutional mandate.

The context and frame of the game is rather simple: a government program, inspired by a constitutional mandate and a policy design, involves a social welfare function that needs to be executed by local officials who aim to improve the well-being of the target population, in this case, the poor, through their privately observed actions. These local officials allocate scarce resources, and that allocation affects the well-being of beneficiaries. In some cases, beneficiaries have room for strategic responses that may affect their own outcomes or even those of local officials.

The behavior of any local official is expected to reflect the social welfare function of the government plan, but such officials, as agents whose behavior is only partially observable to the principal (the government agency), may not act entirely according to the social objective and may include behavioral responses that reflect their own personal social preferences and biases. In particular, preferences toward social, ethnic, or racial equity, among others, can affect the behavior of local officials during the process of receiving applications from and providing social services to the poor.

In various ways, local officials act as bounded dictators who assign resources to beneficiaries of social programs within a certain set of rules but also with some discretion in their actions. Their choices—only partially observable to the principal—affect how funds are allocated and distributed among different target groups subject to discrimination and biases of various kinds. However, the social preferences of the poor can also influence the possibilities of discrimination. Social groups that expect to be discriminated against may be more tolerant of unfair or unequal allocations. If, in equilibrium, such norms are replicated and widespread, local officials may find it morally acceptable to sustain current levels of discrimination without personal costs.

An Experimental Design on Distributive Justice, Altruism, Inequity Aversion, Trust, and Reciprocity

Various dimensions lie at the core of the social exchange that occurs in the process of providing social services to the poor. These dimensions are critical in the interactions among the government program (the principal), the local official (the agent) in charge of executing the program, and the beneficiary (the recipient) of the social service. These dimensions include altruism, distributive justice, aversion to inequity, trust, and reciprocity. Altruism and aversion to inequity are at the core of pro-poor redistributive programs. Voter preferences are thus reflected in the design of government programs, and local officials are expected to implement programs that improve the well-being of the poorest and reduce social inequalities. However, that process can be affected by discrimination against certain groups (for example, racial or ethnic groups). Such discrimination, which in theory should not occur if the programs are designed in accordance with the constitutional mandate, can in fact occur because of the discretionary role that local officials have in the application, approval, and provision process.

Trust and reciprocity are important mechanisms in a relationship that involves the possibility of gains or losses because of coordination failures, interdependence, or externalities. The provision of public goods, or the co-financing of public projects between the state and the community, depends on mutual trust for the optimization of available resources. Reciprocity can either sustain or destroy cooperation in the provision of public goods that are crucial to the poor. Once again, preferences that involve discrimination against certain groups can limit trust or trigger negative reciprocity, reducing the social efficiency of pro-poor programs.

In this study, we conducted standard and modified experiments in the field that have been used widely for detecting and measuring degrees of altruism, inequity aversion, trust, and reciprocity. In treatment and control sessions, we provided information to players about features of their counterparts in the experiment (for example, gender, status, race, ethnicity, origin, occupation, family composition). Through these field experiments, we observed and measured the degrees of discrimination that may affect these dimensions.

However, our protocols included a mild framing in every task where players were told that the game situation was similar to that where people request social services at local public agencies. We expected both the providers and the recipients to be familiar with such interactions, although from a different standpoint. Nevertheless, decisions remained private and confidential, maintaining the discretionary nature of allocation decisions on the part of public officials as well as response strategies on the part of beneficiaries. The five experiments selected and the reasons for including them are as follows:

- *Dictator game* (Forsythe and others 1994; Kahneman, Knetsch, and Thaler 1986). Player 1 decides on the distribution of a fixed amount of Col\$20 and sends a fraction to player 2, who receives that amount. Player 1 keeps the remaining part. This game provides information about pure altruism—that is, willingness to decrease one's well-being for increasing the well-being of another.
- *Ultimatum game* (Güth, Schmittberger, and Schwarze 1982). Player 1 (proposer) decides on the distribution of a fixed amount and sends a fraction to player 2 (responder), who receives that amount. If the responder accepts, the distribution happens; if the responder rejects, both players receive nothing, and the money returns to the experimenter. The ultimatum game provides information on equity, reciprocal fairness, and reciprocity as mechanisms to enforce social norms. Negative reciprocity and conformism can be critical for understanding the social preferences of both local officers and beneficiaries of social programs.
- *Trust game* (Berg, Dickhaut, and McCabe 1995). Both players 1 and 2 are endowed with Col\$8. Player 1 (proposer) can send a fraction of his or her initial endowment to player 2 (responder). The amount sent is tripled before it reaches player 2, who then decides how to split the tripled amount plus the initial endowment with player 1. The trust or investment game offers critical information on trust and trustworthiness, which is critical to augmenting efficiency in the provision of public goods.
- *Third-party punishment* (Fehr and Fischbacher 2004). This game is based on the dictator game but includes a third party, player 3, who receives an additional endowment that he or she can keep or use to punish player 1 if player 3 considers the action of player 1 as punishable due to fairness or justice considerations. Player 3 can punish by spending part of his or her endowment to reduce the payoffs of player 1. This game captures preferences for costly punishment of socially undesirable outcomes and willingness to punish unfair actions.
- *Distributive dictator game.*[10] Player 1 receives a fixed payment of, say, Col\$10 as a salary for performing the following allocation task. Then player 1 ranks five players 2 in the order in which they each will receive a fixed payment or a voucher for Col\$10 determined by a random distribution from one to five possible payments. The random number of vouchers between one and five decides the first N players 2 who will receive the Col\$10. The remaining players will receive nothing. Player 1 observes a card for each of the five players 2 that includes a picture of his or her face and basic information

on the player's demographic and socioeconomic condition. This game measures preferences for distributive justice, mediated by the characteristics of the beneficiaries, including those not associated with deservedness, but rather with discrimination. The results of this game are discussed in much more detail in Cárdenas and Sethi (2009).

For any pair of players, each of these games was conducted as one-shot (one round), with an exit survey containing demographic, behavioral, and psychological questions to control for the individual behavior observed in the experiments. All players 1 made decisions on all five games, and all players 2 were involved in each of the five games. Players 3 participated only in the 3PP game. In the following section, we describe in detail how the experimental sessions were conducted. An annex to this chapter includes a detailed description of the experimental design of one session, information on the lab setting, and the samples. Protocols are available from the authors on request.

Data and Results

The experiments provided evidence of certain patterns of behavior that can be summarized as follows. The average participant showed pro-social behavior[11] toward vulnerable groups that were potential or actual beneficiaries of social services. In particular, we observe significant preferences for distributive justice toward the more vulnerable (favoring the weakest or more in need); we also observe altruism (unselfish transfers toward others at one's own cost) and reciprocal altruism and reciprocity (willingness to treat others as one would expect to be treated). Also we find that trust is followed by reciprocity (people who are trusted show higher levels of reciprocity by attaining positive returns on the initial investment) and that third parties adopt social sanctioning as a strategy to sanction, at a personal cost, unfair allocators. As in most experimental literature with nonstudent samples, the 50/50 split of endowments for the dictator, ultimatum, and third-party punishment games is the most common. However, when our players 1 and 2 were both from target samples 2, such levels of pro-social behavior were statistically larger in favor of the poor, compared with our control samples. Further, when players 2 were from our target sample, pro-sociality increased for all players 1, both target and controls. These differences suggest that our design was successful and internally valid in detecting the increased pro-sociality toward more deserving groups in the players 2 sample compared with the controls.

However, when our senders or players 1 were controls and players 2 were targets, offers and pro-social actions in general were even greater than when players 1 were from our target samples, namely, public servants. This result raises an interesting question: Why would target players 1 (actual public servants) be less generous than their controls? We do not believe that public officials engaged in providing social services to the poor are less pro-social; instead, we believe that they incorporate more strategic factors into their decisions regarding the recipients of transfers. For instance, public officials reward education and shorter time of unemployment among players 2. Further, based on a survey questionnaire for estimating an index of humanitarian-egalitarian preferences and for Protestant work ethic (Fong, Bowles, and Gintis 2005; Katz and Hass 1989), we find that our target public officials showed higher levels of these two indicators than their controls. When explaining variation in offers and pro-social actions by players 1, we find a set of attributes from players 2 that triggered or reduced pro-social behavior from the former to the latter. Women who had more dependents, especially if those dependents were minors, received higher altruistic offers than men. Black and indigenous people received higher or equal offers, but never lower offers, than other racial groups.[12] Occupation, social condition, and current activity seem to affect offers. The unemployed as well as those with less education were treated with more generosity, but street recyclers and street vendors were often sent lower offers, confirming anecdotal evidence of stigmatization and suspicion toward certain activities.

The political conflict manifests itself in the results. People displaced by violence were given higher offers, while ex-combatants were given lower offers, controlling for the rest of the sociodemographic characteristics of these particular samples. In fact, we find evidence of discrimination against ex-combatants, not only in the offers sent to them in the dictator and ultimatum games, but also in the reluctance of third parties to punish unfair behavior toward ex-combatants. This behavior is confirmed by the lower expected offers declared by the ex-combatants themselves. Our target group of players 2 showed higher levels of conformism than their controls. First, they were willing to accept more unfair offers in the ultimatum game—that is, their rejection rates are lower for unfair offers. We also find that, on average, expected offers by players 2 from players 1 were slightly, but consistently, lower than actual offers. However, in all games, the expected and actual offers are positively correlated.

Sample of Participants

We contacted a total of 568 people as players 1, 2, and 3, including both target and control subjects. Of the 568 recruited, 55 people (9.7 percent) did not show up for the game stage, although they had received Col$2,000 as part of the show-up fee, which represented a sign of commitment on the part of the researchers and provided assistance for the cost of transportation to the location of the games. We attempted to contact those who did not show up and found that some had reported false phone numbers, some could not come at the time because of unexpected family or work events, and some believed that the study was a hoax.[13] In fact, almost 18 percent of the individuals recruited to be players 2 did not show up. These people had to make the longest trips across the city to attend the games and were more likely to have doubts regarding the exercise's credibility. Concerned about the possible presence of selection bias, we examined the final sample and compared it to the recruited sample. As shown in table 3A.5 in the annex, only 9 percent of players 1, 18 percent of players 2, and 2 percent of players 3 did not attend the sessions. For players 1, we considered the transport costs as a determinant of attendance and modified the experimental setup; in the first six sessions 18 people did not attend (attendance rate was, on average, 64 percent). Beginning with the seventh session, five individuals did not attend (only 2.5 percent of the recruits). There are no significant differences between those who did not attend and those who did. We also checked the significance of the difference between the characteristics of players 2 who attended and those who did not. Players 2 who did not attend were from the target group, were older, had not lived in Bogotá all their lives, were displaced, were living as a couple, had a lower monthly expenditure level, and belonged to a lower stratum than people who attended the sessions. The people who did not want to participate from the beginning reflect a similar type of self-selection bias found in other studies, largely because we employed a similar recruitment strategy, presenting this as a confidential, economically rewarded academic study.

Summarizing the samples for the five games, table 3.1 presents the number of observations obtained in our sample, the players involved, and the Nash equilibrium predictions for each game based on backward induction for self-oriented (selfish) players. The "maximum social efficiency" in the table corresponds to the maximum amount of money that a pair could earn in a one-shot game, given the feasible action sets. In the case of dictator and ultimatum games, player 1 divides the endowed money (Col$20,000) given to each pair. In the case of the trust game, the maximum efficiency is achieved when player 1 transfers the entire endowment of Col$8,000 to player 2. This amount is tripled and then added to the endowment of Col$8,000 of player 2, yielding the maximum social pie possible for the pair. For the third-party punishment game, the amount corresponds to the amount endowed to the trio of players 1, 2, and 3. Finally, the distributive dictator game yields Col$60,000 if the random number obtained is 5; then all five recipients obtain the Col$10,000 voucher plus the fixed payment to player 1.

Table 3.1 is the benchmark point for each of the games. Depending on the game, the maximum social efficiency is achieved through chance for the DDG—dependent on player 1's choice (TG) or player 2's choice (UG)—but is determined automatically for the DG and 3PP games. Likewise, the level

Table 3.1 Summary of the Sessions

Games	DDG	DG	UG	TG	3PP
Total observations	1,130	729	729	728	486
Players involved in the game	1–6	1, 2	1, 2	1, 2	1, 2, 3
Maximum social efficiency ($Col, thousands)	40	20	20	32	30
Predictions for the offers by player 1[a] assuming self-oriented maximizing players ($Col, thousands)	n.a.	0	1	0	0

Source: Authors' compilation.

Note: US\$1 = Col\$2,490.66 (monthly mean average for May to July, 2006). http://www.banrep.gov.co. DDG = distributive dictator game; DG = dictator game; UG = ultimatum game; TG = trust game; 3PP = third-party punishment game.

a. Nash equilibrium.

of equality achieved depends on player 1's choice (DG, UG, TG, 3PP) or player 2's choice (UG, TG). Players 3 decide on both efficiency and equity when choosing whether to punish players 1.

Based on these benchmarks, in the following section we report the descriptive statistics for the offers sent by players 1, followed by the average behavior of players 2 and 3. Later we explore how the variation in these decisions could be explained by the attributes of the participants in the experiments, using regression analysis.

Average Offers: Target versus Control Groups

Figure 3.1 compares the results of average amounts offered by players 1 to players 2, in percentage of the initial endowment, by type of subsample (target or control), and across the four games that involve sending an amount from an initial endowment (DG, UG, TG, 3PP). The four panels also include the average amount offered by player 1 and the expected offer that player 2 reported before knowing the actual value. Also included is the average reported for these experiments by several international studies, as reported in Cárdenas and Carpenter (2008). The upper-left panel (target-target) corresponds to the interactions in which both player 1 and player 2 were our target sample of public officials and the poor, respectively.

An overview of the amounts offered suggests that for all treatments there is a strong trend toward fairness: in the DG, UG, and 3PP games, player 1 decides how much to send from an initial endowment of Col\$20,000.

Figure 3.1 Offers and Expected Amounts of Money in the Dictator, Ultimatum, Trust, and Third-Party Punishment Games

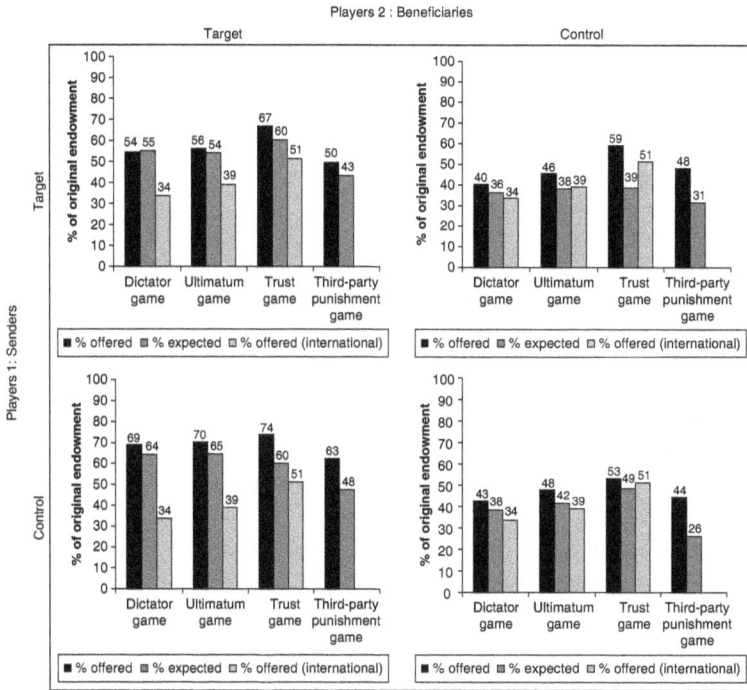

Source: Authors' compilation. International offers were calculated through data presented by Cárdenas and Carpenter (2008).

Offers fell within the range of 40 to 60 percent for these three games. Further, in the ultimatum game, as expected, offers from the dictator were higher given the possibility of punishment by player 2, who could reject the offer and "burn" the entire amount. However, the difference is statistically significant only for the players who were controls (p value = 0.0449), as expected and as seen in the literature, where the fear of rejection of an unfair offer increased the offer made by players 1. When the recipient (player 2) was part of the target sample, the difference is not significant (p value = 0.1519), suggesting that both games were seen in similar ways by target and control players 1: as transfers that express altruistic motivations toward the target players 2. However, both DG and UG offers were larger when the recipient was a target player (p value = 0.000 in both cases, supported by the regression analysis later on).

The trust game illustrates another dimension of pro-sociality, in which player 1 trusts player 2 and expects the latter to reciprocate, creating a larger and fairly distributed pie. Players 1, on average, sent between 50 and 70 percent of their endowment, depending on the treatment, and target players 2 sent larger offers. Both target and control players 1 sent larger offers to target players 2 than to their controls. This suggests that altruistic motivations may also be involved in the trust game.

In the case of the third-party punishment game (3PP), we again observe generosity from players 1, in this case mediated by the possibility that player 3 could punish player 1. If players 1 expect players 3 to sanction their unfair behavior, they should behave in a more generous manner compared to the dictator offers. However, we find an unexpected result. The fear of sanctioning by players 3 decreased the offers from players 1, if compared to dictator offers, by 6 percent (p value = 0.0133) for the entire sample. These differences remain for subsamples, such as only target players 2 (p value = 0.0083) or only target players 1 (p value = 0.0206). The anticipation of punishment may induce players 1 to "save" some earnings to compensate for the expected sanction. In fact, the punishment rates for noncontrol samples reinforce the idea that sanctioning is heavier when players 2 are from the target subsample.

In general, the offers observed are higher than the international averages for such games (figure 3.1). Our interpretation is simple: our framing explicitly asked participants to think of familiar situations in which social services are delivered to vulnerable groups, and our nonrandom sample of players 2 (potential or actual beneficiaries of social services) should, on average, trigger greater levels of generosity from players 1, compared with the canonical design of these games, in which the interactions happen among peers and the framing divides a pie between a pair.[14]

In general, when players 2 belonged to the target group, the amount of money received was higher than the amounts received by the control groups. However, control players 1 sent more money than target players 1 to target players 2. Players 2's expectations also follow this pattern—that is, target players 2 expected more money from control players 1 than from target players 1.

This supports the salience of the experimental design and its internal validity—that is, the sampling strategy and the framing used created a differentiated behavior between target and control groups; therefore, we can assign the differences to the deservedness of players 2 or the pro-sociality of players 2 to certain vulnerable groups. Pro-sociality was higher when players 2 were from the target samples than when they were from the controls. Both control and target players 1 sent higher amounts to target players 2. The experimental protocol, which was framed within the situation of a social service provision program, was successful because players 1 were able to distinguish between control and target players 2. Control players 2 had the same expectations as target players 2, since they expected less money from target players 1 than from control players 1. It remains an open question whether lower expected offers by target players 1 were based on pro-social motivations on the part of players 2 or on lower expectations because of lower pro-social motivations by players 2 about players 1. Moreover, offers and expectations in this project are higher than the international offers when target players 2 are involved in the interaction. Nonetheless, offers for control players 2 do not differ greatly from international reports.

Were Expectations Met Regarding Offers?

In general, the expectations of players 2 regarding the amount of money sent by players 1 were lower than the real amount of money sent for most of the games (figure 3.1), showing some kind of pessimism regarding the pro-sociality of society in general. However, the two variables are positively and significantly correlated. Regression analysis available in the annex supports the conclusions that expectations can help to explain the variation in actual choices. Table 3.2 summarizes the correlation coefficients by player between the expected and actual offers, all significant at 1 percent.

Reciprocity and Reciprocal Altruism

The rate of rejections in the ultimatum game is also a key variable for explaining how social preferences affect behavior. If players 1 expect players 2 to have stronger social preferences toward altruism, fairness,

Table 3.2 Correlations between Offers and Expected Values

Variables	Correlation
Dictator game offered by player 1	0.1398***
Dictator game expected by player 2	
Ultimatum game offered by player 1	0.1318***
Ultimatum game expected by player 2	
Trust game offered by player 1	0.1473***
Trust game expected by player 2	
Third-person punishment game offered by player 1	0.1339***
Third-person punishment game expected by player 2	

Source: Authors' compilation.
*** Significant at 1 percent.

and equity, players 1 should increase their offers in comparison with the dictator game.

Figure 3.2 shows the rejection rates of the ultimatum game for all four treatments. Given that we conducted the game using the strategy method, we were able to capture schedules of decisions by each player 2 for each possible offer from player 1. The average of international rejections is calculated from average data presented by Cárdenas and Carpenter (2008), although it should be compared with caution since data on strategy method are scarce. Therefore, we report only the mean rejection for all offers.

As in the existing literature, rejection rates are quite high for very unfair offers from players 1. The rejection rate decreases as offers increase, reaching the minimum level for the most fair offer of 50/50. The rejection rate increases slightly with offers that are excessively generous (see Henrich and others 2004 for a discussion of hyper-fairness in small-scale societies).

We additionally observe a higher level of rejection rates for the treatment where both players 1 and 2 were controls. In other words, when players 2 were the target (poor), we observe lower levels of rejection, that is, higher levels of conformism with unfair outcomes. In our previous result, we show that players' expectations are correlated with actual offers. If players

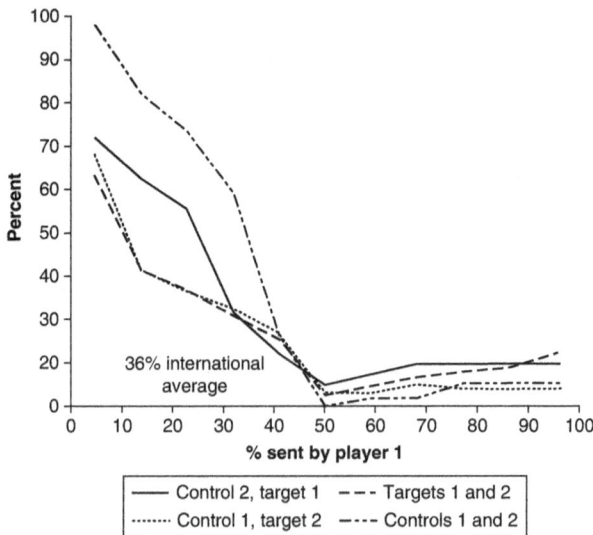

Figure 3.2 Rate of Rejection in the Ultimatum Game

Source: Authors' compilation.

1 think strategically that players 2 are more or less tolerant toward certain offers, the offers in this game will be generally accepted.

Trust and Reciprocity

In figure 3.3, we show the amounts returned by players 2 as a response to different offers sent by players 1. Both are shown in percentages to allow for comparability. The results once again replicate those found in most of the literature (Berg, Dickhaut, and McCabe 1995; Cárdenas and Carpenter 2008). On average, trust from player 1 is rewarded with higher returns from player 2 to player 1. These percentages show that, for all cases, the rate of return on the investment is greater than unity. However, the controls returned higher amounts to players 1 than to target players 2. This could mean that target players 2 claimed more rights to the transferred amounts, because these transactions were framed to capture the provision of social services to the poor. However, when the amounts were low, players 2 (target) were also more generous than their controls when sending back money to players 1.

Third-Party Punishment: Altruistic Punishment

Finally, we present the results for the rates of punishment by players 3. Recall that players 3 only played this game and no other. They were shown

Figure 3.3 Amount Returned by Player 2, Trust Game

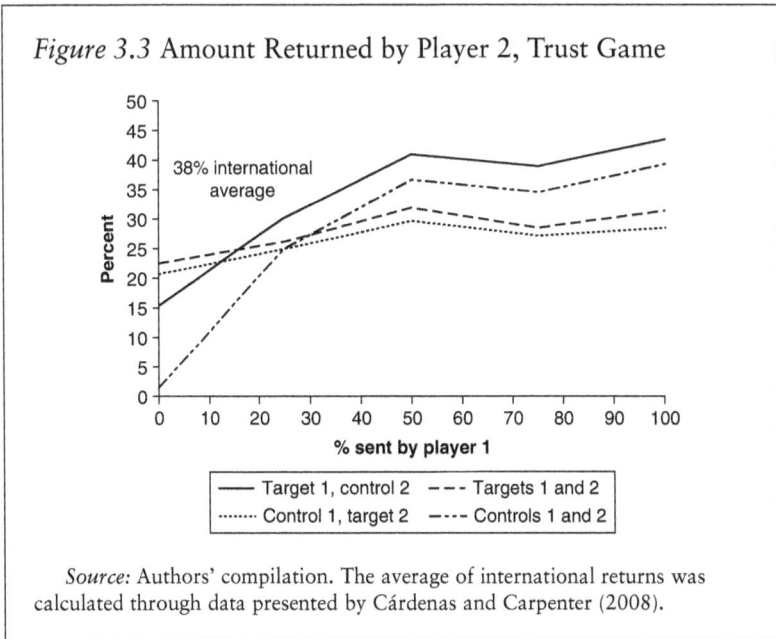

Source: Authors' compilation. The average of international returns was calculated through data presented by Cárdenas and Carpenter (2008).

the offers by players 1 to players 2 and then decided whether to punish at a cost. (They could spend Col$2,000 of their Col$10,000 endowment to have the experimenter take Col$6,000 away from player 1). The sample of players 3 was recruited from the overall population, including both students and nonstudents.

Figure 3.4 shows the rate of punishment observed for different levels of offers by players 1. These data resulted from playing the game by asking players 3 whether they would punish for each possible level of offers from players 1.

The results are also consistent with existing literature on this game (Fehr and Fischbacher 2004; Henrich and others 2006). Third parties were willing to sacrifice their own personal material income to punish unfair behavior by reducing the income of those engaging in unfair actions toward others. The rate of rejection starts at 70 percent when players 1 kept their entire endowment and decreases as offers grew in size. The rate of rejection drops more rapidly for the control-control groups, while remaining steady and higher for the target groups. In fact, even at quite high divisions in favor of players 2, a percentage of players 3 were willing to punish players 1 who would not send most of their endowments. This result completes the overall picture of socially accepted norms of fairness toward the poor and suggests that citizens are willing to reject and even punish unfair behavior.

Figure 3.4 Punish Rate in Third-Party Punishment Game

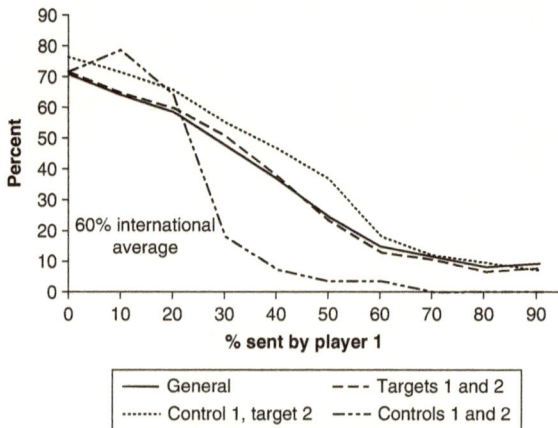

Source: Authors' compilation. The average of international punishment rates was calculated through data presented by Berg, Dickhaut, and McCabe (1995).

Explaining Variations in Pro-Social Behavior

The regression analysis that follows is aimed at explaining the variation in the experimental behavior as a function of the attributes of players 2 and also as a function of the attributes of players 1 observed by players 2. We tested as dependent variables the following, measured as a percentage of the total possible amount in each game:

- Amounts offered by players 1 to players 2 in the DG, UG, TG, and 3PP,
- Punishment rates of players 3,
- Average ranking obtained in the DDG by player 2 from the rankings given by all players 1 who ranked that particular player 2, and
- The same regressions for the amounts expected by players 2 (reported in the annex).

The regressions confirm the statistical differences across treatments (combinations of target and control subsamples for players 1 and 2). They also support the notion that some of the characteristics of the recipients matter for the level of pro-sociality, as supported by the significance of some of the coefficients included as explanatory variables.

Tables 3.3 through 3.7 include several specifications in order to convey how sensitive or robust the results are to different combinations of independent variables. Unfortunately, several of these variables are highly correlated given the high concentration of certain characteristics among vulnerable groups (such as level of education, number of dependent minors, being a female head of household, being displaced). However, we wanted to test whether certain demographic characteristics of players 1 might also play a role in the amounts being offered to players 2. Therefore, we conducted the following regression analyses:

- Dictator game offers by player 1 to player 2 (target and control participants), shown in table 3.3,
- Ultimatum game offers by player 1 to player 2 (target and control participants), shown in table 3.4,
- Trust game offers by player 1 to player 2 (target and control participants), shown in table 3.5,
- Third-party punishment game offers by player 1 to player 2 (target and control participants), shown in table 3.6, and
- Third-party punishment game sanctioning rates by players 3, shown in table 3.7.

A short discussion of the main results is included. In the annex we include other regressions that were conducted, but not reported in the main text.

Dictator game offers by player 1 to player 2 (target and control participants). Specifications 1 and 2, which check for the effects of the basic treatments and attributes of players 2, confirm that players 2 received higher offers when they were part of the target group, but that such increases were lower if player 1 was also a target—that is, an actual public officer. The level of education of player 1 increased the offers, and employees of the health sector were more generous (see table 3.3).

Regarding the attributes of recipients, we find that being female, unemployed, less educated, and with a higher number of minor dependents triggered higher offers, and this result is robust to different specifications. This is consistent with several public policies targeting the more vulnerable groups (many cash transfer programs, for instance, are aimed at single female heads of household).

However, we also find that ex-combatants from the political violence in the country received lower offers than their counterparts, despite the current government and nongovernment social programs aimed at demobilizing these young people. This illustrates a personal bias on the part of players 1. A similar result, but less robust statistically, is found for street recyclers, a group of vulnerable households whose income is based on wandering the streets collecting recyclables and reselling them to major warehouses that supply the recycling industry.

In the lower parts of the table, we also report the cross-effects of player 2 characteristics when player 1 was a target (actual public official) and also for the case of only target players 1, with some interesting results. Public servants rewarded education on the part of player 2 instead of compensating for the lack of it. At the same time, they punished unemployment. These two results might provide some insight into why target players 1 generally offered lower amounts to players 2. As part of their job, these public servants allocate scarce resources to vulnerable groups with a greater purpose, one might think, of bringing these groups out of poverty instead of making purely charitable donations. The latter might be the rationale for the control groups of donors, while public servants would be interested in transferring resources to the poor with the aim of getting them out of poverty (the more educated and currently employed even if under very poor conditions of life). This possible explanation might be reinforced by the fact that public servants made higher offers to target recipients than to controls, showing higher pro-sociality toward vulnerable groups.

Ultimatum game offers by player 1 to player 2 (target and control participants). Once again, the effects of the treatment design with respect to the interaction of target and control players show that target recipients (players 2) triggered higher offers, but that target players 1 (public servants) also made lower offers than control players 1 (see table 3.4). Once again, more educated public officers sent higher amounts.

Table 3.3 Dictator Game Offers by Player 1 to Player 2 (Target and Control Participants)

Method		OLS												
Dependent variable		*Percentage of the allocation offered by player 1 to player 2 in the dictator game*												
Independent variables		*(1)*	*(2)*	*(3)*	*(4)*	*(5)*	*(6)*	*(7)*	*(8)*	*(9)*	*(10)*	*(11)*	*(12)*	*(13)*
	1 if player 1 is a target	−0.055	0.042					−0.314*	0.021	−0.450*				
	1 if player 2 is a target	0.268***	0.289***											
	1 if players 1 & 2 are targets	−0.119*	−0.143**								−0.277	0.160**	−0.293	
Player 1's data: Sociodemographic	1 if player is a woman		−0.002											−0.042
Player 1's data: Sociodemographic	Age		−0.005***											−0.003*
Player 1's data: Sociodemographic	Player's level of education		0.051***											0.028**
Player 1's data: Sociodemographic	Natural logarithm of player's household expenses per capita													0.031
Player 1's data: Sociodemographic	1 if player works in a health institute													0.120***
Player 1's data: Sociodemographic	1 if player works in an education institute													0.035
Player 1's data: Sociodemographic	1 if player works in a nutrition institute													−0.070**
Player 1's data	Player's time worked multiplied by dummy of target player 1		0.007**											
Player 1's data	Player 1's – player 2's household expenses per capita (in Colombian pesos, thousands)		0	0.000**		0.000**	0.000*	0		0	0		0	0.000**

(continued)

Table 3.3 Dictator Game Offers by Player 1 to Player 2 (Target and Control Participants) *(continued)*

Method		OLS												
Dependent variable		Percentage of the allocation offered by player 1 to player 2 in the dictator game												
Independent variables		(1)	(2)	(3)	(4)	(5)	(6)	(7)	(8)	(9)	(10)	(11)	(12)	(13)
Sociodemographic	1 if player 2 is a woman			0.075***		0.065**	0.044	0.084		0.071	0.052		0.062	
	Player 2's age			0.001		0	0.001	0		-0.001	0		0	
	1 if player 2 is single			0.029		0.029	0.021	-0.031		-0.027	-0.008		-0.017	
	1 if player 2 is in common law			0.018		0.022	-0.012	0.009		-0.016	0.042		0.019	
	Player 2's years of education			-0.029**		-0.040***	-0.036***	-0.052***		-0.075***	-0.058***		-0.070***	
	Player 2's number of minor people in charge			0.029***		0.029**	0.009	0.02		-0.005	0.025*		0.017	
	1 if player 2 is unemployed			0.056		0.041	0.046	0.226***		0.232***	0.223***		0.247***	
Discriminatory	1 if player 2 considers herself black				0.039	0.045	0.043		-0.023	0.072		0.037	0.097*	
	1 if player 2 considers herself indigenous				0.068	0.021	0.012		0	0		0	0	
	1 if player 2 is displaced				0.062	-0.033	-0.037		0.214***	0.073		0.061	-0.032	
	1 if player 2 is an ex-combatant				-0.069**	-0.041	-0.031		-0.105	-0.128		-0.072**	-0.025	
	1 if player 2 is a recycling worker				-0.027	-0.091*	-0.024		0.041	-0.012		-0.032	-0.086*	
	1 if player 2 is a street vendor				-0.044	-0.071	-0.02		-0.016	-0.065		-0.028	-0.051	
Games	Percentage of the allocation expected by player 2 from player 1 in the dictator game			0.053	0.135**	0.056	0.002	0.097	0.251***	0.066	0.118	0.377***	0.13	
	Player 2's rank given by player 1 in the distributive dictator game						0.059***							

Table 3.3 Dictator Game Offers by Player 1 to Player 2 (Target and Control Participants) (continued)

Method							OLS						
Dependent variable					Percentage of the allocation offered by player 1 to player 2 in the dictator game								
Independent variables	(1)	(2)	(3)	(4)	(5)	(6)	(7)	(8)	(9)	(10)	(11)	(12)	(13)
1 if player 2 is a woman							-0.041		-0.036				
Player 2's age							0.002		0.003				
1 if player 2 is single							0.072		0.062				
1 if player 2 is in common law							0.038		0.071				
Player 2's years of education							0.052**		0.069**				
Player 2's number of minor people in charge							0.007		0.039				
1 if player 2 is unemployed							-0.180**		-0.180**				
Player 1's – player 2's household expenses per capita (Colombian pesos, thousands)							0.000***		0.000***				
1 if player 2 considers herself black								0.088	-0.026				
1 if player 2 considers herself indigenous								0.097*	0.01				
1 if player 2 is displaced								-0.187**	-0.160*				
1 if player 2 is an ex-combatant								0.051	0.131				
1 if player 2 is a recycling worker								-0.069	-0.096				
1 if player 2 is a street vendor								0	0				
Percentage of the allocation expected by player 1 from player 1 in the dictator game							-0.123	-0.196*	-0.1				

Dummy of target player 1 per player 2's data

(continued)

Table 3.3 Dictator Game Offers by Player 1 to Player 2 (Target and Control Participants) *(continued)*

Method									OLS				
Dependent variable	Percentage of the allocation offered by player 1 to player 2 in the dictator game												
Independent variables	(1)	(2)	(3)	(4)	(5)	(6)	(7)	(8)	(9)	(10)	(11)	(12)	(13)
1 if player 2 is a woman										0		-0.018	
Player 2's age										0.001		0.002	
1 if player 2 is single										0.041		0.047	
1 if player 2 is in common law										0.001		0.027	
Player 2's years of education										0.050*		0.056**	
Player 2's number of minor people in charge										-0.001		0.008	
1 if player 2 is unemployed										-0.176**		-0.216***	
Player 1's – player 2's household expenses per capita (Colombian pesos, thousands)										0.000***		0.000***	
1 if player 2 considers herself black											0.009	-0.06	
1 if player 2 considers herself indigenous											0.075	0.015	
Percentage of the allocation expected by player 2 from player 1 in the dictator game										-0.144	-0.383***	-0.161	
Constant	0.433***	0.252***	0.461***	0.461***	0.526***	0.409***	0.687***	0.454***	0.834***	0.659***	0.364***	0.713***	0.145
Interactions	534	534	534	534	534	487	534	534	534	534	534	534	451
R-squared	0.095	0.189	0.137	0.051	0.151	0.210	0.213	0.100	0.240	0.212	0.080	0.227	0.191

Dummy of target player 1 and target player 2 per player 2's data

Source: Author's compilation.

Note: A cluster with player 1's decisions is included.

* Significant at 10%.

** Significant at 5%.

*** Significant at 1%.

Table 3.4 Ultimatum Game Offers by Player 1 to Player 2 (Target and Control Participants)

	Method	*OLS*												
	Dependent variable	*Percentage of the allocation offered by player 1 to player 2 in the ultimatum game*												
	Independent variables	*(1)*	*(2)*	*(3)*	*(4)*	*(5)*	*(6)*	*(7)*	*(8)*	*(9)*	*(10)*	*(11)*	*(12)*	*(13)*
	1 if player 1 is a target	–0.018	0.045					–0.027	0.110*	–0.056				
	1 if player 2 is a target	0.206***	0.209***											
	1 if player 1 & 2 are targets	–0.116**	–0.118**								–0.027	0.198***	–0.04	
Player 1's data – Sociodemographic	1 if player is a woman		–0.037											–0.007
Player 1's data – Sociodemographic	Age		–0.002											0
Player 1's data – Sociodemographic	Player's level of education		0.042***											0.027***
Player 1's data – Sociodemographic	Natural logarithm of player's household expenses per capita													0.015
Player 1's data – Sociodemographic	1 if player works in a health institute													0.024
Player 1's data – Sociodemographic	1 if player works in an education institute													0.017
Player 1's data – Sociodemographic	1 if player works in a nutrition institute													–0.094**
Player 1's data – Sociodemographic	Player's time worked multiplied by the dummy of target player 1		0.005*											
Player 1's data – Sociodemographic	Player 1's – player 2's household expenses per capita (Colombian pesos, thousands)		0	0.000***		0.000***	0.000***	0		0	0		0	0

(continued)

Table 3.4 Ultimatum Game Offers by Player 1 to Player 2 (Target and Control Participants) *(continued)*

Method				OLS									
Dependent variable			Percentage of the allocation offered by player 1 to player 2 in the ultimatum game										
Independent variables	(1)	(2)	(3)	(4)	(5)	(6)	(7)	(8)	(9)	(10)	(11)	(12)	(13)
Sociodemographic													
1 if player 2 is a woman			0.039**		0.032	0.003	0.054*		0.049	0.04		0.039	
Player 2's age			0		0	0	0.001		0.001	0		0	
1 if player 2 is single			-0.028		-0.029	-0.042	-0.001		-0.001	0.011		0.016	
1 if player 2 is in common law			-0.037		-0.044	-0.063*	-0.037		-0.03	-0.03		-0.015	
Player 2's years of education			-0.016*		-0.022**	-0.023**	-0.039***		-0.045***	-0.045***		-0.051***	
Player 2's number of minor people in charge			0.028***		0.027***	0.016*	0.009		-0.002	0.01		0.01	
1 if player 2 is unemployed			0.057**		0.059*	0.064*	0.046		0.056	0.04		0.058	
Discriminatory													
1 if player 2 considers herself black				0.017	0.038	0.03		-0.026	0.048		-0.014	0.051	
1 if player 2 considers herself indigenous				0.056	0.01	0.004		-0.157**	-0.122		-0.121	-0.133	
1 if player 2 is displaced				0.067**	-0.024	-0.043		0.120**	0.05		0.068**	-0.032	
1 if player 2 is an ex-combatant				-0.060**	-0.027	-0.039		-0.013	-0.026		-0.059**	-0.004	
1 if player 2 is a recycling worker				0.022	0.001	0.008		0.067	0.058		0.034	0.017	
1 if player 2 is a street vendor				-0.045	-0.029	0.136		-0.013	-0.003		-0.011	0.015	
Games													
Percentage of the allocation expected by player 2 from player 1 in the ultimatum game			0.002	0.102*	0.005	-0.001	0.161*	0.282***	0.129	0.180**	0.376***	0.177**	
Player 2's rank given by player 1 in the distributive dictator game						0.024***							

(Player 2's data)

(continued)

Table 3.4 Ultimatum Game Offers by Player 1 to Player 2 (Target and Control Participants) (continued)

Method							OLS					
Dependent variable							Percentage of the allocation offered by player 1 to player 2 in the ultimatum game					
Independent variables	(1)	(2)	(3)	(4)	(5)	(6)	(7)	(8)	(9)	(10)	(11)	(12)	(13)
1 if player 2 is a woman							-0.032		-0.038				
Player 2's age							-0.001		0				
1 if player 2 is single							-0.032						
1 if player 2 is in common law													
Player 2's years of education							0.024		0.006				
Player 2's number of minor people in charge							0.034*		0.039*				
1 if player 2 is unemployed							0.023		0.039*				
Player 1's – player 2's household expenses per capita (Colombian pesos, thousands)							0.02		0.03				
1 if player 2 considers herself black							0.000*		0.000*				
1 if player 2 considers herself indigenous								0.074	0.002				
1 if player 2 is displaced								0.242***	0.135				
1 if player 2 is an ex-combatant								-0.063	-0.117				
1 if player 2 is a recycling worker								-0.052	0.018				
1 if player 2 is a street vendor								-0.035	-0.062				
Percentage of the allocation expected by player 2 from player 1 in the ultimatum game								0	0				
							-0.266**	-0.313***	-0.229**				

Dummy of target player 1 per player 2's data

(continued)

Table 3.4 Ultimatum Game Offers by Player 1 to Player 2 (Target and Control Participants) *(continued)*

Method	OLS												
Dependent variable	Percentage of the allocation offered by player 1 to player 2 in the ultimatum game												
Independent variables	(1)	(2)	(3)	(4)	(5)	(6)	(7)	(8)	(9)	(10)	(11)	(12)	(13)
1 if player 2 is a woman										-0.015		-0.024	
Player 2's age										0		0	
1 if player 2 is single										-0.053		-0.072	
1 if player 2 is in common law										0.014		-0.016	
Player 2's years of education										0.034		0.041*	
Player 2's number of minor people in charge										0.022		0.022	
1 if player 2 is unemployed										0.027		0.017	
Player 1's – player 2's household expenses per capita (Colombian pesos, thousands)										0.000**		0.000**	
1 if player 2 considers herself black											0.066	0.009	
1 if player 2 considers herself indigenous											0.193**	0.148	
Percentage of the allocation expected by player 2 from player 1 in the ultimatum game										-0.297***	-0.465***	-0.302***	
Constant	0.482***	0.290***	0.554***	0.501***	0.586***	0.568***	0.590***	0.437***	0.619***	0.606***	0.385***	0.622***	0.271
Interactions	535	535	535	535	535	489	535	535	535	535	535	535	450
R-squared	0.075	0.189	0.143	0.052	0.148	0.168	0.179	0.096	0.193	0.188	0.099	0.198	0.120

Dummy of target player 2 and target player 1 per player 2's data

Source: Authors.

Note: A cluster with player 1's decisions is included.

* Significant at 10%.

** Significant at 5%.

*** Significant at 1%.

Likewise, having lower levels of education, being unemployed, having more minor dependents, and being female increased the offers sent by players 1. Displaced recipients saw an extra increase in the offers, and ex-combatants saw a reduction, similar to the dictator game offers. Education of recipients (players 2) was rewarded by public officials in the same manner as in the previous analysis of DG offers. Given that the offers in the dictator and ultimatum games do not show significant differences and that the effects of the attributes of the players are similar, the interpretations are equivalent to those given in the previous case.

Trust game offers by player 1 to player 2 (target and control participants). The effects of the sampling treatments remain as in the previous two games. Target recipients received larger offers than the controls, and actual public officers showed more restraint in the amounts sent when the interaction was with a target recipient (see table 3.5).

For players 2, lower levels of education and being unemployed were among the more robust attributes to make a difference, as was being indigenous. Once again, being displaced brought a reward, and being an ex-combatant or street vendor brought a punishment.

Third-party punishment game offers by player 1 to player 2 (target and control participants). The regression results in this case show similar results with respect to pro-sociality and to target and control interactions, indicated by the significance and signs of the first coefficients in table 3.6. However, fewer characteristics of the players seem to explain the variation in the offers. Education, for instance, maintains the negative effect but is no longer significant. That player 2 was in a common-law relationship has a negative effect in several of the specifications, and being an ex-combatant or a street recycler also has a negative effect, although not significant.

Because the third-party punishment game also explores the importance of social norms of fairness in third parties, we regressed the decisions to punish on different levels of fairness elicited from players 1. The results reinforce some of the findings of other games, as shown in table 3.7.

Punishment rates by players 3 in third-party punishment game. As expected, lower offers by players 1 increased the likelihood of punishment by players 3. Moreover, the attributes of players 1 changed the probability. Younger and more educated players 1 saw a higher probability of being sanctioned. The level of education of the punisher (player 3) also increased the likelihood.

Consistent with the previously discussed games, when player 2 was an ex-combatant, we observe less pro-social behavior, in this case on the part of players 3. Ceteris paribus, the likelihood of player 1 sanctioning an unfair offer is lower when the affected recipient was part of that particular group.

Table 3.5 Trust Game Offers by Player 1 to Player 2 (Target and Control Participants)

						OLS							
Method													
Dependent variable					Percentage of the allocation offered by player 1 to player 2 in the trust game								
Independent variables	(1)	(2)	(3)	(4)	(5)	(6)	(7)	(8)	(9)	(10)	(11)	(12)	(13)
1 if player 1 is a target	0.097	0.141**					0.102			0.159	0.126**	0.127	
1 if player 2 is a target	0.219***	0.211***						-0.012					
1 if player 1 & 2 are targets	-0.176***	-0.184***							-0.182				
1 if player is woman		-0.062*											-0.063
Age		-0.001											0
Player's level of education		0.039***											0.029**
Natural logarithm of player's household expenses per capita													
1 if player works in a health institute													-0.01
1 if player works in an education institute													0.02
1 if player works in a nutrition institute						0			0				-0.109**
Player's time worked multiplied by dummy of target player 1		0.006	0		0	0	0		0	0			-0.107**
Player 1's – player 2's household expenses per capita (Colombian pesos, thousands)		0	0		0	0	0	0	0	0	0	0	0

(continued)

Table 3.5 Trust Game Offers by Player 1 to Player 2 (Target and Control Participants) *(continued)*

Method							OLS						
Dependent variable						Percentage of the allocation offered by player 1 to player 2 in the trust game							
Independent variables	(1)	(2)	(3)	(4)	(5)	(6)	(7)	(8)	(9)	(10)	(11)	(12)	(13)
Sociodemographic													
1 if player 2 is a woman			0.03		0.029	0.009	0.074*		0.061	0.065		0.090**	
Player 2's age			0.001		0.001	0.001	0.003*		0.001	0.002		0.002	
1 if player 2 is single			-0.022		-0.02	-0.026	0.048		0.056	0.009		0.02	
1 if player 2 is in common law			0.019		0.018	-0.006	0.054		0.029	0.028		-0.014	
Player 2's years of education			-0.024**		-0.027**	-0.026*	-0.037**		-0.063***	-0.029		-0.036*	
Player 2's number of minor people in charge			0.009		0.002	-0.006	0.034**		0.014	0.029**		0.018	
1 if player 2 is unemployed			0.128***		0.102***	0.100**	0.123**		0.091*	0.127***		0.143***	
Discriminatory													
1 if player 2 considers herself black				0.034	0.047	0.035		-0.036	0.044		0.028	0.089*	
1 if player 2 considers herself indigenous				0.124**	0.079	0.062		0.135*	0.235**		0.253***	0.243***	
1 if player 2 is displaced				0.108***	0.021	0.005		0.207*	0.055		0.111***	0.018	
1 if player 2 is an ex-combatant				-0.045	-0.011	-0.01		-0.130**	-0.144		-0.046	0.005	
1 if player 2 is a recycling worker				0.076	0.049	0.071		-0.007	-0.051		0.079	0.062	
1 if player 2 is a street vendor				-0.131**	-0.164***	-0.167		-0.119	-0.142**		-0.119*	-0.148**	
Games													
Percentage of the allocation expected by player 2 from player 1 in the trust game			0.068	0.097**	0.072	0.069	0.151*	0.134	0.132	0.218***	0.263***	0.215***	
Player 2's rank given by player 1 in the distributive dictator game						0.030***							

(continued)

(Row group label, left margin: Player 2's data)

Table 3.5 Trust Game Offers by Player 1 to Player 2 (Target and Control Participants) (continued)

Method							OLS					
Dependent variable						Percentage of the allocation offered by player 1 to player 2 in the trust game						
Independent variables	(1)	(2)	(3)	(4)	(5)	(6)	(7)	(8)	(9)	(10)	(11)	(12)	(13)
1 if player 2 is a woman							−0.073		−0.055			
Player 2's age							−0.002		0.001			
1 if player 2 is single							−0.074		−0.088			
1 if player 2 is in common law							−0.014		0.009			
Player 2's years of education							0.031		0.066**			
Player 2's number of minor people in charge							−0.033*		−0.017			
1 if player 2 is unemployed							0.011		0.024			
Player 1's – player 2's household expenses per capita (Colombian pesos, thousands)							0		0			
1 if player 2 considers herself black								0.101	0.017			
1 if player 2 considers herself indigenous								−0.006	−0.149			
1 if player 2 is displaced								−0.126**	−0.052			
1 if player 2 is an ex-combatant								0.112	0.186*			
1 if player 2 is a recycling worker								0.105	0.144			
1 if player 2 is a street vendor								0	0			
Percentage of the allocation expected by player 2 from player 1 in the trust game							−0.101	−0.051	−0.076			

Dummy of target player 1 per player 2's data

(continued)

Table 3.5 Trust Game Offers by Player 1 to Player 2 (Target and Control Participants) *(continued)*

Method									OLS				
Dependent variable													
					Percentage of the allocation offered by player 1 to player 2 in the trust game								
Independent variables	(1)	(2)	(3)	(4)	(5)	(6)	(7)	(8)	(9)	(10)	(11)	(12)	(13)
1 if player 2 is a woman										-0.068		0.092*	
Player 2's age										-0.001		-0.001	
1 if player 2 is single										-0.046		-0.059	
1 if player 2 is in common law										0.015		0.056	
Player 2's years of education										0.001		0.011	
Player 2's number of minor people in charge										-0.026		-0.023	
1 if player 2 is unemployed										0.012		-0.031	
Player 1's – player 2's household expenses per capita (Colombian pesos, thousands)										0.000*		0.000*	
1 if player 2 considers herself black											0.01	-0.052	
1 if player 2 considers herself indigenous											-0.1129**	-0.163*	
Percentage of the allocation expected by player 2 from player 1 in the trust game										-0.221**	-0.258***	-0.212**	
Constant	0.528***	0.360***	0.632***	0.582***	0.619***	0.567***	0.512***	0.591***	0.694***	0.536***	0.504***	0.519***	0.726**
Interactions	537	537	537	537	537	491	537	537	537	537	537	537	450
R-squared	0.042	0.118	0.114	0.078	0.135	0.144	0.140	0.095	0.173	0.149	0.091	0.171	0.083

Dummy of target player 1 and target player 2 per player 2's data

Source: Authors.

Note: A cluster with player 1's decisions is included.

* Significant at 10%.

** Significant at 5%.

*** Significant at 1%.

Table 3.6 Third-Party Punishment Game Offers by Player 1 to Player 2 (Target and Control Participants)

Method							OLS						
Dependent variable	Percentage of the allocation offered by player 1 to player 2 in the third-party punishment game												
Independent variables	(1)	(2)	(3)	(4)	(5)	(6)	(7)	(8)	(9)	(10)	(11)	(12)	(13)
1 if player 1 is a target	-0.006	0.036											-0.06
1 if player 2 is a target	0.138***	0.134**											-0.001
1 if player 1 & 2 are targets	-0.123**	-0.115**					-0.301*	-0.03	-0.294	-0.192	0.002	-0.182	0.016
1 if player is a woman		-0.071**											
Age		-0.001											
Player's level of education		0.033***											
Natural logarithm of player's household expenses per capita													0.002
1 if player works in a health institute													0.048
1 if player works in an education institute													0.027
1 if player works in a nutrition institute													-0.078*
Player's time worked multiplied by dummy of target player 1		0.006*											
Player 1's – player 2's household expenses per capita (Colombian pesos, thousands)	0	0	0.000**		0.000**	0.000*	0	0	0	0	0	0	0.000**

Player 1's data · Sociodemographic

(continued)

Table 3.6 Third-Party Punishment Game Offers by Player 1 to Player 2 (Target and Control Participants) *(continued)*

Method						OLS								
Dependent variable				Percentage of the allocation offered by player 1 to player 2 in the third-party punishment game										
Independent variables		*(1)*	*(2)*	*(3)*	*(4)*	*(5)*	*(6)*	*(7)*	*(8)*	*(9)*	*(10)*	*(11)*	*(12)*	*(13)*
Sociodemographic	1 if player 2 is a woman			0.092***		0.088**	0.080***	0.105**		0.101*	0.075*		0.064	
	Player 2's age			0.003**		0.002	0.002	0.003		0.006	0.004		0.004	
	1 if player 2 is single			0.013		0.023	0.024	-0.026		0.002	-0.036		-0.035	
	1 if player 2 is in common law					-0.02	-0.037	-0.142*		-0.174*	-0.151*		-0.142*	
	Player 2's years of education			0.005		-0.002	-0.0018	-0.035		-0.013	-0.031		-0.028	
	Player 2's number of minor people in charge			0.005		-0.003	-0.01	-0.041		-0.051	-0.036		-0.05	
	1 if player 2 is unemployed			0.081**		0.057	0.051	0.075		0.102	0.072		0.091	
Discriminatory (Player 2's data)	1 if player 2 considers herself black				-0.006	-0.011	-0.019		-0.114	-0.086		-0.133**	-0.097	
	1 if player 2 considers herself indigenous				-0.049	-0.017	0.001		-0.171	0.01		-0.125	-0.045	
	1 if player 2 is displaced				0.077**	0.058	0.058		0.05	0.086		0.112***	0.084*	
	1 if player 2 is an ex-combatant				-0.090***	-0.035	-0.073		0.003	0.067		-0.060*	-0.009	
	1 if player 2 is a recycling worker				-0.062	-0.018	-0.03		0.045	0.207		-0.004	0.018	
	1 if player 2 is a street vendor				0.007	0.005	0.163		0.045	0.036		0.056	0.048	
Games	Percentage of the allocation expected by player 2 from player 1 in the third-party punishment game			0.073	0.097*	0.074	0.057	0.190*	0.233**	0.190*	0.202**	0.248***	0.198**	
	Player 2's rank given by player 1 in the distributive dictator game						0.001							

(continued)

Table 3.6 Third-Party Punishment Game Offers by Player 1 to Player 2 (Target and Control Participants) (continued)

Method							OLS						
Dependent variable							Percentage of the allocation offered by player 1 to player 2 in the third-party punishment game						
Independent variables	(1)	(2)	(3)	(4)	(5)	(6)	(7)	(8)	(9)	(10)	(11)	(12)	(13)
1 if player 2 is a woman							-0.024		-0.036				
Player 2's age							0		-0.005				
1 if player 2 is single							0.065		0.041				
1 if player 2 is in common law							0.146*		0.184*				
Player 2's years of education							0.060*		0.028				
Player 2's number of minor people in charge							0.057		0.053				
1 if player 2 is unemployed							0.005		-0.078				
Player 1's – player 2's household expenses per capita (Colombian pesos, thousands)							0.000**		0.000***				
1 if player 2 considers herself black								0.176*	0.124				
1 if player 2 considers herself indigenous								0.15	-0.014				
1 if player 2 is displaced								0.056	-0.001				
1 if player 2 is an ex-combatant								-0.102	-0.144				
1 if player 2 is a recycling worker								-0.083	-0.239*				
1 if player 2 is a street vendor								0	0				
Percentage of the allocation expected by player 2 from player 1 in the third-party punishment game							-0.200*	-0.214*	-0.19				

Dummy of target player 1 per player 2's data

(continued)

Table 3.6 Third-Party Punishment Game Offers by Player 1 to Player 2 (Target and Control Participants) *(continued)*

Method		*OLS*												
Dependent variable		*Percentage of the allocation offered by player 1 to player 2 in the third-party punishment game*												
Independent variables		*(1)*	*(2)*	*(3)*	*(4)*	*(5)*	*(6)*	*(7)*	*(8)*	*(9)*	*(10)*	*(11)*	*(12)*	*(13)*
Dummy of target player 1 and target player 2 per player 2's data	1 if player 2 is a woman										0.006		0.01	
	Player 2's age										–0.001		–0.002	
	1 if player 2 is single										0.074		0.068	
	1 if player 2 is in common law										0.160*		0.155*	
	Player 2's years of education										0.026		0.028	
	Player 2's number of minor people in charge										0.053		0.058*	
	1 if player 2 is unemployed										0.025		–0.04	
	Player 1's – player 2's household expenses per capita (Colombian pesos, thousands)										0.000**		0.000**	
	1 if player 2 considers herself black											0.214**	0.156*	
	1 if player 2 considers herself indigenous											0.106	0.035	
	Percentage of the allocation expected by player 2 from player 1 in the third-party punishment game										–0.235**	–0.269***	–0.228**	
	Constant	0.428***	0.324***	0.312***	0.481***	0.359***	0.450***	0.532***	0.499***	0.338	0.509***	0.466***	0.504***	0.46
	Interactions	428	428	428	428	428	388	428	428	428	428	428	428	282
	R-squared	0.044	0.140	0.128	0.072	0.136	0.160	0.175	0.134	0.200	0.178	0.124	0.194	0.102

Source: Authors.

Note: A cluster with player 1's decisions is included.

* Significant at 10%.

** Significant at 5%.

*** Significant at 1%.

Table 3.7 Punishment Rates by Players 3 in Third-Party Punishment Game

Method		Probit	
Dependent variable		Punishment rate: 1 if player 3 pays for punishing player 1	
		dF/dx	
Independent variables	(1)	(2)	(3)
Player 1's data			
% of money sent by player 1	−0.873*	−0.877*	−0.898*
1 if player 1 is a woman	−0.005		0.005
Age	−0.002		−0.004**
Player's level of education	0.038*		0.037*
Player 2's data — Sociodemographic			
1 if player 2 is a woman		0.038	0.024
Player 2's age		−0.003***	−0.003
1 if player 2 is single		0.06	0.073***
1 if player 2 is in common law		0.119	0.145
Player 2's years of education		−0.64*	−0.059*
1 if player 2 is unemployed		0.059	0.068
1 if player 2 has 4 or more people in charge		−0.019	−0.005
Player 2's stratum		0.032	0.027
Player 2's data — Discriminatory			
1 if player 2 considers herself black		−0.038	−0.059
1 if player 2 considers herself indigenous		−0.02	−0.003
1 if player 2 is displaced		−0.023	−0.034
1 if player 2 is an ex-combatant		−0.141**	−0.135**
1 if player 2 is a recycling worker		0.021	0.07
1 if player 2 is a street vendor		−0.017	0.059
Player 3's data			
1 if player 3 is a woman			−0.043
Age			0.002
Player's level of education			0.032**
Player's number of minor people in charge			−0.013
Preferences for fairness and income distribution			−0.031***
Interactions		4,760	
R-squared	0.2039	0.2099	0.238

Source: Authors.
Note: A cluster with player 3's decisions is included.
* Significant at 10%.
** Significant at 5%.
*** Significant at 1%.

Lessons Based on the Results

Several lessons may be derived from this study. Some of them relate to using these methods to explore questions such as the economics of poverty, discrimination, and pro-social behavior that can be of use for other organizations and researchers. Some lessons relate to the design and implementation of pro-poor social policies and the role of public servants as deliverers of services targeted to the poor when there is room for discretionary power.

Our framed experiment offers a context of pro-sociality toward poor or vulnerable groups. We expected our recipients to trigger generosity and pro-sociality in general among service providers, both public officials and controls. A study by Pablo Brañas (2006) confirms that the framing of dictator game experiments and the attributes of the recipients matter greatly. Having actually poor recipients and even going to the extreme of having the donations of the dictators convert into medicines for poor nations resulted in very high offers, and about two-thirds of players 1 sent their entire endowment.

Our study falls in between the conventional designs of unframed games among anonymous students and the strongly framed Brañas design. Nevertheless, what is remarkable in our design is not that we observe higher-than-average levels of generosity, but the degree of variation observed toward the same groups of beneficiaries and the fact that our target groups of public officials and the poor displayed several behaviors that seem to respond to the individual attributes of senders and recipients.

Do social preferences affect the behavior of public officials? We think that they do. In general, citizens and public officials whose work is related to the provision of social services to the poor do manifest pro-social behavior, confirming that fairness, altruism, trust, and social punishment are mechanisms and traits that determine behavior when dealing with the more vulnerable. However, such behavior is affected by the characteristics of the recipients of the social services and, in some cases, by the attributes of the providers. In some cases, the factors that trigger greater levels of altruism and fairness are consistent with social policy, and in others they are not, which raises concerns.

In particular, citizens (public officials and nonpublic officials) favor women, particularly those in households with lower levels of education and more minor dependents. This seems to be a reasonable strategy if strengthening human capital among the poor is seen as a cost-effective strategy and if women are seen as guarantors of building such human capital within the household. Also, people seem to favor displaced people, also consistent with the country's political context and a recent constitutional mandate by the constitutional court.

However, certain attributes of recipients decreased pro-social behavior by players 1. Those attributes are related to occupation, marital status, and social background, none of which should result in differentiated or discriminatory treatment; being an ex-combatant, a street recycler, a street vendor, or in a common-law relationship decreased generosity from players 1. People in common-law relationships also expected lower offers, confirming the actual amounts sent, but with no legal or moral foundation for such behavior and expectations. These attributes do not necessarily decrease the deservedness of the recipients of social services, but they do seem to shape the preferences of public officials and nonpublic officials when making their choices.

Such results raise the question of whether social programs should monitor the level and quality of social services toward certain groups. Then again, it might be important to reduce or hide the collection of information on social services applicants that might be irrelevant to the allocation or delivery of such services when public servants make micro decisions about allocating scarce resources (for example, assigning available spaces in medical attention, education, child care, or nutrition services).

The levels of conformism expressed in lower expected offers and lower levels of rejection of unfair offers for our target group (the poor) also deserve some attention. Such conformism can create an equilibrium of lower levels of commitment in the provision of certain social services. We wonder whether placing greater emphasis on explaining the rights of the most vulnerable groups in society could increase the demand for fairness in the delivery of services by creating stronger social norms in favor of fairness.

Certain groups emerged as being subject to discriminatory treatment and of particular importance. The population of street dwellers and homeless persons working in informal garbage recycling activities is significant in major cities,[15] and that population is particularly vulnerable with regard to enrollment in social services, basic conditions of the household, and access to health and education. Meanwhile, our results confirm a cultural stigma toward them that deserves further attention. Despite the stigma, their activity and income are based not on altruistic transfer (such as begging) but rather on self-employment and the provision of environmental services (recycling and reduction of disposed garbage); furthermore, they have been working with governmental and nongovernmental organizations to strengthen self-governing institutions such as cooperatives and associations.

As for ex-combatants, the social punishment and lower pro-social behavior observed toward this group, after controlling for their age, gender, and level of education, deserve some attention. A state program exists to reinsert these young people into civil life based on welfare programs, but such programs contradict the social norm of redistributive justice that seems to be present in the society and is clearly manifested across our samples. Favoring displaced people and punishing ex-combatants reflect the social climate of the country with respect to the search for peace and negotiations within an ongoing conflict.

Annex: Methodology

This annex adds information regarding the methods used, the demographic characteristics of the samples, and the recruitment strategies employed.

Design of the Sessions

Table 3A.1 shows the sequence and components of the experimental sessions. The original design proposed for the study involved 24 people per session. Unfortunately, this design was very difficult to implement because a large number of people failed to show up at the appointed time and location. Four sessions of 24 participants each were conducted under the 24-participant design for a total of 96 people. After that, we split the design in two and ran sessions with 12 people each from then on (designs II and III in the table). Design III is essentially the same as design II, except that more people were recruited and attended the sessions, and these persons were allowed to participate.

These changes did not affect the design of the basic protocol or the instructions. First, the DDG game, where one player 1 makes decisions based on five players 2, remained unaltered throughout. Second, all other games (DG, UG, TG, and 3PP) involved the same number of interactions and decisions across the designs.

Table 3A.2 shows the sequence and components of a single experimental session run with 12 players.

Table 3A.1 Stages of the Field Sessions

Design	Sessions	Number of sessions	Number of people	People by roles		Total participants
I	1, 2, 4	3	24	Player 1	10	72
				Player 2	10	
				Player 3	4	
II	3, 5–12	9	12	Player 1	5	108
				Player 2	5	
				Player 3	2	
	13–21[a]	18	12	Player 1	5	216
				Player 2	5	
				Player 3	2	
III	22–28[b]	13	12 or 13	Player 1	5 + 1	163
				Player 2	5	
				Player 3	2	
Total						559

Source: Authors' compilation.
a. Each one of 24 people.
b. Each one of 26 people.

Table 3A.2 Stages for One Field Session

Stage	Activity	Location	Data produced
Stage I	Recruitment of 5 players 2 Build cards A-B-C-D-E players 2 from demographics	Streets, centers for the attention of target populations	Invitation, photo, pre-game demographics player 2, received Col$2,000 for transportation as part of their show-up fee player 2 cards
Stage II	Recruitment of 5 players 1 Game decisions (5 activities) players 1 Build Cards 1-2-3-4-5 players 1 from demographics	Service providers (health centers, public schools, daycare centers, community kitchens) Workplace (80%) or campus lab (off-hours) (20%)	Invitation, pre-game demographics player 1, received Col$4,000 (show-up fee) Game choices players 1 player 1 cards
Stage III	Recruitment of 2 players 3 Game decisions (Activity-5) players 3 Matching of choices by players 1, players 3 Payments and exit survey players 3	Workplace, streets, campus	Pre-game demographics player 3 Game choices players 3 Game outcomes Receipts (Col$4000, show-up fee) and post-game survey
Stage IV	Game decisions (5 activities) players 2 Matching of choices by players 1, players 2 Payments and exit survey players 2	Campus (70%) or centers for the attention of targeted populations (30%)	Game choices players 2 Game outcomes Receipts and post-game survey, Col$2,000 for bus
Stage V	Payments and exit survey players 1	Workplace	Receipts and post-game survey

Source: Authors' compilation.
Note: Session involved 12 participants.

Lab Setting

Figure 3A.1 describes the basic setup of the experimental design for one of the activities (the ultimatum game, or activity 2). All other games were conducted in the same manner. In this case, based on the card of player 2, player 1 decided how much to send to player 2 of the Col$20,000 given as the endowment for the pair. Player 2 decided whether to accept or reject the offer. Depending on that decision, the funds were allocated as initially proposed, and, if the offer was rejected, no payment was made to either player.

Players 1 were in one location, and they were informed that players 2 were in another location (see figure 3A.2). They did not see each other at any time, and their identities and decisions were kept confidential. Players 1 were seated at a desk and recorded their decisions privately on a decisions sheet (paper). Players 2 were invited the next day to come to campus. At that time, Players 2 were seated in a waiting room and called one at a time to a desk where a monitor verbally asked for decisions and recorded them on a decisions sheet. The monitor then wrote the decisions of each player 2 in each activity. At the end of the five activities, all

Figure 3A.1 Lab Setting for the Ultimatum Game

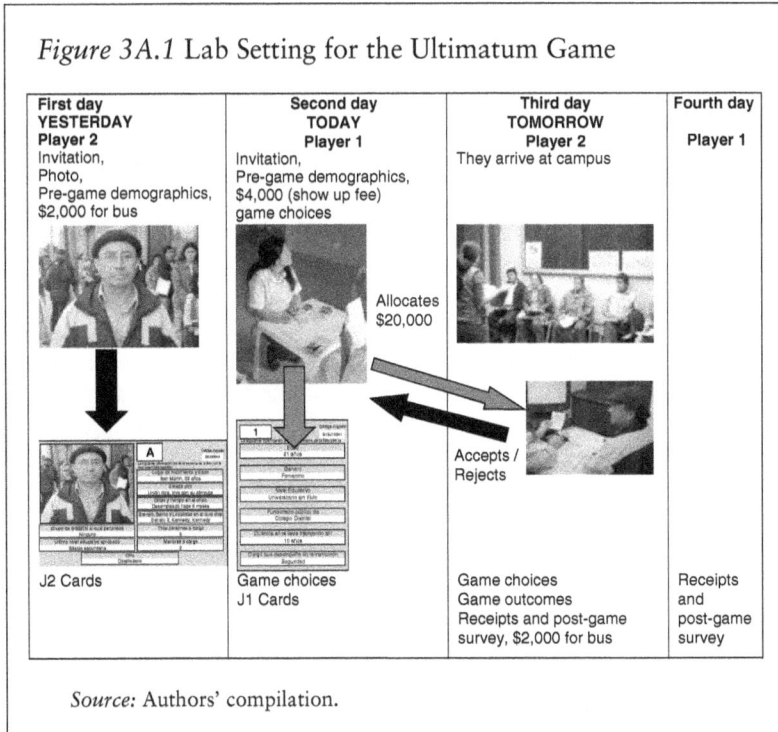

First day YESTERDAY Player 2 Invitation, Photo, Pre-game demographics, $2,000 for bus	Second day TODAY Player 1 Invitation, Pre-game demographics, $4,000 (show up fee) game choices	Third day TOMORROW Player 2 They arrive at campus	Fourth day Player 1
	Allocates $20,000		
		Accepts / Rejects	
J2 Cards	Game choices J1 Cards	Game choices Game outcomes Receipts and post-game survey, $2,000 for bus	Receipts and post-game survey

Source: Authors' compilation.

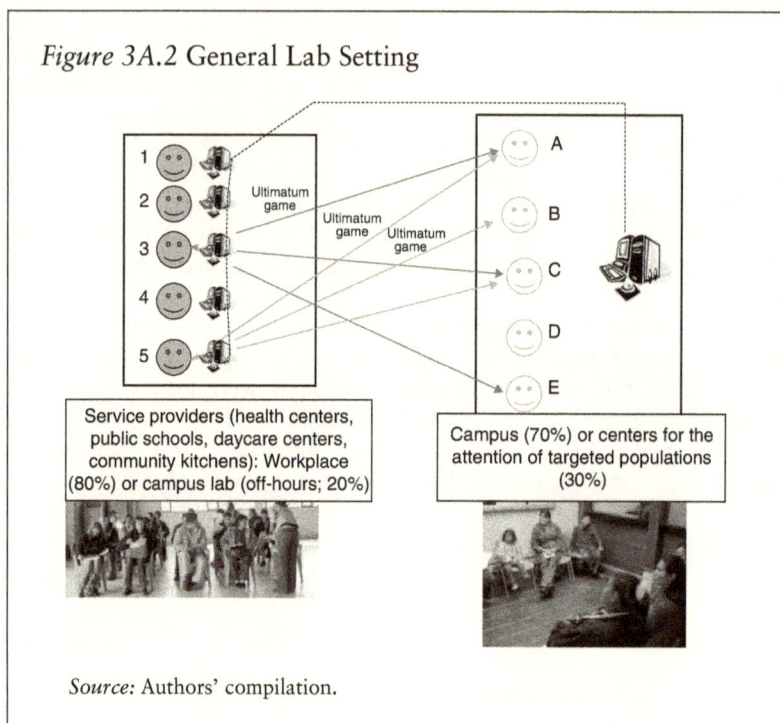

Figure 3A.2 General Lab Setting

Service providers (health centers, public schools, daycare centers, community kitchens): Workplace (80%) or campus lab (off-hours; 20%)

Campus (70%) or centers for the attention of targeted populations (30%)

Source: Authors' compilation.

decisions were matched for determining the earnings in each interaction and activity. For the ultimatum game, each player 1 sent three different offers to three players 2.

At the end of the session, we selected randomly for each player at least one activity that would be paid in cash on top of the show-up fee that was paid to cover the transportation costs of each participant. On average, players were paid for more than one activity, and this was common information for all players. Prior to making their decisions, players 1 and 2 received information about the other player in the particular interaction through the cards mentioned above.

The information that each player had about the other player in each interaction is shown in table 3A.3. Based on this information, the players were asked to make their decisions in each of the games. Recall that each participant played the same game with three different people.

Sampling and Recruitment

We conducted these experiments among the groups described in the proposal, including local officials and beneficiaries of social services as well

Table 3A.3 Information for the Players

What Player 1 observed in Player 2 card	What Player 2 observed in Player 1 card
Photo	Age
Birthplace and age	Gender
Marital status	Education level (highest degree obtained)
Occupation and time in it	Service provider (health, education, child care, nutrition)
District, location, and district stratification	Years spent working
Number of dependents	Position
Dependents that are minors	
Last year of education	
SISBEN	

Source: Authors' compilation.

as control groups. In most cases, the role of player 1 was assigned to local officials and comparable control subjects, and the role of recipients was played by people sampled from poor populations who were current or potential beneficiaries of social services.

We use the terms "target" and "control" for our experiment participants. By "target," we refer to those individuals involved in the direct process of application and delivery of social services. In the case of players 1, the target sample refers to those employed in the public service agencies that interact directly with the potential or actual beneficiaries of social services to the poor. These include white-collar and blue-collar employees at the four types of agencies (education, health, child care, and nutrition programs). Players 2 are persons who are applying for, are eligible to apply for, or are receiving these kinds of social services. As for the controls, we recruited citizens of the city with different levels of education, income, occupation, and location of residence to serve as control groups for players 1, 2, and 3.

We recruited participants by visiting neighborhoods where potential beneficiaries apply for these social services or where they actually receive them. We additionally recruited local officials or employees for these government programs. Examples include health services for the poorest citizens, public preschool and day care centers, and community kitchens and nutritional government programs. The following groups were included in the subject pool:

- Potential applicants and current beneficiaries of social protection services,
- Local officials in Bogotá's agencies that provide social services such as education, health, day care, and nutrition,

- Surveyors usually hired by private contractors who conduct the SIS-BEN survey in large cities and metropolitan areas, and
- Controls (other government officials and citizens with demographic characteristics equivalent to those of the groups above).

The map in figure 3A.3 shows the locations of the public agencies where we recruited players 1.

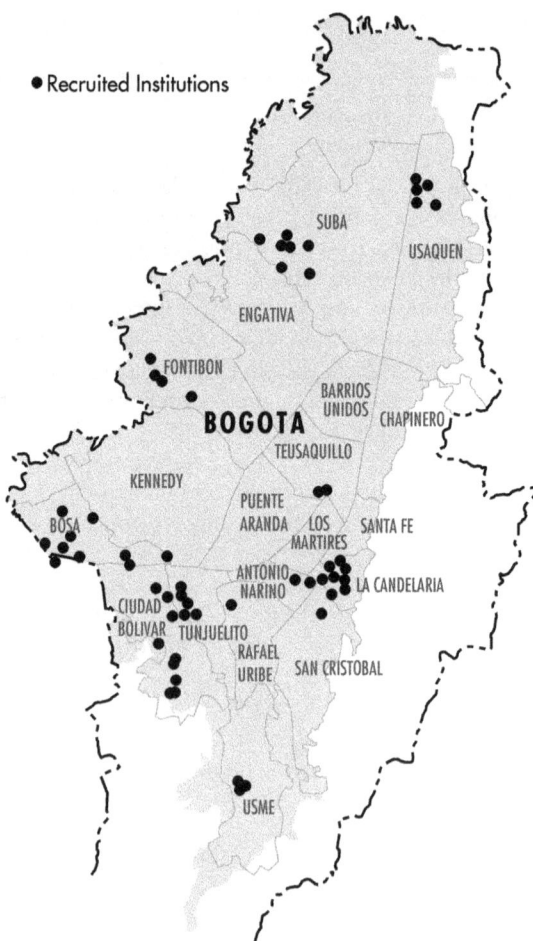

Figure 3A.3 Recruitment of Players 1 in Bogotá, Colombia, by Geographical Location

Source: Authors' compilation.

In the case of local officials, the confidentiality and privacy of data were a major concern, as we were asking individuals to reveal their preferences regarding fairness, altruism, and discrimination. Therefore, the identities of the local officials or their decisions were never revealed to the other players and could not be observed by their superiors. In fact, we tried to recruit more than one officer from each service provider we visited in the sample.

For players 2, recruitment took place among the poor and more vulnerable groups around these and other locations in the city. Table 3A.4 shows the geographic location (*localidad*) of the participants' households, and table 3A.5 shows the attendance of participants, by the role played. To give an idea of their locations and occupations, tables 3A.6 through 3A.8 show the composition of the sample, by type of player, for both the target and the control groups.

Table 3A.4 Geographical Location of Participants' Households (percent)

Location	N	Player 3	Player 2	Player 1
Antonio Nariño	20	0.0	85.0	15.0
Barrios Unidos	6	33.3	16.7	50.0
Bosa	17	5.9	58.8	35.3
Candelaria	1	0.0	100.0	0.0
Chapinero	54	25.9	59.3	14.8
Ciudad Bolívar	33	0.0	51.5	48.5
Engativá	43	32.6	7.0	60.5
Fontibón	26	19.2	7.7	73.1
Kennedy	35	25.7	17.1	57.1
Mártires	5	20.0	40.0	40.0
Puente Aranda	15	20.0	20.0	60.0
Rafael Uribe	14	0.0	50.0	50.0
San Cristóbal	38	0.0	71.1	28.9
Santafé	39	10.3	64.1	25.6
Suba	43	30.2	18.6	51.2
Teusaquillo	25	28.0	20.0	52.0
Tunjuelito	37	0.0	40.5	59.5
Usaquén	36	33.3	16.7	50.0
Usme	11	0.0	45.5	54.5
Alrededores	15	40.0	20.0	40.0
Total	513	17.7	38.0	44.2

Source: Authors' compilation.

Table 3A.5 Players Who Attended the Sessions by Role

Player role	N	% of total recruited	% target group	% control group
1	227	90.80	75.33	24.67
2	195	82.28	84.10	15.90
3	91	97.85	100	
Total	513	568 recruited		

Source: Authors' compilation.

Table 3A.6 Players 1 by Groups

Target group			Control group		
Local officers	N	%		N	%
Mayor's office	3	1.75	College Students	27	48.21
Education[a]	31	18.13	Private sector[e]	9	16.07
Health[b]	34	19.88	Government (Central)[f]	10	17.86
Nutrition[c]	28	16.37	Government (District)[g]	10	17.86
Child Care[d]	44	25.73			
Surveyers SISBEN	31	18.13			
Total	171	100		56	100

Source: Authors' compilation.
a. Public schools and CADELs (Local Administrative Center for Education).
b. ARSs (Administradora del Régimen Subsidiado), UPAs (Unidad Primaria de Atención), UBAs (Unidad Básicas de Atención), CAMIs (Centros de Atención Médica Inmediata).
c. Community kitchens and COLs (Local Operative Center).
d. *Hogares comunitarios*, daycare centers, kindergarten, Casas Vecinales, nursery schools.
e. Universities and NGOs.
f. DNP (Departamento Nacional de Planeación).
g. SGD (Secretaría de Gobierno Distrital), SHD (Secretaría de Hacienda Distrital).

In the following three tables we show the composition of our sample for Players 1, 2 and 3 for both the target and controls to give an idea of the locations and occupations they have.

Table 3A.7 Players 2 by Groups

Target group			Control group		
	N	%		N	%
Displaced people	43	26.22	Students	27	87.10
People with disabilities	4	2.44	Private sector[a]	4	12.90
Indigenous people	1	0.61	Black	6	19.35
Ex-combatant	34	20.73	SISBEN	3	9.68
Recycler	18	10.98			
Street vendor	12	7.32			
Black	25	15.24			
SISBEN	107	65.24			
Total	164			31	

Source: Authors.
a. Universities and NGOs.

Table 3A.8 Players 3 by Groups

Target group			Control group		
Officers	N	%		N	%
Government (central)[a]	38	90.48	Students	30	61.22
Government (district)[b]	1	2.38	Private sector[d]	13	26.53
Congress	1	2.38	Street	6	12.24
International organizations[c]	2	4.76			
Total	42	100		49	100

Source: Authors' compilation.
a. Ministerio de Comunicaciones, Ministerio de Hacienda, Ministerio de Minas y Energía, Super Intendencia Financiera, DIAN (Dirección de Impuestos y Aduanas Nacionales), CGR (Contraloría General de la República), FOSYGA (Fondo de Solidaridad y Garantías).
b. SGD (Secretaria de Gobierno Distrital).
c. CEPAL (Comisión Económica para América Latina).
d. Universities and NGOs.

To give an idea of the socioeconomic status of the players recruited, table 3A.9 shows the household expenditures (in Colombian pesos and U.S. dollars) reported by players in both the target and control subsamples.

Table 3A.10 presents the kind of aid and welfare benefits that players 2 were receiving from the government through different social services programs. It is based on the demographic survey filled out for each participant.

Table 3A.9 Players' Monthly Household Expenditures by Role (US$)

Role player	Target			Control		
	1	2	3	1	2	3
Mean	293.22	135.19	678.25	906.10	580.10	1,147.70
Minimum	20.08	7.23	120.45	120.45	120.45	100.38
Maximum	3,613.50	401.50	2,409.00	4,015.00	2,409.00	6,022.50
Standard deviation	309.11	698.14	502.21	817.35	490.16	1,434.74

Source: Authors' compilation.
Note: US$1 = Col$2,490.66 (Monthly mean average for May to July 2006, according to http//:www.banrep.gov.co).

Table 3A.10 Welfare Benefits of Target Population (Players 2)

	Target	Control
1. Possession of an aid program certificate (percent)		
SISBEN certificate	52.63	9.67
Ex-combatant certificate	29.82	0
Displaced aid program certificate	11.40	0
Familias en Acción program	3.51	0
2. Use of welfare programs (percent)		
People receiving benefits from public programs	79.27	29.03
Education[a]	56.92	88.89
Nutrition[b]	29.23	0
Health[c]	84.62	33.33
Child care[d]	17.05	0

Source: Authors' compilation.
a. Public schools and CADELs (Local Administrative Center for Education).
b. Community kitchens and COLs (Local Operative Center).
c. ARSs (Administradora del Régimen Subsidiado), UPAs (Unidad Primaria de Atención), UBAs (Unidad Básicas de Atención), CAMIs (Centros de Atención Médica Inmediata).
d. *Hogares comunitarios*, daycare centers, kindergarten, Casas Vecinales, nursery schools.

Sociodemographic Characteristics of Players

Tables 3A.11 and 3A.12 present a series of characteristics for the sample of participants. Recall that only the information in the card was known to the other player.

Table 3A.11 Players 2 Characteristics Observed by Players 1

	Target	Control
Age		
Mean	31.98	22.39
Max	16	18
Min	65	32
SD	12.87	3.56
Marital status (%)		
Single	39.63	96.77
Married	7.93	3.23
Union	36.59	0
Divorced	3.66	0
Widow	12.20	0
Activity (%)		
Working	51.22	16.13
Studying	15.85	83.87
Looking for a job	21.95	0
Home work	7.93	0
Disabled	1.83	0
Other	1.22	0
Employment (%)		
Private sector	27	100
Unskilled worker	1.12	0
Government worker	2.25	0
Home worker	6.74	0
Professional worker	1.12	0
Independent worker	59.55	0
No payment	2.25	0
Years in that activity		
Mean	4.78	10.26
Max	40	21
Min	0	0.02
SD	8.29	7.67
Strata (%)		
0	13.50	0
1	26.99	3.23
2	25.77	9.68
3	17.79	54.84
4	15.95	19.35
5	0	6.45
6	0	6.45
Dependents		
Mean	1.98	0
Max	7	0
Min	0	0
SD	1.85	0
Children		
Mean	1.54	0
Max	6	0
Min	0	0
SD	1.58	0

	Target	Control
Gender (%)		
Female	57.93	58.06
Male	42.07	41.94
Race (%)		
Black	15.24	19.35
Indigenous	7.93	0
Mestizo	76.83	80.65
SISBEN (%)		
Yes	65.24	9.68
No	34.76	90.32
SISBEN group (%)		
0	43.40	0
1	39.62	0
2	13.21	33.33
3	3.77	33.33
4	0	33.33
Education: level[a]		
Mean	2.62	5.35
Max	6	8
Min	0	4
SD	0.79	0.80
Education: years		
Mean	8.15	17.26
Max	18	20
Min	0	15
SD	3.57	0.77
Other (%)		
Displaced people	38.39	0
People with disabilities	3.57	0
Ex-combatant	30.36	0
Indigenous	0.89	0
Recycler	16.07	0
Street vendor	10.71	0

Source: Authors' compilation.

Note: SD = standard deviation.

a. 1 = primary (incomplete); 2 = secondary (high school incomplete); 3 = tertiary (technical, college incomplete or complete).

Table 3A.12 Players 1 Characteristics Observed by Players 2

1	Código Jugador
	8/15/10041
La siguiente información es de la persona de la foto que la	
Edad	
21 años	
Género	
Femenino	
Nivel Educativo	
Universitario sin título	
Funcionario público de	
Colegio Distrital	
Cuántos años lleva trabajando allí	
10 años	
Cargo que desempeña en la institución	
Seguridad	

Only Target	N	%
Officers	176	77.53
Education[a]	35	19.89
CADEL		22.86
CED		60.00
Health[b]	34	19.31
CAMI		17.65
UBA		29.41
UPA		26.47
Nutrition[c]	28	15.91
COL		21.95
DABS		39.29
IDIPRON		25.00
Child Care[d]	54	30.68
jardinDABS		61.11
hogarICBF		38.89
Surveyers SISBEN	31	13.66

	Target	Control
Age		
Mean	34.3	25.9
Max	17	17
Min	55	54
SD	8.43	8.79
Gender		
Women	57.93	58.06
Male	42.07	41.94
Education: level		
Mean	4.46	5.71
Max	8	8
Min	2	3
SD	1.63	1.36
Education: years		
Mean	14.53	17.45
Max	20	20
Min	4	12
SD	3.91	1.66
Years in the activity		
Mean	5.49	3.48
Max	33	22
Min	0.08	0.03
SD	5.88	4.88
Private sector[e]	18.13	6.90
Position		
For the government[f]	81.87	93.10
Blue collar	36.43	7.14
White collar	63.57	92.59
Students	0.00	48.21

Source: Authors' compilation.

Note: SD = standard deviation.

a. Public schools, CADELs (Local Administrative Center for Education) and CED (Centro de Educacion para el Desarrollo: Education Programs).

b. ARSs (Administradora del Régimen Subsidiado), UPAs (Unidad Primaria de Atención), UBAs (Unidad Básicas de Atención), and CAMIs (Centros de Atención Médica Immediata).

c. Community kitchens and COLs (Local Operative Center).

d. Community kitchens, COL (Local Operative Center), DABS (Departamento Administrativo de Bienestar Social: Welfare Programs), and IDIPRON (Instituto para la Protección de la Niñez y la Juventud: Youth and Childhood Protection).

e. Universities and NGOs.

f. DNP (Departamento Nacional de Planeación), SGD (Secretaría de Gobierno Distrital), SHD (Secretaría de Hacienda Distrital).

Payments

Each player received his or her earnings from at least one of the five games and at most three games, randomly selected. The final frequency of each game paid to each player is reported in table 3A.13. Since in the 3PP game

Table 3A.13 Frequency of Payments by Game

Role player	Game				
	DDG	DG	UG	TG	3PP
1	19.33	14.29	18.07	13.03	39.08
2	59.09	14.05	16.94	12.81	39.26
3	n.a.	n.a.	n.a.	n.a.	100.00
Total	33.04	11.89	14.69	10.84	48.95

Source: Authors' compilation.
Note: n.a. = not applicable. DDG = distributive dictator game; DG = dictator game; UG = ultimatum game; TG = trust game; 3PP = third-party punishment game.

Table 3A.14 Earnings by Role[a]

Role player	Mean	Maximum	Minimum	Sum	Standard deviation
1	3.71	10.40	0.00	862	1.80
2	6.60	16.00	0.00	1,504	3.07
3	3.84	4.00	3.20	354	0.32
Total	4.93	16.00	0.00	2,719	2.69

Source: Authors' compilation.
a. An activity was not paid for when the participant did not attend the session. Earnings do not include the show-up fee (Col$4,000 = US$1.60) paid to each participant.

we needed to pay at least one player 3, and we wanted to pay all players when a game was selected, all players 1 and 2 involved in the 3PP were paid. Those players who were not paid for the 3PP were paid for one of the other activities.

The final earnings, without show-up fee, are reported in table 3A.14. Overall, US$2,700 was paid to the 513 people who participated. Every player also received a show-up fee of Col$4,000 (US$1.6).

Social Efficiency and Equity across Games

Table 3A.15 reports the social efficiency and equity statistics for each of the games and for the two major types of (player 1–player 2) interactions, by sample. These interactions consisted of target-target, control-control, target-control, and control-target.

Table 3A.15 Social Efficiency and Equity in the Dictator, Ultimatum, Trust, and Third-Party Punishment Games

General		DDG	DG	UG	TG	3PP
Number of observations		557	558	559	444	2,118
Real social efficiency	Mean	100%	89%	83%	93%	91%
	Maximum	1.00	1.00	1.00	1.00	1.00
	Minimum	1.00	0.00	0.50	0.73	0.00
	Standard deviation	0.00	0.30	0.13	0.11	0.18
Player 2's equity	Mean	54%	62%	61%	36%	53%
	Maximum	1.00	1.00	1.00	0.66	1.00
	Minimum	0.00	0.00	0.00	0.00	0.00
	Standard deviation	0.28	0.24	0.17	0.15	0.24
Target: Players 1 and 2		DDG	DG	UG	TG	3PP
Number of observations		364	360	363	283	1,370
Real social efficiency	Mean	100%	89%	83%	92%	91%
	Maximum	1.00	1.00	1.00	1.00	1.00
	Minimum	1.00	0.00	0.50	0.73	0.00
	Standard deviation	0.00	0.30	0.13	0.11	0.18
Player 2's equity	Mean	52%	62%	61%	35%	52%
	Maximum	1.00	1.00	1.00	0.66	1.00
	Minimum	0.00	0.00	0.00	0.00	0.00
	Standard deviation	0.27	0.23	0.17	0.15	0.24

(continued)

Table 3A.15 Social Efficiency and Equity in the Dictator, Ultimatum, Trust, and Third-Party Punishment Games *(continued)*

Control: Players 1 and 2		DDG	DG	UG	TG	3PP
Number of observations		52	57	53	28	190
Real social efficiency	Mean	100%	80%	76%	99%	88%
	Maximum	1.00	1.00	1.00	1.00	1.00
	Minimum	1.00	0.00	0.50	0.73	0.00
	Standard deviation	0.00	0.30	0.12	0.05	0.24
Player 2's equity	Mean	42%	61%	57%	32%	48%
	Maximum	1.00	1.00	0.93	0.66	1.00
	Minimum	0.00	0.30	0.13	0.00	0.00
	Standard deviation	0.25	0.21	0.16	0.12	0.22
Control: Players 1 – Target: Players 2		DDG	DG	UG	TG	3PP
Number of observations		98	99	99	84	380
Real social efficiency	Mean	100%	94%	87%	93%	94%
	Maximum	1.00	1.00	1.00	1.00	1.00
	Minimum	1.00	0.00	0.50	0.73	0.00
	Standard deviation	0.00	0.22	0.12	0.11	0.14
Player 2's equity	Mean	70%	71%	68%	44%	62%
	Maximum	1.00	1.00	1.00	0.66	1.00
	Minimum	0.00	0.10	0.35	0.00	0.00
	Standard deviation	0.28	0.23	0.16	0.16	0.24

Source: Authors.
Note: DDG = distributive dictator game; DG = dictator game; UG = ultimatum game; TG = trust game; 3PP = third-party punishment game.

Notes

The authors want to acknowledge the help of the many people who contributed to this project, which enabled them to achieve sampling across the city, recruit participants, conduct the experimental sessions, explore archives, and understand the provision of social services to the poor. They are grateful to the following organizations and individuals: Fundación Enséñame a Pescar; Dangely Bernal, Pilar Cuervo, Álvaro Castillo, Hernando Ramírez, Dora Alarcón, and Fernando Arrázola (Consultorio Jurídico y Facultad de Derecho, Universidad de los Andes); Rocío Marín (Defensoría del Pueblo); Sandra Carolina Vargas (Facultad de Economía, Universidad de los Andes); Natalia Marín (Foro Joven); Yezid Botiva (SEI Consultores); Teresa Ortiz (Jardín Infantil Gimnasio Británico); Luz Mélida Hernández (Fundación Bella Flor); Carlos Betancourt and Germán Nova (Secretaría de Hacienda Distrital); Mauricio Castillo and Luis Hernando Barreto (Contraloría General de la República); Jeannette Avila (Departamento Administrativo de Bienestar Social); and the following students from the Universidad de los Andes, who volunteered at different stages of the project: Pablo Andrés Pérez, Stybaliz Castellanos, Juan Carlos Reyes, Andrés Felipe Sarabia, Gustavo Caballero, Gloria Carolina Orjuela, Orizel Llanos, and Fabián García. Finally, the authors wish to express their gratitude to Hugo Ñopo and Andrea Moro, who provided valuable comments on previous drafts.

1. All but the last experiment involve a player 1 (provider) and a player 2 (beneficiary). For the third-party punishment game, a third player decides whether to punish at a personal cost player 1 when the latter has acted unfairly against player 2. The strategy method is used for games where players 2 have to make choices contingent on the decisions by players 1. We asked players 2 and 3 to elicit their responses to every possible scenario or choice by player 1, before realizing the actual decisions. Thus we gathered rich information about reciprocal responses by players 2 and 3.

2. At the time of the experiments, the exchange rate was about US$1 = Col$2,490 (Colombian pesos). The minimum wage at the time was about US$5.5 a day, about Col$13,300 a day.

3. See Chaudhuri and Sethi (2003) for a survey of the Arrow-Phelps literature on stereotypes and statistical discrimination.

4. Sistemas Únicos de Información sobre Beneficiarios en América Latina.

5. Régimen Subsidiado en Salud, based on SISBEN rankings.

6. http://www.ramajudicial.gov.co; http://200.21.19.133/sentencias/.

7. "Writ of protection of constitutional rights."

8. The constitutional court has made several rulings based on the mechanism of the *tutela* commanding public institutions to guarantee social services to the poor. We find the following types of arguments: (1) individuals who argue that their rights and the principle of equality have been violated as a result of being classified into the SISBEN indexing system; (2) displaced people who argue for equal treatment when asking for social services such as health care and medicines, education for their children, housing and economic stabilization programs, and child care; (3) displaced people who argue that they should be registered as displaced (to obtain the *Sistema Único de Registro de Desplazados*); (4) people who argue that they have been denied treatment for no reason by health care institutions.

The Colombian ombudsman (Defensoría del Pueblo) has heard various allegations in which poor people claimed to be the subject of social exclusion in the provision of social services. Out of 1,123 accusations, 100 describe circumstances in which poor people could have experienced discrimination by local officials involved in providing social services. Among the cases of alleged discrimination, 52 percent involved health care institutions, 20 percent involved educational institutions, 20 percent featured problems with SISBEN surveyors, 6 percent involved claims with institutions that provide nutrition, and 2 percent involved disputes with child care institutions. Those who alleged discrimination possessed the following sociodemographic characteristics (totals add up to more than 100 percent because of multiple characteristics): 64 percent were women, 46 percent were unemployed or working at home, 9 percent were displaced, 30 percent were handicapped, and 7 percent were from other parts of the country or were indigenous or Afro descendants.

9. *Reinsertados* is a common name used to identify ex-combatants from irregular armed forces who are in the process of being reinserted into civil life through government programs that provide various kinds of support.

10. The design for this game has benefitted greatly from the valuable exchange with Catherine Eckel (University of Texas at Dallas).

11. Including traits and mechanisms related to other-regarding preferences such as altruism, reciprocal altruism, reciprocity, fairness, trust, and altruistic (social) punishment.

12. This result, however, needs to be explored further because we initially used the self-reported ethnic or racial affiliation, which might involve subreporting of affiliation with minorities or groups that have been historically discriminated against.

13. We have, however, data for the 55 people who did not attend, because we collected basic demographic information at the time of recruitment such as age, gender, and education level.

14. Brañas (2006) is an exception.

15. The National Association of Recyclers (http://www.anr.org.co/) has estimated that about 50,000 families depend on money earned by recycling garbage from the streets.

References

Arrow, Kenneth J. 1973. "The Theory of Discrimination." In *Discrimination in Labor Markets*, ed. Orley Ashenfelter and Albert Rees. Princeton, NJ: Princeton University Press.

Becker, Gary S. 1971. *The Economics of Discrimination*. Chicago: University of Chicago Press.

Berg, Joyce, John Dickhaut, and Kevin McCabe. 1995. "Trust, Reciprocity, and Social History." *Games and Economic Behavior* 10 (1995): 122–42.

Bertrand, Marianne, and Sendhil Mullainathan. 2004. "Are Emily and Greg More Employable Than Lakisha and Jamal? A Field Experiment on Labor Market Discrimination." *American Economic Review* 94 (4): 991–1013.

Bowles, Samuel. 2004. *Microeconomics: Behavior, Institutions, and Evolution*. Princeton, NJ: Princeton University Press.

Bowles, Samuel, and Herbert Gintis. 2000. "Walrasian Economics in Retrospect." *Quarterly Journal of Economics* 115 (4): 1411–39.

Brañas, Pablo. 2006. "Poverty in Dictator Games: Awakening Solidarity." *Journal of Economic Behavior and Organization* 60 (3): 306–20.

Camerer, Colin F., and Ernst Fehr. 2004. "Measuring Social Norms and Preferences Using Experimental Games: A Guide for Social Scientists." In *Foundations of Human Sociality: Economic Experiments and Ethnographic Evidence from fifteen Small-Scale Societies*, ed. Joseph Henrich and others. Oxford, U.K.: Oxford University Press.

Cárdenas, Juan-Camillo, and Jeffrey Carpenter. 2008. "Behavioural Development Economics: Lessons from Field Labs in the Developing World." *Journal of Development Studies* 44 (3, March): 337–64.

Cárdenas, Juan-Camillo, and Rajiv Sethi. 2009. "Resource Allocation in Public Agencies: Experimental Evidence." Working Paper, Columbia University, New York. http://www.columbia.edu/~rs328/rankings.pdf.

Chaudhuri, Shubham, and Rajiv Sethi. 2003. "Statistical Discrimination with Neighborhood Effects: Can Integration Eliminate Negative Stereotypes?" Game Theory and Information EconWPA 0312001, Columbia University, Barnard College, New York.

Fehr, Ernst, and Urs Fischbacher. 2004. "Third-Party Punishment and Social Norms." *Evolution and Human Behavior* 25 (2): 63–87.

Fehr, Ernst, and Simon Gachter. 2002. "Altruistic Punishment in Humans." *Nature* 415 (10 January): 137–40.

Fong, Christina, Samuel Bowles, and Herbert Gintis. 2005. "Behavioural Motives for Income Redistribution." *Australian Economic Review* 38 (3): 285–97.

Fong, Christina M., and Erzo F. P. Luttmer. 2008. "What Determines Giving to Hurricane Katrina Victims? Experimental Evidence on Racial Group Loyalty." Department of Social and Decision Sciences, Carnegie Mellon University (May).

Forsythe, Robert, Joel L, Horowitz, N. E. Savin, and Martin Sefton. 1994. "Fairness in Simple Bargaining Experiments." *Games and Economic Behavior* 6 (3): 347–69.

Gaviria, Alejandro, and Román Ortiz. 2005. "Inequidad racial en la afiliación al régimen subsidiado en salud." Unpublished mss., Universidad de los Andes, Facultad de Economía, Bogotá.

Gintis, Herbert, Samuel Bowles, Robert T. Boyd, and Ernst Fehr, eds. 2005. *Moral Sentiments and Material Interests: The Foundations of Cooperation in Economic Life, Economic Learning, and Social Evolution.* Cambridge, MA: MIT Press.

Güth, Werner, Rolf Schmittberger, and Bernd Schwarze. 1982. "An Experimental Analysis of Ultimatum Bargaining." *Journal of Economic Behavior and Organization* 3 (4): 367–88.

Henrich, Joseph, Robert Boyd, Samuel Bowles, Colin Camerer, Ernst Fehr, and Herbert Gintis, eds. 2004. *Foundations of Human Sociality: Economic Experiments and Ethnographic Evidence from fifteen Small-Scale Societies.* Oxford: Oxford University Press.

Henrich, Joseph, R. McElreath, A. Barr, J. Ensminger, C. Barrett, A. Bolyanatz, J. C. Cardenas, and others. 2006. "Costly Punishment across Human Societies." *Science* (23 June): 1767–70.

Irarrázaval, Ignacio. 2004. "Sistemas únicos de información sobre beneficiarios en América Latina." Paper presented at the VII Hemispheric Meeting of the Inter-American Development Bank Poverty and Social Protection Network, November 11.

Kahneman, Daniel, Jack L. Knetsch, and Richard Thaler. 1986. "Fairness as a Constraint on Profit Seeking: Entitlements in the Market." *American Economic Review* 76 (4): 728–41.

Katz, Irwin, and R. Glen Hass. 1989. "Racial Ambivalence and American Value Conflict: Correlational and Priming Studies of Dual Cognitive Structures." *Journal of Personality and Social Psychology* 55 (6): 893–905.

Núñez, Jairo, and Silvia Espinosa. 2005. "Exclusión e incidencia del gasto social." Documento CEDE 2005-16, Universidad de los Andes, Facultad de Economía, Bogotá.

Phelps, Edmund S. 1972. "The Statistical Theory of Racism and Sexism." *American Economic Review* 62 (4): 659–61.

4

Discrimination and Social Networks: Popularity among High School Students in Argentina

Julio Elías, Víctor Elías, and Lucas Ronconi

This chapter seeks to understand peer popularity and to assess the extent of discrimination in the formation of networks during adolescence in Argentina. Are teenagers of some particular ethnic origin less likely to be accepted by their peers? Does parental income matter for popularity? Are foreign-born teenagers excluded? Does physical attractiveness matter? The importance of this issue is underscored by several studies and in the media, suggesting that discrimination is a problem in Argentine society (Braylan and Jmelnizky 2004; Villalpando and others 2006).

To answer these questions, we asked high school students to select and rank 10 classmates with whom they would like to form a team to perform school activities and then used this information to construct a measure of

Julio Elías is with the Banco Central de la República Argentina and the Universidad del CEMA, Víctor Elías is with the Universidad Nacional de Tucumán, and Lucas Ronconi is with the Universidad Torcuato Di Tella. The authors would like to thank Adriana Boyer, Lucas Sal, and Olga Seeber for their excellent research assistance as well as Hugo Ñopo Aguilar, Alberto Chong, and Andrea Moro for their valuable comments and suggestions. They also benefited from the comments of Marina Bassi, Laura Ripani, Alejandro Rodríguez, John Dunn Smith, and Máximo Torero, and of seminar participants at the Universidad de San Andrés and at the meetings of the Latin American Research Network on "Discrimination and Economic Outcomes" in Washington, DC, and Mexico in 2006. They are grateful to Raquel Gómez for her hospitality and help as a research network coordinator.

popularity. Next, we collected information on students' characteristics, including physical attractiveness, ethnic origin, skin color, nationality, previous academic performance, personality traits, parental socioeconomic background, and other family characteristics. We then explored the effect of these characteristics on popularity.

Being popular during adolescence is relevant for at least three reasons. First, school peer effects are important for academic achievement (see Zimmerman 2003). Second, peer popularity affects the development of social skills, which in turn appear to be important for success during adulthood. For instance, Galeotti and Mueller (2005) find that adults who are highly ranked by their classmates during high school earn significantly higher wages during adulthood, and Kuhn and Weinberger (2005) find that people who occupy leadership positions in high school subsequently earn more during adulthood. Third, attaining status in the groups to which we belong is a goal of social life (see, for example, Becker, Murphy, and Werning 2005).

This study has two distinctive features. First, and contrary to most empirical work that relies on experiments where the environment is artificial, we study real school classes.[1] School authorities asked students to select classmates with whom to form a team, mentioning that, based on their expressed preferences, teams would be formed to conduct activities during the rest of the year. Second, to the best of our knowledge, the micro data sets available to study discrimination in Argentina do not include information on factors such as skin color, ethnicity, or physical attractiveness.[2] The findings reported here are based on a rich set of student characteristics that were collected to explore the existence of discrimination against different traits and to avoid potential omitted-variable bias.

The chapter proceeds as follows. The first section describes the survey design and procedures, the second presents the data and discusses the measures of popularity and beauty, the third presents results on the main determinants of students' popularity, the fourth discusses some features of popularity and social networks, the fifth discusses expected sorting by groups, and the sixth provides some estimates of the potential benefits of joining a network. A final section concludes.

Survey Design and Procedures

The sample frame consists of schools with students attending third grade in the *polimodal* (that is, equivalent to the last year in high school) in Florencio Varela and Hurlingham (two municipalities located in greater Buenos Aires) and in the city of Tucumán.[3] According to the 2001 census, approximately 1.3 million individuals 16–17 years of age were living in Argentina. The selected sample frame imposes two potential biases with respect to the population. First, only 40 percent of the population under study resides in the selected provinces (35 percent in Buenos Aires and 5 percent in Tucumán). Second, not all teenagers are enrolled in high school. According to the Ministry of Education, approximately three-quarters were enrolled in high school in 2001.[4] The figure is 73 percent for Greater Buenos Aires and 65 percent for Tucumán. Dropouts have different characteristics than those enrolled in high school (for example, they are poorer on average), which suggests the inadequacy of extrapolating the results of the study to them.

Almost 1,000 schools offer *polimodal* in Greater Buenos Aires, including 30 located in the municipality of Florencio Varela and 23 in Hurlingham. In the city of Tucumán, 88 schools offer *polimodal*. The survey was performed in nine schools in Greater Buenos Aires (six in Florencio Varela and three in Hurlingham) and seven schools in Tucumán.

Data were collected in the following manner. First, a survey was conducted in the classroom, where the "tutor"[5] gave students a questionnaire asking them to rank classmates according to their preference for forming a team.[6] Based on this information, different measures of popularity were constructed.

Two important aspects of the survey are worth emphasizing. First, the survey was conducted in March (the first month of the school year in Argentina), and students were told that, based on their expressed preferences, teams would be formed at some point during the year to conduct activities at school and that teams would meet on a regular basis. Second, in all schools where the survey was conducted, the authorities were planning to form teams and act on this information. Therefore, the environment was not artificial.

After collecting the first questionnaire, the tutor gave students a second questionnaire, which included questions about socioeconomic background, nationality, race, ethnicity, and personality. Finally, students received a third questionnaire, which asked them to name and rank, separately, the three female and male classmates that they considered to be physically the most attractive. At this point, the tutor asked students to fill out the questionnaire responsibly, mentioning that the results would remain strictly confidential and would be used by researchers to analyze the role that beauty and other factors play among adolescents.

The second source of information was school records. Information was collected on students' grades during the previous year, whether the student was a beneficiary of the Becas program, and the year in which the student enrolled in the school.[7]

The annex to this chapter presents an English translation of the three questionnaires, which were designed with the following (sometimes conflicting) objectives: maintaining simplicity, collecting relevant information, avoiding nonresponses, and increasing the reliability of answers. Discussions with schoolteachers and authorities were extremely helpful in designing the questionnaires.

Data

This section describes the measures used for popularity and beauty and presents the data for schools located in Buenos Aires and in Tucumán.

Popularity and Beauty

Measures of popularity and beauty were created by focusing on the ranking sections of the survey (first and third questionnaires). As students ranked their order of preference for 10 classmates as members of a group to perform school activities, it is possible to derive measures of peer popularity based either on the rankings that students received from their classmates or simply on whether they were chosen.[8]

There are alternative ways to measure popularity and beauty. One of the most common measures of popularity in network analysis is the number of times each student is chosen by his or her classmates divided by class size. In this study, an analogous measure is constructed that also incorporates the extra information coming from the student's position in the ranking.

First, the position of the student in the average ranking is considered as a measure of popularity. To construct this measure, a ranking from 1 to 11 is considered, where the eleventh position is assigned to students who were not nominated in the first 10 positions by their classmates. Under this assumption, the average ranking for student i is given by the following:

$$\bar{r}_i = \sum_{b=1}^{11} \frac{N_{b,i} w_b}{ClassSize_i - 1} \tag{4.1}$$

where $w_1 = 1$, $w_2 = 2$, ... $w_{10} = 10$, and $w_{11} = 11$, $N_{b,i}$ is the number of times student i was nominated in the b position by his or her classmates, w_b is the ranking position, and $ClassSize_i$ is the total number of students in the class. An advantage of this simple measure is that a monotonic transformation of the ranking variable, w_b, does not affect the qualitative results.

Additionally, a dichotomous variable approach is applied to perform the analysis, which can be considered as a monotonic transformation of the student ranking variable, w_b. As a consequence, similar results are obtained. However, this approach is helpful in analyzing other important aspects of the same problem. Within this approach, two alternatives are considered. First, popularity is defined as a dichotomous variable that indicates whether the student was chosen by at least 50 percent of his or her classmates. That is,

$$d_i = \begin{cases} 1 & if & \dfrac{\sum\limits_{h=1}^{10} N_{h,i}}{ClassSize - 1} \geq 0.5 \\[20pt] 0 & Otherwise \end{cases} \qquad (4.2)$$

A second alternative considered for each student in the class is whether he or she was chosen separately by each of his or her classmates in the first five places for forming a group. That is,

$$d_{i,j} = \begin{cases} 1 & if & \text{student } j \text{ chose student } i \text{ in the first five places} \\[10pt] 0 & Otherwise \end{cases} \qquad (4.3)$$

For example, in a class of 20 students, there will be 19 observations for each student, indicating whether he or she was chosen by each of the members of the class. In this example, there will be a total of 380 observations just for this class. A valuable feature of this approach is that it permits an investigation of how the rater's characteristics affect the individual's selection of peers.

Finally, the standard deviation of the ranking of each student is computed. That is,

$$\sigma_{\bar{r}i} = \sqrt{\sum_{h=1}^{11} \frac{N_{h,i}(w_h - \bar{r}_i)^2}{ClassSize_i - 1}} \qquad (4.4)$$

The standard deviation is low for students who are either very popular or very unpopular and is high for those who are liked by some, but not all, of their classmates. This measure permits an analysis of the degree of homogeneity of preferences within a classroom.

Using the information obtained by the third questionnaire, a formula similar to equation 4.1 is applied to construct a proxy for beauty. In this case, however, h goes from 1 to 4, since students were asked to rank only the three physically most attractive classmates. That is, the measure of beauty is defined as follows:

$$B_i = \frac{\sum\limits_{h=1}^{4} N_{h,i} w_h}{ClassSize_i - 1} \qquad (4.5)$$

where $w_1 = 3$, $w_2 = 2$, $w_3 = 1$, and $w_4 = 0$ and $N_{h,i}$ is the number of times student i was ranked in the h position by his or her classmates.

Schools Located in Buenos Aires

In Buenos Aires, the survey was conducted in nine schools—six in Florencio Varela and three in Hurlingham. Four out of the nine schools are public, and two are located in the municipality of Florencio Varela. The total number of students in the selected schools is 641, and the average class size is 26 students. Although 62 students were absent on the day the survey was conducted, there was a 100 percent participation rate among those who were present. Therefore, 579 students completed the surveys. The average age is 17 years old, less than half of the students are male, and almost all of the students were born in Argentina (only one student in the sample is foreign born—in neighboring Paraguay).

Table 4.1 presents basic statistics, the number of responses, and correlations for the main independent variables that enter into the preliminary specification. A valuable feature of this study is that a very high percentage of students answered each question. With the exception of ethnicity, which was answered by only 65 percent of students,[9] all of the remaining questions were answered by more than 90 percent of students. Approximately 45 percent of the sample has white skin. With respect to ethnic origin, 87 percent of the students who answered the question mentioned European origins, 18 percent Native American, 4 percent Middle Eastern, 2 percent Asian, and 1 percent African (students were asked to select all ethnic origins that apply). Out of a set of four goods (car, computer, access to Internet, and air conditioning), students have, on average, 1.6 goods. Each student has, on average, 2.6 siblings. The average grade the previous year is 7 out of 10 for math and 7.7 out of 10 for literature, and 19 percent of the sample receives a Beca scholarship. The average parental education is 9.7 years of schooling.

It is difficult to determine whether this is a representative sample of the population because there are no other surveys with information about skin color or ethnicity. However, it is possible to compare other characteristics such as parental education. The Encuesta de Calidad de Vida (ECV) was conducted by the National Institute of Statistics in 2001. The average parental education of teenagers 16 to 17 years of age, who were enrolled in *polimodal* and living in Greater Buenos Aires (which includes both Hurlingham and Florencio Varela) was 9.9 years of schooling in 2001, slightly higher than in the sample we study.

Panel A of table 4.1 presents the correlations between the main independent variables included in our specification. As expected, the measure of wealth (hereafter, parental wealth) is highly correlated with parents' average education, with a correlation coefficient of 0.46, and is negatively correlated with whether the student receives a scholarship and number of siblings, with correlation coefficients of –0.32 and –0.23, respectively. Parental wealth and parents' average education are also positively correlated with whether the student is white and has European ethnicity.

Table 4.1 Descriptive Statistics, Buenos Aires

A. Mean, Standard Deviation, and Correlations of Selected Individual Characteristics

	Parental wealth	Parental education	Has scholarship	Literature grade	Math grade	Beauty	White skin	Native American ethnicity	European ethnicity	Foreign-born parents	Number siblings
Mean	1.59	9.74	0.19	7.72	6.97	0.28	0.45	0.18	0.87	0.09	2.6
Standard deviation	1.37	3.75	0.39	1.47	2.09	0.40	0.50	0.38	0.33	0.28	1.8
Number responses	568	578	641	532	530	641	572	371	371	545	564
Parental education	0.46										
Has scholarship	-0.32	-0.29									
Literature grade	-0.11	-0.03	0.11								
Math grade	-0.05	-0.02	0.11	0.33							
Beauty	0.07	-0.05	0.07	0.09	0.02						
White skin	0.18	0.19	-0.03	-0.02	-0.02	0.05					

(continued)

Table 4.1 Descriptive Statistics, Buenos Aires *(continued)*

A. Mean, Standard Deviation, and Correlations of Selected Individual Characteristics *(continued)*

	Parental wealth	Parental education	Has scholarship	Literature grade	Math grade	Beauty	White skin	Native American ethnicity	European ethnicity	Foreign-born parents	Number siblings
Native American ethnicity	−0.13	−0.20	0.08	0.01	0.09	−0.06	−0.15				
European ethnicity	0.16	0.14	−0.02	0.03	−0.01	0.07	0.20	−0.59			
Foreign-born parents	0.02	−0.08	0.01	0.04	−0.01	0.01	−0.06	0.11	−0.11		
Number siblings	−0.23	−0.19	0.12	−0.10	−0.02	0.01	−0.10	0.09	−0.06	0.04	1.00

B. Mean and Standard Deviation of Selected Individual Characteristics

Variable	Number of responses	Mean	Standard deviation
Age	579	17.1	0.71
Gender (male = 1)	641	0.47	0.50
Nationality (Argentine = 1)	576	0.99	0.05
African ethnicity	371	0.01	0.09
Asian ethnicity	371	0.02	0.15
Middle East ethnicity	371	0.04	0.19

Source: Authors' compilation.

Regarding school performance, math grades are highly correlated with literature grades, with a correlation coefficient of 0.33. Hereafter, the average grade is used as a measure of a student's academic performance.

The overall standard deviation is 0.5 for white skin, 1.37 for parental wealth, and 3.75 for parental education. The within-school class standard deviation for these variables is 0.47, 1.07, and 3.09, respectively. These figures show that heterogeneity within the school class is high with respect to race and socioeconomic status, implying that this is an appropriate environment in which to study peer discrimination.[10]

Schools Located in Tucumán

The survey was also conducted in seven schools in Tucumán. Two out of the seven schools are public. The total number of students in the selected schools is 375, and the average class size is 28.8 students. While 32 students were absent the day the survey was conducted, there was a 100 percent participation rate among those who were present. Therefore, information is available for 343 students. The average age in the sample is 16.8 years old, slightly lower than in the sample for Buenos Aires, and only two students in the sample are foreign born.

Table 4.2 presents basic statistics for the sample of Tucumán, the number of responses, and correlations for the main independent variables that enter into the specifications. As in the case of Buenos Aires, the response rate was very high. Most questions, including ethnicity, were answered by more than 95 percent of the students. Approximately 44 percent of the sample has white skin, almost the same as the 45 percent found for Buenos Aires. With respect to ethnic origin, the percentage of the students who reported European and Native American origin is much lower than in Buenos Aires. In Tucumán, 64 percent of students reported European origin, compared with 87 percent in Buenos Aires, and 13 percent reported Native American origin, compared with 18 percent in Buenos Aires. In contrast, the proportion reporting Middle Eastern origin is much higher, 12 percent compared with 4 percent in Buenos Aires. Students have an average of 2.4 siblings. The average grade the previous year is 6.4 out of 10 for math and 7.4 out of 10 for literature; only 8 percent of the sample receives a Beca scholarship.

Students have, on average, 2.1 out of four goods (car, computer, access to Internet, and air conditioning), and the average parental education in the sample is 13 years of schooling. Clearly, the Tucumán sample has a higher socioeconomic status than the Buenos Aires sample. This difference is explained, in part, by the fact that the average income and education in the capital city of Tucumán are higher than in both Hurlingham and Florencio Varela. But five of the seven schools surveyed in Tucumán are private, which suggests that the sample we study in Tucumán over-represents students with high socioeconomic status. This is confirmed by the fact

Table 4.2 Descriptive Statistics, Tucumán

A. Mean, Standard Deviation, and Correlations of Selected Individual Characteristic

	Parental wealth	Parental education	Has scholarship	Literature grade	Math grade	Beauty	White skin	Native American ethnicity	European ethnicity	Foreign-born parents	Number siblings
Mean	2.13	13.05	0.08	7.37	6.40	0.31	0.44	0.13	0.64	0.03	2.40
Standard deviation	1.40	3.8	0.27	1.51	1.99	0.51	0.50	0.33	0.48	0.17	1.32
Number responses	342	343	375	339	336	375	343	343	343	336	343
Parental education	0.39										
Has scholarship	-0.14	-0.15									
Literature grade	0.28	0.15	-0.19								
Math grade	0.20	0.20	-0.21	0.40							
Beauty	-0.04	0.10	0.00	-0.06	-0.06						
White skin	0.14	0.12	-0.02	0.05	0.03	0.09					
Native American ethnicity	-0.12	-0.07	0.05	0.03	0.00	-0.14	-0.16				

(continued)

Table 4.2 Descriptive Statistics, Tucumán (continued)

A. Mean, Standard Deviation, and Correlations of Selected Individual Characteristics (continued)

	Parental wealth	Parental education	Has scholarship	Literature grade	Math grade	Beauty	White skin	Native American ethnicity	European ethnicity	Foreign-born parents	Number siblings
European ethnicity	0.18	0.25	0.07	0.12	0.04	-0.08	0.06	0.00			
Foreign-born parents	0.10	0.04	-0.04	0.00	0.02	0.13	-0.05	0.04	-0.05		
Number siblings	-0.04	0.03	0.01	-0.07	-0.06	0.09	0.00	0.01	0.03	0.00	1.00

B. Mean and Standard Deviation of Selected Individual Characteristics

Variable	Number of responses	Mean	Standard deviation
Age	343	16.78	0.53
Gender (male = 1)	375	0.36	0.48
Nationality (Argentine = 1)	343	0.99	0.08
House is of corrugated iron	332	0.01	0.09
African ethnicity	343	0.01	0.08
Asian ethnicity	343	0.03	0.18
Middle East ethnicity	343	0.12	0.32

Source: Authors' compilation.

that, in the ECV, the average parental education is 10.8 among teenagers 16 to 17 years of age attending school and living in Greater Tucumán (which includes the city of Tucumán).[11]

Panel A of table 4.2 presents, for Tucumán, the correlations among the main independent variables included in the specification. As in the case of Buenos Aires, parental wealth is positively correlated with average parental education and negatively correlated with whether the students are on scholarship and the number of siblings, but they are lower in absolute terms than for Buenos Aires. Parental wealth and average parental education are also positively correlated with whether the student is white and with European ethnicity.

As in Buenos Aires, heterogeneity within the school class is high with respect to race and socioeconomic status. The overall and within-school class standard deviation is 0.5 and 0.48, respectively, for the variable white skin, 1.4 and 1.23 for parental wealth, and 3.8 and 3.4 for parental education.

Empirical Results

This section investigates the effects of individual characteristics, such as skin color, beauty, ethnic origin, and family wealth on student popularity. The analysis assumes that student rankings depend on a set of individual characteristics. In addition, in ranking their classmates, students may differ in their valuation of each relevant characteristic. Hence, there is a distribution of valuations over each characteristic in the population.

A student's ranking is therefore determined by his or her characteristics and by the value that his or her classmates (that is, the raters) place on each of these characteristics. The following empirical model, which serves as a baseline for the estimations, summarizes such considerations:

$$r_{i,j} = x_i'\alpha_j + \beta_{1,j}B_i + u_{i,j} \tag{4.6}$$

where $r_{i,j}$ is the ranking assigned to student i by student j, with values from 1 to 11, x_i is a vector of individual characteristics, B_i is a measure of beauty of the student, and $u_{i,j}$ is a disturbance, representing the other forces affecting $r_{i,j}$ that are not explicitly measured.

Using equation 4.6, equation 4.7 gives the average ranking of student i:

$$\bar{r}_i = x_i'\bar{\alpha} + \bar{\beta}_1 B_i + \bar{u}_i \tag{4.7}$$

where the upper bar denotes the mean over the school class.

According to equation 4.7, the partial effect of a student characteristic (for example, beauty, race) on its average ranking is equal to the class average valuation of that characteristic. An important implication of this analysis is that, by using the average student ranking as a measure of popularity, it is only possible to recover the population's average valuation placed on each characteristic.

In addition, the average valuations may also vary across different classes according to unobservable or observable class characteristics, such as average parental wealth and whether the class is mixed. This implies that the average ranking for student i in class k is given by the following:

$$\overline{r}_{ik} = x'_{ik}\overline{\alpha}_k + \overline{\beta}_{1,k}\overline{B}_{ik} + \overline{u}_{ik} \tag{4.8}$$

where the subscript k reflects variations in average valuations across school classes.

Estimating equation 4.8 raises some econometric problems. First, the error term in the linear regression model is heteroskedastic because the number of students differs by class, and the distribution itself may vary across classes. This problem is solved by computing clustered standard errors, where the clusters correspond to school classes.

Second, in estimating the effect of beauty on student average ranking, the measure of beauty is likely to have measurement error for at least two reasons. First, students only selected and ranked the three most attractive female and male classmates, not the entire class. Second, students did not provide an absolute measure of beauty for the selected classmates.

Different versions of equation 4.8 are estimated below. First, a common effect of individual characteristics on student average ranking is assumed. Then, variations on coefficients across classes are allowed according to whether the school is mixed. In order to check the robustness of our estimates to different definitions of popularity, a probit model is also run, using student popularity as defined in equation 4.2 as the dependent variable. Finally, a modified version of equation 4.6 is used to investigate how the beauty and academic performance of the rater affect his or her valuations of each individual characteristic.

Baseline Effects of Individual Characteristics on Popularity

In table 4.3 students are categorized according to their average ranking as very popular (top 20 percent of the class), moderately popular (between 20 and 80 percent), and unpopular (bottom 20 percent of the class). The table presents the mean of parental wealth, parental education, beauty, school performance, and race for these three groups. Results for Buenos Aires and Tucumán are presented separately.

In both provinces, highly popular students are, on average, physically more attractive and have better grades than unpopular students. When looking at differences in race, wealth, and parental education across groups, the sign of the differences varies according to the sample. In Buenos

Table 4.3 Wealth, Parental Education, School Performance, Race, and Beauty According to Student's Average Ranking, Buenos Aires and Tucumán

	Buenos Aires			Tucumán		
	Very popular (top 20%)	Moderately popular (between 20% and 80%)	Unpopular (bottom 20%)	Very popular (top 20%)	Moderately popular (between 20% and 80%)	Unpopular (bottom 20%)
Parental wealth	1.45	1.52	2.05	2.51	2.05	1.91
Parental education	9.21	9.71	10.52	13.53	13.00	12.60
Literature grade	8.04	7.76	7.10	7.62	7.39	7.00
Math grade	7.39	7.00	6.27	6.75	6.38	6.07
Beauty	0.40	0.28	0.10	0.51	0.28	0.14
White skin	0.45	0.46	0.41	0.39	0.46	0.46
Native American ethnicity	0.21	0.19	0.12	0.09	0.14	0.14
European ethnicity	0.89	0.86	0.91	0.63	0.62	0.69
Foreign parents	0.09	0.08	0.07	0	0.03	0.03

Source: Authors' compilation.

Aires, high-ranked students are, on average, poorer than low-ranked students, and their parents' average education is also lower. In Tucumán, the opposite is observed: students with a high average ranking are, on average, wealthier, and their parents are, on average, more educated. Since average wealth in the sample of Buenos Aires is lower than in the sample of Tucumán, this suggests that the relationship between average ranking and wealth may vary with the level of wealth, displaying a U-shaped relationship between average ranking and income. Regarding race, the percentage of students in Buenos Aires with Native American ethnicity is larger among high-ranked students than among low-ranked students, while in Tucumán the reverse is true. In addition, in Tucumán the percentage of students with white skin is lower among high-ranked students than among low-ranked students.

Table 4.4 presents estimates of the effects of individual characteristics on student popularity assuming a homogeneous effect across school classes. All regressions are run by ordinary least squares (OLS). The dependent

Table 4.4 Estimates of the Effects of Individual Characteristics on Student's Average Ranking, Buenos Aires and Tucumán

	All I	*Buenos Aires* II	*Tucumán* III
Age	0.037	0.097*	−0.104**
	(0.044)	(0.055)	(0.048)
Gender (male = 1)	−0.168	−0.309**	0.118
	(0.118)	(0.129)	(0.239)
Not born in the school province	0.549**	0.791***	−0.062
	(0.235)	(0.212)	(0.473)
Not born in the school district	−0.101	−0.147**	0.145
	(0.069)	(0.064)	(0.271)
Average grade	−0.195***	−0.179***	−0.199***
	(0.033)	(0.037)	(0.069)
Beauty	−0.377***	−0.297***	−0.501***
	(0.099)	(0.101)	(0.167)
Native American ethnicity	−0.063	−0.335	0.003
	(0.116)	(0.217)	(0.152)
European ethnicity	−0.111	−0.538**	−0.030
	(0.112)	(0.248)	(0.135)
African ethnicity	0.190	0.583*	0.466***
	(0.143)	(0.315)	(0.134)

(continued)

Table 4.4 Estimates of the Effects of Individual Characteristics on Student's Average Ranking, Buenos Aires and Tucumán *(continued)*

	All I	Buenos Aires II	Tucumán III
Asian ethnicity	0.227* (0.136)	–0.268 (0.217)	0.284* (0.167)
Middle Eastern ethnicity	0.081 (0.083)	–0.101 (0.176)	0.030 (0.128)
Did not report ethnicity	–0.038 (0.142)	–0.494* (0.253)	
Skin color (white = 1)	–0.022 (0.069)	–0.073 (0.094)	0.082 (0.093)
Parental wealth	–0.022 (0.031)	–0.005 (0.042)	–0.046 (0.047)
Parents' average education	–0.018** (0.009)	–0.016 (0.013)	–0.025** (0.010)
Number of siblings	0.019 (0.020)	0.037* (0.020)	–0.024 (0.050)
Foreign parents	0.037 (0.156)	–0.045 (0.174)	0.623* (0.333)
Observations	840	509	331
R^2	0.45	0.48	0.48
F	10.71	16.36	

Source: Authors' compilation.

Note: The samples for Buenos Aires and Tucumán comprise all the students who completed the surveys for whom all the variables included in the regression are available. The dependent variable is the Student's Average Ranking (see equation 4.1). All regressions include the following controls: school class dummies, student's numbers of years living in the school district, whether the student has a scholarship, whether the student lives with both parents, whether the student's parents are married, whether the student's parents were born outside the school province, and measures of the student's personality. Clustered standard errors are reported in parentheses below each coefficient, where clusters correspond to school classes.

* Significant at 10 percent.
** Significant at 5 percent.
*** Significant at 1 percent.

variable is the average student ranking as defined in equation 4.1. The first column presents results using the pooled sample. Columns 2 and 3 present results for Buenos Aires and Tucumán, respectively.

All specifications include school class dummies. The table reports only the variables that turn out to be important in the analysis, and the regressions include the following controls that are not reported in the table because they are not statistically significant: the number of years the student has been living in the school district, whether the student has a scholarship, whether the student lives with both parents, whether the student's parents are married, whether the student's parents were born outside the province in which the school is located, and measures of the student's personality. Clustered standard errors are reported in parentheses below each coefficient, where clusters correspond to school classes.

The results paint a consistent picture when looking across samples for two factors as the main determinants of a student's average ranking. These two factors are academic performance (average grade) and beauty. Both factors have a negative sign, which means that students with better grades and those perceived as more beautiful are ranked in a higher position (that is, are more popular). Both variables are statistically significant at the 1 percent level in all samples.

Consider first the effect of average grade on student popularity. The coefficients on this variable are very similar across samples, –0.18 for the sample of Buenos Aires and –0.2 for the sample of Tucumán, implying that a five-point increase in grades leads to a gain of approximately one position in the ranking.[12] Regarding the effect of beauty, the magnitude of the effect in the sample of Tucumán is larger than in the sample of Buenos Aires—by a factor of 1.7. This issue is discussed in more detail below.

There does not appear to be a strong and consistent effect of ethnicity and skin color on the average ranking of students. Skin color is not significantly correlated with popularity in any of the specifications. Regarding ethnic origin, in the pooled sample, only Asian ethnicity has a negative effect on popularity, and the effect is only significant at the 10 percent level. When looking at the sample of Buenos Aires, having European ethnicity significantly increases popularity, while having African ethnicity decreases popularity (significant at the 10 percent level). In Buenos Aires, however, those who did not report their ethnicity are more popular. Given that individuals who did not report ethnicity are more likely to be part of a minority, the estimated positive effect of European ethnicity may be biased upward. For Tucumán, where 95 percent of students reported ethnicity, African and Asian ethnicity is negatively correlated with popularity (although in the latter case the effect is only significant at the 10 percent level).

Regarding the effects of average parental education, the coefficients are negative and statistically significant in the pooled sample and in Tucumán (that is, students with more-educated parents are more popular). Parental wealth, in contrast, has no significant effect on popularity. Since the variables of wealth and average parental education are highly correlated (a correlation coefficient of 0.46 and 0.39 for the samples of Buenos Aires and Tucumán, respectively), it is hard to disentangle the effect. Finally, no correlation is found between popularity and parental nationality (except in Tucumán, where students with foreign-born parents are less popular, although the effect is only significant at the 10 percent level).

The effect of physical attractiveness on popularity would be biased if beauty were correlated with the error term. Physical attractiveness is measured based on the rankings provided by students, not by external evaluators. If students rank their classmates based not only on their physical attractiveness but also on other traits unobservable to the econometrician, the estimated effect of beauty would capture the effects of both physical attractiveness and the unobserved factor. Personality traits, such as extroversion, represent factors that are usually unobserved by the econometrician but could be correlated with both beauty and popularity (Anderson and others 2001).

To deal with this concern, students were explicitly asked to rank their classmates based on their physical appearance, and information was also collected on personality traits such as extroversion and conscientiousness. In particular, students were asked to report what they like to do when they meet with their friends (that is, talk a lot, tell jokes, listen), and what they plan to do after finishing high school (that is, study, work, work and study, don't know).[13] The estimates presented in table 4.4 control for these factors. Therefore, it is unlikely that the effect of physical attractiveness on popularity captures personality traits.

Furthermore, using the sample of mixed schools, four additional measures of physical attractiveness are generated, as defined in equation 4.4, but varying the group of raters according to their gender as follows: considering the rankings generated (1) by females only, (2) by males only, (3) by students of the same gender as the rated student, and (4) by students of the opposite gender as the rated student. Even though this strategy does not fully solve the concern that students select their most attractive classmates based on unobservable factors other than beauty, the underlying premise is that the criteria used by the rater to assess beauty in an "objective" way may vary according to the gender of the student rater or in relation to the gender of the rated student. That is, the omitted-variable bias may vary with the gender of the rater of beauty. Although it is a priori unknown how the bias varies with the different measures of beauty (that is, whether males or females are more "objective" raters), at least it is possible to analyze the extent to which the magnitude and the statistical significance of the coefficients are affected by the use of these different measures of beauty.

Table 4.5 presents the correlations between the different measures of physical attractiveness for the whole sample, as well as separately for Buenos Aires and Tucumán. As the table shows, the four additional measures of beauty are highly correlated with the measure of beauty generated using all students in the school class as raters (correlation coefficients range from 0.84 to 0.92). However, the correlation between the measures of beauty when the group of raters is restricted to male students or to female students is much lower, 0.65 for the whole sample. Thus it seems that both measures offer different information or measure different things.

Table 4.5 Matrix Correlation of Different Measures of Beauty, Buenos Aires and Tucumán

A. Whole Sample

		Measure of beauty computed using raters			
		Males	*Females*	*Opposite gender*	*Same gender*
Measure of beauty computed using raters	Females	0.65			
	Opposite gender	0.82	0.85		
	Same gender	0.83	0.80	0.65	
	Total class	0.87	0.91	0.91	0.86

Number of observations is 778.

B. Buenos Aires

		Measure of beauty computed using raters			
		Males	*Females*	*Opposite gender*	*Same gender*
Measure of beauty computed using raters	Females	0.61			
	Opposite gender	0.81	0.84		
	Same gender	0.81	0.77	0.62	
	Total class	0.84	0.92	0.91	0.85

Number of observations is 573.

C. Tucumán

		Measure of beauty computed using raters			
		Males	*Females*	*Opposite gender*	*Same gender*
Measure of beauty computed using raters	Females	0.69			
	Opposite gender	0.83	0.87		
	Same gender	0.85	0.83	0.69	
	Total class	0.91	0.89	0.92	0.88

Source: Authors' compilation.
Note: Number of observations is 205.

Table 4.6 presents estimates of the effect of beauty on popularity using the four additional measures of beauty defined above. Each column corresponds to one of the four measures of beauty. As the table shows, the

Table 4.6 Estimates of the Effects of Individual Characteristics on Student's Average Ranking Using Different Measures of Beauty: Mixed Schools, Whole Sample

	Raters			
	Females	Males	Same gender of rated	Opposite gender of rated
Beauty	−0.366***	−0.242**	−0.322***	−0.279**
	(0.074)	(0.108)	(0.075)	(0.113)
Observations	633	633	633	633
R^2	0.46	0.44	0.46	0.45

Source: Authors' compilation.

Note: The sample comprises all the students from mixed schools in Buenos Aires and Tucumán who filled out the surveys for whom all the variables included in the regression are available. The dependent variable is the student's average ranking (see equation 4.1). Each column corresponds to a different measure of beauty as defined in the text. All regressions include the same controls as in table 4.4. Clustered standard errors are reported in parentheses below each coefficient, where clusters correspond to school classes.

** Significant at 5 percent.

*** Significant at 1 percent.

results are practically unaffected, and the effect of beauty on popularity is positive and statistically significant, independent of the measure of beauty used. However, the magnitude of the effect varies depending on the gender of the rater. In particular, the coefficient when beauty is rated by male students is much lower than when beauty is rated by female students.

Finally, in order to check the robustness of the results to an alternative definition of popularity, a probit model is also run, using as the dependent variable whether the student was chosen by at least half of the class (see equation 4.2). The results of the probit model, presented in table 4.7, confirm the previous findings. Academic performance and beauty appear as the main determinants of student popularity in all three samples. Parental education is also positively correlated with popularity, and parental wealth, skin color, and ethnicity are not significant factors (except for Native American ethnicity, which is positively correlated with popularity, although only in the pooled sample and at the 10 percent level).

Heterogeneity in the Effects of Individual Characteristics on Student Popularity: Mixed versus Single-Sex Schools

Table 4.8 investigates how the effects of average grade, beauty, and average parental education vary according to whether the school is mixed.

Table 4.7 Probit Model for the Probability of Being Chosen by at Least 50 Percent of the Class, Tucumán and Buenos Aires

	All I	Buenos Aires II	Tucumán III
Age	0.020 (0.074)	–0.035 (0.088)	0.087 (0.140)
Gender (male = 1)	0.272*** (0.093)	0.514*** (0.124)	–0.003 (0.155)
Not born in the school province	–0.455** (0.218)	–0.603* (0.309)	0.189 (0.388)
Not born in the school district	0.162 (0.099)	0.262** (0.125)	–0.113 (0.258)
Average grade	0.164*** (0.034)	0.175*** (0.046)	0.146*** (0.056)
Beauty	0.520*** (0.110)	0.583*** (0.154)	0.552*** (0.161)
Native American ethnicity	0.243* (0.146)	0.609** (0.272)	0.221 (0.221)
European ethnicity	0.105 (0.130)	0.598* (0.316)	0.037 (0.163)
Asian ethnicity	–0.615 (0.380)	–	–0.324 (0.393)
Middle Eastern ethnicity	0.040 (0.197)	0.900** (0.425)	–0.109 (0.236)
Did not report ethnicity	0.090 (0.163)	0.672* (0.343)	–
Skin color (white = 1)	–0.027 (0.094)	0.094 (0.124)	–0.183 (0.155)
Parental wealth	0.026 (0.040)	–0.002 (0.057)	0.072 (0.063)
Parents average education	0.031** (0.014)	0.038** (0.019)	0.041* (0.023)
Number of siblings	–0.029 (0.028)	–0.029 (0.036)	–0.012 (0.054)
Foreign parents	0.183 (0.199)	0.276 (0.218)	–0.494 (0.515)

(continued)

Table 4.7 Probit Model for the Probability of Being Chosen by at Least 50 Percent of the Class, Tucumán and Buenos Aires *(continued)*

	All I	Buenos Aires II	Tucumán III
Observations	836	502	329
R^2	0.0791	0.1188	0.0861

Source: Authors' compilation.

Note: The table reports the marginal effects of a probit regression. The samples for Buenos Aires and Tucumán comprise all the students who completed the surveys for whom all the variables included in the probit model are available. The dependent variable is whether the student was chosen by at least 50 percent of the class (see equation 4.2). The model includes the same set of variables as in table 4.4. Z-values are reported in parentheses below each coefficient.

* Significant at 10 percent.
** Significant at 5 percent.
*** Significant at 1 percent.

Table 4.8 Estimates of the Effects of Individual Characteristics on Student's Average Ranking for Mixed and Single-Sex Schools, Buenos Aires and Tucumán

	Pooled sample		Buenos Aires		Tucumán	
	Mixed schools I	Single- sex schools II	Mixed schools III	Single- sex schools IV	Mixed schools IV	Single- sex schools VI
Average grade	−0.18***	−0.26***	−0.18***	−0.13**	−0.11	−0.28***
	(0.04)	(0.08)	(0.04)	(0.06)	(0.09)	(0.11)
Beauty	−0.41***	−0.07	−0.29***	−0.76	−0.62***	−0.11
	(0.11)	(0.16)	(0.10)	(0.79)	(0.17)	(0.24)
Parents' average education	−0.02**	−0.00	−0.02*	0.04	−0.02	−0.02
	(0.01)	(0.02)	(0.01)	(0.06)	(0.02)	(0.02)
Observations	633	207	453	56	180	151
R^2	0.46	0.42	0.50	0.53	0.52	0.40

Source: Authors' compilation.

Note: All regressions include the same set of variables as in table 4.4, but we only report the coefficients of average grades, beauty, and average parental education. Clustered standard errors are reported in parentheses below each coefficient, where clusters correspond to school classes.

* Significant at 10 percent.
** Significant at 5 percent.
*** Significant at 1 percent.

The table presents separate regressions for mixed and single-sex schools for the pooled sample and for Tucumán and Buenos Aires separately. Eight out of the 38 school classes in the sample are single sex, with four classes including only females and four classes including only males. The same specifications are run as in table 4.4, but table 4.8 reports only the coefficients of the variables of interest: average grade, beauty, and average parental education.

When looking across samples, the effects of average grade and beauty appear to be different according to whether the school is mixed. For the pooled sample, columns 1 and 2 suggest that the effect of average grade is statistically significant in both kinds of schools, but is much larger among single-sex schools.

An interesting result is that beauty only matters in mixed schools. Moreover, for the Tucumán sample, average grade does not affect student popularity among mixed schools, while beauty has a strong positive effect. In contrast, among single-sex schools in Tucumán, the effect of academic performance is strong, while beauty has no statistically significant effect on popularity. Since the effect of beauty is more important in mixed schools, this result suggests that mating may be driving the relationship between popularity and beauty.

Heterogeneity in Individual Valuations According to Beauty and Academic Performance of the Rater

This section investigates how the beauty of the rater affects his or her valuations of beauty, academic performance, and parental education of fellow students. In order to learn about the distribution of valuations across students, we use a probit model to estimate the determinants of the probability that student i will be chosen in the first five places by student j to form a group (see equation 4.3). In this specification, students' beauty, academic performance, and parental education enter, not only alone, but also interacted with the beauty variable of the rater (that is, the beauty of student j). Table 4.9 reports the marginal effects of the probit model.

The interaction terms between beauty of the rater and beauty of the rated student are positive and statistically significant for the sample of Buenos Aires, meaning that more-beautiful students place a higher value on the beauty of other students when choosing classmates to form a group. The same is true for the effect of beauty of the rater on the valuation of parental education: more-beautiful students place a higher value on the parental education of other students when choosing classmates to form a group.

When the effect of academic performance of the rater on his or her valuation of the traits of other students in forming a group is considered, it is found that the higher the average grade of the rater, the lower the value placed on beauty; the higher the value placed on academic performance, the lower the value placed on parental education.

Table 4.9 The Effect of Beauty and Academic Performance of the Rater on Her/His Valuations of Student's Individual Characteristics, Tucumán and Buenos Aires

| | All | Buenos Aires | Tucumán | All | Buenos Aires | Tucumán |
	I	II	III	IV	V	VI
Average grade	0.018*** (0.002)	0.017*** (0.003)	0.017*** (0.003)	-0.004 (0.005)	-0.005 (0.007)	-0.011 (0.008)
Beauty	0.033*** (0.006)	0.010 (0.009)	0.055*** (0.008)	0.112*** (0.028)	0.124*** (0.046)	0.087** (0.034)
Average parental education	-0.002** (0.001)	-0.003** (0.001)	-0.001 (0.001)	0.010*** (0.003)	0.011** (0.005)	0.014*** (0.004)
Beauty of the rater * Beauty	0.026*** (0.009)	0.061*** (0.016)	0.001 (0.011)	n.a.	n.a.	n.a.
Beauty of the rater * Average grade	-0.002 (0.002)	-0.004 (0.003)	-0.006** (0.003)	n.a.	n.a.	n.a.
Beauty of the rater * Average parental education	0.002** (0.001)	0.004* (0.002)	0.004*** (0.002)	n.a.	n.a.	n.a.

(continued)

Table 4.9 The Effect of Beauty and Academic Performance of the Rater on Her/His Valuations of Student's Individual Characteristics, Tucumán and Buenos Aires (continued)

| | All | Buenos Aires | Tucumán | All | Buenos Aires | Tucumán |
	I	II	III	IV	V	VI
Average grade of the rater * Beauty	n.a.	n.a.	n.a.	-0.009** (0.004)	-0.012** (0.006)	-0.004 (0.005)
Average grade of the rater * Average grade	n.a.	n.a.	n.a.	0.003*** (0.001)	0.003*** (0.001)	0.004*** (0.001)
Average grade of the rater * Average parental education	n.a.	n.a.	n.a.	-0.001*** (0.000)	-0.002** (0.001)	-0.002*** (0.001)
Observations	24,318	13,812	10,506	21,596	12,069	9,527

Source: Authors' compilation.

Note: n.a. = not applicable. In the table we report the marginal effects of a probit regression. The dependent variable is whether student i was chosen in the first five places by student j to form a group (see equation 4.4). In this specification, the student's beauty, academic performance, and parental education now enter not only alone, but also interacted with the beauty variable of the rater (i.e., beauty of student j). We only report the variables of interest; the model also includes the same set of variables as in table 4.4. Z-values are reported in parentheses below each coefficient.

* Significant at 10 percent.
** Significant at 5 percent.
*** Significant at 1 percent.

Popularity and Social Networks

It is plausible that discrimination or segregation in the formation of social networks during the school years against a particular group of people hinders their acquisition of social skills and that lack of social competencies is subsequently penalized in the labor market. The formation of social networks calls attention to the importance of popularity and non-anonymity in an individual's chances of joining a network. It is possible to proxy how difficult it will be for a student to form a group and the degree of homogeneity of preferences within a class by looking at students' average ranking and its variability, measured by the standard deviation of the student ranking.

Figure 4.1 shows the relationship between the average ranking and the standard deviation of the ranking for each student in the pooled sample.[14] As the figure shows, there is a strong positive relationship between the average ranking and its standard deviation. One interpretation of this relationship is that most people agree on whom they do not want to have in a group, but the degree of agreement over potential teammates decreases as the student's expected ranking increases. In other words, there is agreement over the position of students at the bottom of the ranking; as the

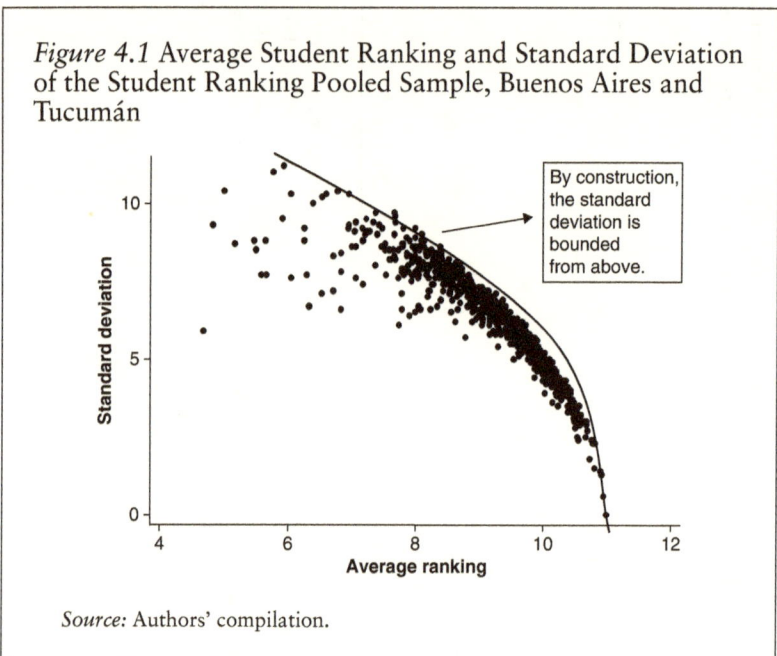

Figure 4.1 Average Student Ranking and Standard Deviation of the Student Ranking Pooled Sample, Buenos Aires and Tucumán

By construction, the standard deviation is bounded from above.

Source: Authors' compilation.

expected position in the ranking increases, however, disagreement among peers also increases.

Moreover, this suggests that factors that adversely affect students' average ranking, such as having low academic performance or not being beautiful, not only reduce the student's expected position in the ranking, but also increase agreement among peers about the student's undesirability as a potential group member. This evidence, together with the previous estimates, suggests that a high degree of segregation by beauty and academic performance should be expected on the part of the members of a group or network.

Expected Sorting

In order to identify potential differences in characteristics and behavior between students who could easily join a network and those who may have difficulty joining one, groups of two students were formed by matching students who chose each other as their first choice in forming a group. Using this simple matching function, in the case of Tucumán, 80 groups of two students each were formed, a total of 160 students. In the case of Buenos Aires, 146 groups of two students each were formed, a total of 292 students. These students were then compared with 215 students in Tucumán and 349 students in Buenos Aires who were not considered to have a group.

Table 4.10 presents the mean academic performance, beauty, and parents' average education by group according to whether the student has a match. As the table shows for both the Buenos Aires and Tucumán samples, the students who have a match have, on average, higher grades and are perceived by their peers as being more beautiful. The gaps in academic performance between groups are large: 0.3 and 0.4 for Buenos Aires and Tucumán, respectively.

Table 4.11 presents correlations between the student characteristics and the characteristics of the first-choice student for all students and for those students who have a match separately. As the table shows, there is a strong correlation between the student's academic performance and the academic performance of the student's first choice. The same is true for beauty, parents' average education, and gender. Again, this suggests that a high degree of positive sorting in academic performance and beauty can be expected.

The Benefits of Networks

The previous section identifies differences in characteristics between members and nonmembers of a group or network, and this evidence could help to assess the potential benefits of being a member of a network. In order

Table 4.10 Average Grade, Beauty, and Average Parental
Education of Matched Students and Not Matched Students,
Buenos Aires and Tucumán

	N	Average grade	Beauty	Parents' average education
All				
Matched	452	7.30	0.32	10.7
Not matched	564	7.04	0.25	11.2
Buenos Aires				
Matched	292	7.50	0.32	9.6
Not matched	349	7.20	0.23	9.9
Tucumán				
Matched	160	7.10	0.32	12.8
Not matched	215	6.70	0.28	13.2

Source: Authors' compilation.
Note: The matched group is composed of those students who have chosen each
other as first choice in forming a group. The not-matched group is composed of all the
remaining students.

to have a rough estimate of the potential benefit of being part of a group
or network, we examine student performance at school. Student performance can be considered a measure of the quality of schooling and, within
certain approximations, could have an effect on wages similar to that of
the quantity of schooling.

Table 4.10 shows that the average school performance is 0.26 higher
for members than for nonmembers of a group, representing a 4 percent
difference in school quality that could be considered an achievement of
the group or network. In Argentina, with an average schooling of 10 years
for the labor force, this 4 percent increase in schooling quality represents
an increase of 0.40 years of schooling, where perfect substitution between
quality and quantity dimensions of schooling is assumed. Considering a
value of 12 percent for the return to schooling in Argentina (see Savanti
and Patrinos 2005), the group or network will obtain a benefit of a 4.8
percent increase in wages. Heckman, Layne-Farrar, and Todd (1996) suggest, however, that it is more appropriate to consider how schooling quality affects the rate of return to schooling. Under this assumption, if a third
of the 12 percent rate of return to schooling is due to schooling quality,
then the expected increase in wages will be only 1.6 percent.

Some estimates of network benefits offer potentially useful comparisons
with those rough estimates. For example, Angrist and Lavy (1997) study

Table 4.11 Correlations between Student Characteristics and the Characteristics of Her or His First-Choice Student to Form a Group: Average Grade, Beauty, Average Parental Education, and Gender, Buenos Aires and Tucumán

A. Buenos Aires

| Characteristic of student | Characteristic of student's first choice | | | |
	Average grade	Beauty	Parents' average education	Gender
All students				
Average grade	0.30	0.05	−0.04	−0.04
Beauty	0.01	0.28	−0.03	−0.12
Parents' average education	−0.08	−0.05	0.17	0.01
Gender	−0.03	−0.15	0.05	0.78
Matched students				
Average grade	0.49	0.07	−0.07	0.06
Beauty	0.07	0.39	−0.04	−0.13
Parents' average education	−0.07	−0.04	0.18	0.02
Gender	0.06	−0.13	0.02	0.84

B. Tucumán

| Characteristic of student | Characteristic of student's first choice | | | |
	Average grade	Beauty	Parents' average education	Gender
All students				
Average grade	0.26	−0.03	0.12	0.05
Beauty	−0.07	0.23	−0.01	0.23
Parents' average education	0.15	−0.03	0.15	0.03
Gender	−0.05	0.06	0.05	0.85
Matched students				
Average grade	0.49	0.01	0.22	0.03
Beauty	−0.01	0.12	−0.02	0.19
Parents' average education	0.25	−0.02	0.29	0.07
Gender	0.00	0.19	0.07	0.89

Source: Authors' compilation.

the effects of an education reform in Morocco that replaced instruction in French with instruction in Arabic; the reform led to a 17 percent decline in the wages of those who did not know French. The authors also mention that immigrants in Germany who knew German had wages 30 percent higher than their counterparts who did not know German; knowledge of a language is here understood as a way of being able to join a network (see, for example, Gresenz, Rogowski, and Escarce 2007). Other studies about "local externalities" mentioned by Banerjee and Duflo (2005) indicate that social learning could increase the adoption rate of new technologies by 17 percent in agriculture.

Conclusions

As established in the Argentine Federal Education Law, one of the main objectives of the education system is to provide real equality of opportunities to every individual and to eradicate all forms of discrimination in the classroom. Furthermore, the school, as an agency of socialization, attempts to inculcate these values in its pupils. In turn, students are expected to change their behavior, thus contributing to the eradication of discrimination in other social environments.

This chapter studies the determinants of peer popularity among students attending their last year of school in Buenos Aires and Tucumán. As this population has spent at least 12 years attending school, analyzing how they rank their classmates provides valuable information for assessing whether there is any evidence of some form of peer discrimination in the school system.[15]

The importance of this issue is underscored by several studies suggesting that discrimination is a problem in Argentine society. Reviewing the literature, Braylan and Jmelnizky (2004) show that most allegations involve discrimination based on nationality, ethnic origin, socioeconomic status, and physical appearance. While estimates of the magnitude of the phenomenon are lacking, most observers believe that discrimination is a major problem.

The findings of this chapter, however, suggest that students do not rank their classmates based on their skin color, parental wealth, or nationality (although there is some evidence of discrimination against African and Asian ethnicity, the results are not robust across specifications). Comparing these results with the reports on discrimination in other social environments suggests that either the school system has improved over time in its efforts to eradicate peer discrimination (that is, younger generations are less likely to discriminate than older generations) or individuals change their behavior over the life cycle. In either case, it is clear that the school system is not reproducing major forms of peer discrimination observed in other social environments. Adolescents who have dark skin and those whose parents are poor or were born in neighboring countries do not appear to be discriminated against by their classmates.

Physical appearance and previous academic performance, in contrast, are strong predictors of popularity. The finding that students have a preference for higher achievers should not necessarily be a reason for concern. Students selected their classmates with the expectation that groups were going to be formed and that those groups would meet to conduct school activities. Assuming that having higher achievers in a group increases its productivity, the finding can be interpreted as evidence that students are interested in improving their performance. Alternatively, it can be interpreted as evidence of meritocracy.

The evidence that beauty matters is more troubling. On the one hand, beauty is an irrelevant trait for carrying out school-related activities. On the other hand, students are likely to select their teammates not only with the objective of improving academic performance, but also with the objective of mating. From this perspective, it becomes difficult to consider "lookism" as a form of prejudice.

There is nonetheless an instrumental reason why policy makers should be concerned about the finding that beauty is a major determinant of peer popularity among adolescents. As social-psychological studies have found, being highly ranked by one's peers during high school enhances confidence, self-esteem, and oral and interpersonal skills, and labor economists have found that social skills are an important determinant of success in the labor market.

Annex. Three Questionnaires

This annex presents the English version of the three questionnaires. Students received the Spanish version.

Questionnaire 1

First and last name: ....

List the 10 classmates with whom you would like to form a group to do activities at school. Rank them beginning with your first choice. (Write their first and last name, no nicknames please!)

First: ....

Second: ....

Third: ....

Fourth: ....

Fifth: ....

Sixth: ....

Seventh: ....

Eighth: ....

Ninth: ....

Tenth: ....

Questionnaire 2

First and last name: ....

Age: ....

Gender (Mark the correct answer with X):

☐ Male

☐ Female

If you were born in Argentina, in which province: .... and locality: ....

If you were born in another country, in which country? ....
....

For how many years have you been living in the current neighborhood?
....

Which grade did you get last year in literature? .... in mathematics?
....

Which material is your house made of?

☐ Corrugated iron

☐ Wood

☐ Bricks

Do your parents have a car?

☐ No

☐ Yes

Do you have a computer at home?

☐ No

☐ Yes

Do you have access to the Internet at home?

☐ No

☐ Yes

Is there air conditioning at home?

☐ No

☐ Yes

Do you live with your parents?

☐ No

☐ Yes

Are they married?

☐ No

☐ Yes

How many brothers and sisters do you have? ....

What is your mother's maximum educational attainment? (Mark only one box)

☐ College graduate

☐ Some college

☐ High school graduate

☐ High school dropout

☐ Primary school graduate

☐ Primary school dropout

☐ Don't know

What is your father's maximum educational attainment? (Mark only one)

☐ College graduate

☐ Some college

☐ High school graduate

☐ High school dropout

☐ Primary school graduate

☐ Primary school dropout

☐ Don't know

In which province/country was your mother born? (Name country if foreign born) ....

In which province/country was your father born? (Name country if foreign born) ....

Do you have any of the following ethnic origins? (Check all boxes that apply)

☐ African

☐ Asian

☐ European

☐ Native American

☐ Middle East

Do you consider yourself? (Check only 1 box)

☐ White

☐ Olive-skinned

☐ Dark

☐ Other

When you meet with friends, do you like to: (Check all boxes that apply)

☐ Talk a lot

☐ Listen

☐ Tell jokes

☐ None of the above

What do you plan to do after finishing high school?

☐ Study and work

☐ Just study

☐ Just work

☐ Do not know

How important are friends to finding a good job?

☐ Very important

☐ Important

☐ Not important at all

☐ Do not know

Do you think there is discrimination in the labor market?

☐ Yes

☐ No

☐ Do not know

On a scale from 1 to 5 (where 1 indicates very important and 5 indicates not important),

How important are the following characteristics to finding a good job?

Education: ....

Physical beauty: ....

Skin color: ....

Parents' wealth: ....

Other: ....

Questionnaire 3

First and last name: ....

Which are the three female classmates you consider the most physically attractive?

(Please answer seriously. This information is useful to analyze the role of beauty among adolescents. Your answer will remain strictly confidential).

The most beautiful female classmate is: ....

The second most beautiful is: ....

The third most beautiful is: ....

And, which are the three male classmates you consider the most physically attractive?

The most handsome male classmate is: ....

The second most handsome is: ....

The third most handsome is: ....

Notes

1. For experimental evidence in Argentina, see Mobius and Rosenblat (2006).

2. The evidence presented in Villalpando and others (2006) and Braylan and Jmelnizky (2004) is based either on allegations or on the opinion of the authors. Additionally, while we focus on peer discrimination among adolescents, these studies are broader and analyze the whole Argentine society. For a discussion about adolescents and peer rejection in the United States, see Fisher, Scyatta, and Fenton (2000).

3. These jurisdictions were chosen simply because the authors possessed the technical capacities to conduct the survey in these places.

4. http://www.me.gov.ar (accessed December 12, 2004).

5. In Argentina, the tutor (*preceptor* in Spanish) is a school authority in charge of several chores at school such as controlling students' behavior and attendance and organizing school events.

6. A figure of 10 nominations was chosen because that is the number used in the National Longitudinal Study of Adolescent Health conducted across schools in the United States. This survey has been the source of information for most empirical studies on popularity and friendship networks among students.

7. The Becas is a federal program where students with poor parental background receive a fellowship equal to 400 pesos per year in exchange for attending school; only students enrolled in public schools are eligible.

8. Developmental psychologists usually distinguish between "sociometrically" and "perceived" popular students. The latter refers to students who are considered popular by their classmates but are not necessarily liked. This variable is usually obtained by asking students to point out which classmates they consider to be the most popular. Our measure captures sociometric popularity. For further discussion, see Cillessen and Rose (2005). The data do not allow us to measure peer rejection, because school authorities refused to collect this information.

9. Students who did not report their ethnicity are less likely to have white skin, are on average poorer, and have less educated parents. Given the positive correlation between these variables and European ethnicity, it is likely that students who did not report their ethnicity are part of a minority group.

10. If schools were totally segregated by race, for example, it would be impossible to detect peer discrimination because students could only choose among classmates who all have the same race.

11. People who reside in the city of Tucumán, however, are on average richer and have more schooling than those who reside in Greater Tucumán, but outside the city. Therefore, the extent to which our sample over-represents students from higher-income families in the city of Tucumán is somewhat overstated by the above figures.

12. Similar results are obtained including separate regressors for the math and literature grade. Both variables are negative and statistically significant. We also include a dummy equal to 1 if the student achieves the best grade in the class. This indicator is not significant in any of the samples.

13. Extroversion refers to energy and the tendency to seek stimulation and the company of others. Conscientiousness refers to a tendency to show self-discipline and aim for achievement, with planned rather than spontaneous behavior. It is not obvious how to properly measure these two concepts (John and Srivastava 1999), and the information we were able to collect is limited. Therefore, it is likely that the proxies we use for extroversion and conscientiousness have measurement error.

14. By construction, the standard deviation of the student ranking is bounded from above with an inverted U-shaped function. Consider the two extreme cases: an individual with the lowest possible average ranking has mean 1 and standard deviation 0, and an individual with the highest possible average ranking has mean 11 and standard deviation 0 as well.

15. An interesting extension of this study would be to analyze whether teachers or school authorities discriminate. Another line of inquiry would be to analyze whether the government allocates more resources to schools located in richer jurisdictions. For a discussion for Argentina, see Braslavsky and Filmus (1987).

References

Anderson, Cameron, Oliver John, Dacher Keltner, and Ann Kring. 2001. "Who Attains Social Status? Effects of Personality and Physical Attractiveness in Social Groups." *Journal of Personality and Social Psychology* 81 (1): 116–32.

Angrist, Joshua, and Victor Lavy. 1997. "The Effect of a Change in Language of Instruction on the Returns to Schooling in Morocco." *Journal of Labor Economics* 15 (1): S48–76.

Banerjee, Abhijit, and Esther Duflo. 2005. "Growth Theory through the Lens of Development Economics." Unpublished mss., Massachusetts Institute of Technology, Cambridge, MA.

Becker, Gary, Kevin Murphy, and Ivan Werning. 2005. "The Equilibrium Distribution of Income and the Market for Status." *Journal of Political Economy* 113 (2): 282–310.

Braslavsky, Cecilia, and Daniel Filmus. 1987. *La discriminación educativa en la Argentina*. Buenos Aires: Miño Dávila.

Braylan, Marisa, and Adrián Jmelnizky. 2004. *Informe sobre antisemitismo en la Argentina*. Buenos Aires: Delegación de Asociaciones Israelitas Argentinas and Centro de Estudios Sociales.

Cillessen, Antonius, and Amanda Rose. 2005. "Understanding Popularity in the Peer System." *Current Directions in Psychological Science* 14 (2): 102–05.

Fisher, Celia, Wallace Scyatta, and Rose Fenton. 2000. "Discrimination Distress during Adolescence." *Journal of Youth and Adolescence* 29 (6): 679–95.

Galeotti, Andrea, and Gerrit Mueller. 2005. "Friendship Relations in the School Class and Adult Economic Attainment." IZA Discussion Paper 1682. Institute for the Study of Labor (IZA), Bonn, Germany.

Gresenz, Carole R., Jeannette A. Rogowski, and José Escarce. 2007. "Social Networks and Access to Health Care among Mexican Americans." NBER Working Paper W13460, National Bureau of Economic Research, Cambridge, MA.

Heckman, James, Anne Layne-Farrar, and Petra Todd. 1996. "Human Capital Pricing Equations with an Application to Estimating the Effect of Schooling Quality on Earnings." *Review of Economics and Statistics* 78 (4): 562–610.

John, Oliver, and Sanjay Srivastava. 1999. "The Big-Five Trait Taxonomy: History, Measurement, and Theoretical Perspectives." In *Handbook of Personality: Theory and Research*, 2d ed, ed. L. A. Pervin and Oliver John. New York: Guilford.

Kuhn, Peter, and Catherine Weinberger. 2005. "Leadership Skills and Wages." *Journal of Labor Economics* 23 (3): 395–436.

Mobius, Markus, and Tanya Rosenblat. 2006. "Why Beauty Matters." *American Economic Review* 96 (1): 222–35.

Savanti, Maria Paula, and Harry A. Patrinos. 2005. "Rising Returns to Schooling in Argentina, 1992–2002: Productivity or Credentialism?" Policy Research Working Paper 3714, World Bank, Washington, DC.

Villalpando, Waldo, Daniel Feierstein, Norma Fernández, Ana González, Horacio Ravenna, and María Sonderéguer. 2006. *La discriminación en Argentina: Diagnósticos y propuestas.* Buenos Aires: Eudeba.

Zimmerman, David. 2003. "Peer Effects in Academic Outcomes: Evidence from a Natural Experiment." *Review of Economics and Statistics* 85 (1): 9–23.

5

An Experimental Study of Labor Market Discrimination: Gender, Social Class, and Neighborhood in Chile

David Bravo, Claudia Sanhueza, and Sergio Urzúa

No matter how much has been done to study labor market discrimination, whether racial, ethnic, or gender, the issue of its detection (identification) is still unsettled. Conventional regression analyses suffer from important limitations due to the omission of relevant variables. The presence of unobservable variables limits the scope of these results (Altonji and Blank 1999; Neal and Johnson 1996; Urzúa 2008). In addition, experimental studies have been criticized for failing to measure discrimination correctly (Heckman 1998; Heckman and Siegelman 1993).

In this chapter, we study the Chilean labor market and identify the presence (or absence) of gender discrimination using an experimental design. This empirical strategy allows us to transcend the limitations of earlier works and represents the first experimental study of its kind in Chile and

David Bravo is with the Centro de Microdatos, Departamento de Economía, Universidad de Chile; Claudia Sanhueza is with the Instituto Latinoamericano de Doctrina y Estudios Sociales (ILADES), Universidad Alberto Hurtado; and Sergio Urzúa is with the Department of Economics and the Institute for Policy Research, Northwestern University. The authors would like to thank Andrea Moro and Hugo Ñopo for their helpful comments, Verónica Flores and Bárbara Flores for their excellent research assistance, and staff of the Survey Unit of the Centro de Microdatos for their outstanding performance.

the region. Our approach also enables us to address the identification of socioeconomic discrimination associated with individual characteristics such as name and place of residence.

Why is Chile an interesting case? Chile offers a perfect example of a labor market in which females seem to be discriminated against. Despite the fact that the average years of schooling of female workers in Chile are not statistically different from those of male workers, average wages of male workers are 25 percent higher.[1] In fact, several studies have suggested that gender discrimination is a factor in determining wages in the Chilean labor market.[2] Estimates obtained using standard Blinder-Oaxaca decompositions give "residual discrimination" a significant role in the total wage gap.[3] The evidence also shows stable and systematic differences in the returns to education and experience by gender along the conditional wage distribution. Additionally, Montenegro (2001) shows that "residual discrimination" is higher for women with more education and experience. Furthermore, Chilean female labor force participation is particularly low, 38.1 percent, compared with Latin America's regional average of 44.7 percent.[4]

However, the evidence suggesting the presence of gender discrimination is subject to important qualifications. Specifically, observed gender differences in labor market outcomes could be interpreted as the manifestation of gender differences in unobserved characteristics that determine labor market productivity. In this context, the estimates of gender differences would be erroneously interpreted as evidence of discrimination. This is a concern affecting most of the applied literature studying discrimination.[5]

Our empirical approach deals explicitly with the issue of unobserved characteristics and is based on a simple and clear identification strategy for the analysis of discrimination. Specifically, we submitted more than 11,000 fictitious curriculum vitae (CVs) to real job vacancies that were published weekly in a widely read newspaper in Santiago (Chile's capital city) during 2006. For each classified ad, we submitted a set of strictly equivalent CVs—with regard to qualifications and employment experience of applicants—varying only their gender, name and surname, and place of residence. We then measured labor market discrimination using differences in call response rates obtained for the various demographic groups. Having full control over the information contained in each CV, we generated "identical" individuals, thus addressing the concerns about potential biases caused by unobserved variables affecting labor market productivity across gender.

The first section reviews the relevant literature for this study; the second presents all of the methodological information associated with implementation of the experiment, which began in the last week of March 2006; a third reports the main results; and a final section presents the main conclusions and policy lessons.

Literature Review

Labor market discrimination is said to arise when two identically productive workers are treated differently on the grounds of their race or gender, when race or gender do not in themselves have an effect on productivity (Altonji and Blank 1999; Heckman 1998). However, no two individuals are identical, and several unobservable factors determine individual performance in the labor market (see Bravo, Sanhueza, and Urzúa 2009 for a review of this literature).

The empirical literature deals with these problems using two alternative methodologies: regression analysis and field experiments.[6] The traditional regression analysis approach typically uses Blinder-Oaxaca decompositions (Blinder 1973; Oaxaca 1973) to determine how much of the wage differential between groups of workers, by race or gender, is unexplained. This unexplained part is usually interpreted as discrimination. Most of the evidence of gender discrimination in Chile comes from the regression analysis approach (see, for example, Montenegro 2001; Montenegro and Paredes 1999; Paredes and Riveros 1994). However, the lack of several control variables, such as cognitive and noncognitive skills, labor market experience, schooling attainment, family background characteristics, and preferences for nonmarket activities, limits the scope of these studies.

In a more recent attempt to disentangle the determinants of differences in the labor market, Núñez and Gutiérrez (2004) study the returns to the socioeconomic background of origin (or "class") in Chile. They measure "class" by the individual's surname, which is classified as low and high social class depending on its origin (for example, Basque or Spanish European ancestry). They use a data set that allows them to reduce the role of unobservable factors by limiting the population under study (homogeneous population). The data also contain a rich set of labor market productivity measures. The class wage gaps obtained by an Oaxaca-Ramson decomposition amount to approximately 25 to 35 percent.

The study presented in this chapter is much more closely related to the literature of experimental studies for the analysis of discrimination in the labor market.[7] This literature started in Europe in the 1960s and 1970s and was subsequently used by the International Labour Organisation in the 1990s. More recently, experimental techniques have been published in leading economic journals (for example, Bertrand and Mullainathan 2004).

Experimental approaches can be divided into two types: audit studies and natural experiments. The latter take advantage of unexpected changes in policies or events (Antonovics, Arcidiacono, and Walsh 2004, 2005; Goldin and Rouse 2000; Levitt 2004; Newmark, Bank, and Van Nort 1996). In Chile, as far as we know, there are no studies using these kinds of variations.

Two strategies have been used to carry out audit studies. The first takes a personal approach, in which individuals are sent to job interviews or apply for jobs over the telephone. The second sends written applications for real job vacancies.

The first procedure is the most subject to criticism. It has been argued that it is impossible to ensure that false applicants are identical. Also, testers have sometimes been told that they are involved in a study of discrimination and that their behavior could bias the results (see Heckman and Siegelman 1993).

The first experiments to use written applications sent unsolicited job applications to "potential employers"; these experiments tested preferential treatment in employer responses and not the hiring decision. Later came experiments in which curriculum vitae were sent in response to real announcements. Although the latter technique overcomes the criticisms of the personal approaches and tests the hiring decision,[8] it does not overcome a common problem in the audit studies mentioned by Heckman and Siegelman (1993) and Heckman (1998), which is that audits are crucially dependent on the distribution of unobserved characteristics for each racial group and the audit standardization level. Thus there may still be unobservable factors that determine productivity, but not discrimination. Riach and Rich (2002) accept this criticism but point out that it is difficult to imagine how firms' internal attributes could enhance productivity. They conclude that, since Heckman and Siegelman (1993) do not explain what could be behind those gaps, the argument has "not been proven."

The study presented here mainly follows the line of work developed by Bertrand and Mullainathan (2004), which measures racial discrimination in the labor market by means of posting fictitious curriculum vitae for job vacancies published in Boston and Chicago newspapers. They randomly gave half of the CVs African American names and half European ("white") names. Additionally, they measured the effect of applicant qualification on the racial gap; for this, the CVs were differentiated between high qualifications and low qualifications.

Their findings are as follows: the curriculum vitae associated with white names received 50 percent more calls for an interview than those with African American names, and whites were more affected by qualification level than blacks. Additionally, the authors find some evidence to suggest that employers were inferring social class based on applicants' names.

Experimental Design

The experiment consisted of submitting more than 11,000 CVs of fictitious individuals for real job vacancies that appeared weekly in the newspaper with the highest circulation in Chile. Each week, the team selected 60 job vacancies from the newspaper. Eight CVs, four corresponding to men and four to women, were submitted for each vacancy. The details of the experimental design are presented here.

Definition of Demographic Cells

We defined eight relevant demographic cells for the categories of interest for our study. The cells were defined to serve the objectives of the study. To study discrimination by gender, we separated men and women. To study socioeconomic discrimination, we included two variables: surname and municipality of residence. To reduce the number of observations required in each case, we separated these last variables into the two extremes: (a) socioeconomically rich and poor municipalities and (b) surnames associated with the upper classes and lower classes.

Since we have three dichotomous variables, the final number of demographic cells is eight, as shown in table 5.1.

We chose approximately 60 job vacancies each week. Eight CVs were sent for each job vacancy, in other words, one for each demographic cell. So 480 CVs were submitted each week: 240 from men and 240 from women.

A group of names, surnames, and municipalities was established to satisfy the requirements of each cell, with the names and municipalities chosen randomly for each vacancy. Figure 5.1 presents the final structure of the fictitious CVs used in our experiment.

Source of Job Vacancies

The main source of job vacancies in Santiago is the newspaper used in our experiment, which publishes around 150 job vacancies every Sunday, with a repeat rate of around 30 percent.[9] The ads are also available on the newspaper's Web site.

To prepare the fieldwork, we first carried out a detailed analysis of the type of job vacancies published by the newspaper. In the month of January and the first three weeks of March 2006, we analyzed all vacancies published. As a result of this preliminary study, we created a CV bank based on three categories: professionals, technicians (skilled workers), and unskilled workers. Other markedly male or female categories were rejected.

Table 5.1 Demographic Cells for the Analysis of Discrimination

	Men		Women	
Municipality	*Upper-class surname*	*Lower-class surname*	*Upper-class surname*	*Lower-class surname*
High-income municipality				
Low-income municipality				

Source: Authors' compilation.

Figure 5.1 The Design of the Fictitious CVs

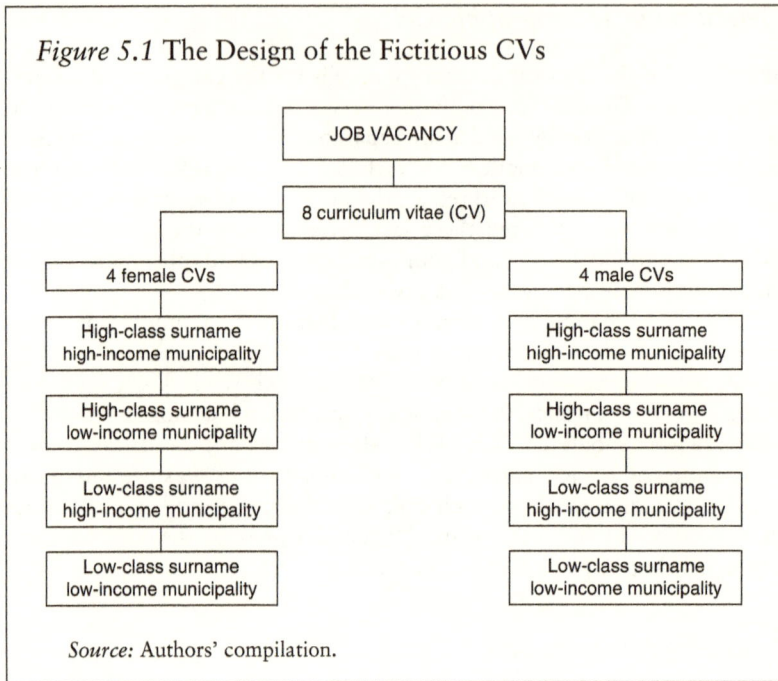

```
                        ┌──────────────────┐
                        │   JOB VACANCY    │
                        └────────┬─────────┘
                        ┌────────┴──────────┐
            ┌───────────┤ 8 curriculum vitae (CV) ├───────────┐
            │           └───────────────────┘                 │
   ┌────────┴────────┐                            ┌───────────┴─────┐
   │   4 female CVs  │                            │    4 male CVs   │
   └────────┬────────┘                            └───────────┬─────┘
   ┌────────┴─────────────┐                      ┌────────────┴────────┐
   │ High-class surname   │                      │ High-class surname  │
   │ high-income municipality │                  │ high-income municipality │
   └────────┬─────────────┘                      └────────────┬────────┘
   ┌────────┴─────────────┐                      ┌────────────┴────────┐
   │ High-class surname   │                      │ High-class surname  │
   │ low-income municipality │                   │ low-income municipality │
   └────────┬─────────────┘                      └────────────┬────────┘
   ┌────────┴─────────────┐                      ┌────────────┴────────┐
   │ Low-class surname    │                      │ Low-class surname   │
   │ high-income municipality │                  │ high-income municipality │
   └────────┬─────────────┘                      └────────────┬────────┘
   ┌────────┴─────────────┐                      ┌────────────┴────────┐
   │ Low-class surname    │                      │ Low-class surname   │
   │ low-income municipality │                   │ low-income municipality │
   └──────────────────────┘                      └─────────────────────┘
```

Source: Authors' compilation.

Creation of CV Banks

Job vacancies were grouped into three skill levels: professionals, technicians, and unskilled workers. An individual was assigned responsibility for each category, and he or she was in charge of selecting the weekly vacancies, as well as the production, submission, and supervision of the CVs submitted.

A database of fictitious CVs was created for each of the skill levels. Three specialized teams generated CV prototypes using as examples real CVs available on two public Web sites.[10] In producing the CVs, the instruction was to comply with the profile of the most competitive applicant for the vacancy selected. Each set of eight CVs was constructed so that their qualification level and employment experience were equivalent. In this way, we ensured that the applicants were equally eligible for the job in question.[11]

Classification of Municipalities

In order to facilitate the fieldwork, we concentrated our efforts on job vacancies for the metropolitan urban region, which is divided into 34 municipalities. We used the socioeconomic classification of households (based on the 2002 census) to classify municipalities into high-income and low-income municipalities. The classification process was the following:

1. Using data from CASEN 2003, we computed the proportion of the households by socioeconomic level within each municipality.
2. We defined as high-income municipalities the top five municipalities with the largest proportion of households in the top socioeconomic level.
3. We defined as low-income municipalities the top 15 municipalities with the smallest proportion of the population in the top socioeconomic level and the greatest proportion in the two bottom socioeconomic levels.

In order to examine the impact of socioeconomic level of the municipality of origin, we excluded all municipalities of intermediate socioeconomic groups. The final list of the municipalities included in each group is presented in table 5.2.

Table 5.2 Selected Municipalities, by Income Level

Selected municipalities	
High-income municipalities	*Low-income municipalities*
Vitacura	Pedro Aguirre Cerda
	Pudahuel
	Conchalí
Providencia	Quilicura
	San Joaquín
	Lo Prado
La Reina	San Ramón
	Lo Espejo
	Renca
Las Condes	Recoleta
	San Bernardo
	La Granja
Ñuñoa	Cerro Navia
	El Bosque
	La Pintana

Source: Authors' compilation.

Table 5.3 Selected Surnames, by Social Origin

Selected surnames	
Upper-class surnames	*Lower-class surnames*
Rodrigo Recabarren Merino	Valeska Angulo Ortiz
Susan Abumohor Cassis	Pablo Ayulef Muñoz
Javiera Edwards Celis	Rosmary Becerra Fuentes
Pedro Ariztia Larrain	Clinton Benaldo Gonzalez

Source: Authors' compilation.

Classification and Selection of Names and Surnames

The names and surnames included on the CVs were classified and selected following the procedure described by Núñez and Gutiérrez (2004). Specifically, a sample of names and surnames was taken from the alumni register of the Faculty of Economics and Business of the Universidad de Chile. Subsequently, a group of individuals classified (based on their personal perception) these names and surnames into high social class, middle social class, and lower social class. For the purposes of the fieldwork, only the names and surnames classified as upper class and lower class were considered. An example of the surnames used in each category is presented in table 5.3.

Description of the Fieldwork

The research team handled the weekly selection of job vacancies that appeared in the newspaper every Sunday and constructed the targeted CVs for each vacancy. This process involved compiling the competitive CVs and ensuring their equivalence so that the only differentiating elements were the gender of the applicant, social level, name and surname, and municipality of residence. The team also included three other research assistants, including a sociologist and an economist, who randomly reviewed the CVs sent and supervised the procedure.

The job vacancies selected and the set of eight CVs submitted to each job vacancy were entered weekly into a specially designed Web page that allowed us to review all of the vacancies, together with their respective sets of CVs. An information technology expert entered that information into the Web page.

A central aspect of our study was the procedure by which we kept records of each of the received contacts (phone calls and e-mails) associated with each CV and job vacancy. To receive these contacts, a fully dedicated team of males and females was ready to take the calls 24 hours a day from Monday to Sunday. Eight mobile telephones, each with a different number, were assigned to each of the CVs in the set; this ensured that the recruiters did not encounter repeated telephone numbers. The people in charge of receiving the calls recorded the day, name of the applicant, the vacancy, and the phone number of the firm that selected the CV. Each report was entered into the Web page of the project, which allowed us to supervise the calls received.

In parallel, job vacancy responses were also received by e-mail, as some job vacancies requested electronic contact information. To handle these cases, we generated a generic e-mail for each CV. All e-mail addresses were checked every three days. As with the phone calls, the e-mails were reported and entered into the Web page of the project.

The Identity of Fictitious Applicants

Once the names and surnames were classified by categories (upper class and lower class), they were mixed so as not to use real names. Additionally, each fictitious applicant had a fictitious national identification number. To ensure the equivalence of each set of CVs, the age of the applicants was set at between 30 and 35 years of age, and applicants were listed as married with at least one child and no more than two children.

Ensuring the Equivalence of Fictitious Applicants between Cells

In order to ensure the equivalence of the eight fictitious applications submitted to each vacancy, we also controlled for additional differences that otherwise might have contaminated our results:

- Regarding the educational background of the applicants, those with university education were considered Universidad de Chile graduates and, when necessary, reported graduate degrees from the same university.
- The secondary school of the applicant and the home address were determined by the applicant's municipality of residence. A bank of school names in each municipality was used for this purpose. To ensure consistency, we randomly assigned secondary schools conditional on the assigned municipality.
- Each CV in a set had a unique telephone number; however, these numbers were allowed to repeat themselves among different groups of CVs.
- The employment experience of the applicants was equivalent within each category (professional, technician, unskilled worker), but different across categories. Thus professionals with greater time spent in the educational system had fewer years of employment experience; meanwhile, unskilled workers had a longer track record in the labor market. To maintain this equivalence, we also assigned the number of jobs and employment history (absence of employment gaps) for each fictitious

Table 5.4 Assignment of Previous Labor Market Experience, by Skill Level

Category	Employment experience	Number of jobs
Professionals	7 to 12 years	2 to 3
Technicians	8 to 13 years	4 to 5
Unskilled workers	12 to 17 years	5 to 7

Source: Authors' compilation.

applicant within skill categories. Table 5.4 presents the assignment of employment experience and number of previous jobs held.

- Graduate degrees of applicants were equivalent within the set of eight CVs. Graduate degrees had to be from the same university (Universidad de Chile). Training courses also had to be from equivalent institutions (technical institutes).
- As a general rule, high-quality CVs were submitted to each vacancy. In other words, the variables of employment history, education, and training were drawn up to be attractive to firms.
- The salary expectations, which generally had to be included in job applications, were based on actual remuneration of professionals and technicians (from the Web page www.futurolaboral.cl). The starting point was a salary level required by a good candidate (percentile 75 of that distribution), and expected remuneration was subsequently reduced to average levels. Each set of eight CVs sent for a vacancy had the same reference salary level, which varied only slightly (in some cases, the level was given as a range and in others it was given as a specific reference).
- Although we worked to ensure that the fictitious CVs were equivalent, we also sought to ensure that they looked as if they were made by different people, such as having different fonts and different organization of the information. (See the annex for examples of CVs.)

Findings

The CV mailing process started during the last week of March 2006. Table 5.5 presents weekly information on the number of classified ads published, the number of CVs submitted, and the response rates. After 20 weeks, we had submitted 11,016 CVs, with an average response rate of 14.65 percent a week. This rate is higher than that obtained by Bertrand and Mullainathan (2004).

The response rate varied from week to week. For example, the response rate was only 6.15 percent during the third week (April 10–16) but reached 24.63 percent during the sixth week (May 1–7). There are several reasons

Table 5.5 Distribution of Responses, by Week

Week		Total number of ads	CVs sent	Total number of calls	General response rate (%)
1	March 24–31	56	448	60	13.39
2	April 3–9	63	504	71	14.09
3	April 10–16	65	520	32	6.15
4	April 17–23	61	488	60	12.30
5	April 24–30	61	488	92	18.85
6	May 1–7	67	536	132	24.63
7	May 8–14	73	584	116	19.86
8	May 15–21	72	576	75	13.02
9	May 22–28	74	592	98	16.55
10	May 29–June 4	74	592	83	14.02
11	June 5–11	72	576	135	23.44
12	June 12–18	78	624	87	13.94
13	June 19–25	73	584	90	15.41
14	June 26–July 2	76	608	77	12.66
15	July 3–9	73	584	63	10.79
16	July 10–16	69	552	84	15.22
17	July 17–23	68	544	101	18.57
18	July 24–30	75	600	93	15.50
19	July 31–August 6	66	528	45	8.52
20	August 7–13	61	488	30	6.15
	Average	69	551	81	14.65
	Total	1,377	11,016	1,624	

Source: Authors' compilation.

for this variation. First, the response rate could be correlated directly with the overall quality of the CVs sent; thus, for those weeks with a low response rate, the quality of the CVs might not have been as good as the CVs sent by real applicants. As explained, in this event the complete set of eight CVs was of low quality, and our results were not affected by this phenomenon. Second, national holidays during some of the weeks could have influenced firms' efforts to contact potential employees. For example, the low response rate of April 10–16 was most likely a result of Holy Week (a Catholic holiday). Finally, the variation in response rates could also be attributed to labor market conditions. Bertrand and Mullainathan (2004) report similar variations in their response rates, apparently associated with different labor market conditions.

Table 5.6 presents the same variables as in table 5.5, but breaking down the information by type of job category (that is, professionals, technicians, and unskilled workers). In the annex, we list the type of qualifications within the three job categories. The average weekly response rate by type of employment shows the same evolution as the overall response rate. Unskilled workers and technicians have a higher response rate than professionals. More precisely, the average response rate for professionals is 12.1 percent compared with 14.2 percent for unskilled workers and 18.1 percent for technicians.

Since we recorded when each fictitious CV was submitted and when it received a callback, we can study the time to receive a phone call (or e-mail). Figure 5.2 presents the distribution of time to receive a phone call. More than 60 percent of the contacts were made before the tenth day. The average number of days before any contact was made is approximately 12 days overall: 14 days for professionals and unskilled workers and 8 days for technicians (see table 5.7).

The résumés were submitted by physical mail, e-mail, and fax. Table 5.8 shows the average number of days that passed before a contact was made, by method of submission. On average, CVs submitted by physical mail received a callback by the eighteenth day, and CVs submitted by e-mail received a callback by the eighth day.

We now examine the average response rate by the three dimensions considered in this chapter.

Gender Effects

Table 5.9 presents the results for response rates by gender. The results show similar overall rates for males and females: 14.9 and 14.6 percent for men and women, respectively. The implied difference is small and not statistically significant (applying a test where the null hypothesis is the equality of the two proportions). In other words, men and women seem to have the same probability of being contacted for a follow-up.

When the gender-based difference is examined by type of occupation, the response rate of women is statistically lower than the response rate of men only for unskilled workers. When analyzing the data by type of surname, women register a slightly higher response rate than men in the upper-class group (15.3 versus 15.1 percent, respectively). However, this difference is not statistically significant. The differences between male and female response rates are also not significant among CVs with lower-class surnames and CVs from high-income municipalities. Among low-income municipalities and technicians, the response rate of women is statistically higher than that of men.

Table 5.6 Number of CVs Sent, Number of Calls, and Response Rate, by Week and Type of Employment

Week	Number of CVs sent			Number of calls received			Response rate (%)		
	Professionals	Technicians	Unskilled	Professionals	Technicians	Unskilled	Professionals	Technicians	Unskilled
1 March 24–31	120	136	192	8	11	41	6.7	8.1	21.4
2 April 3–9	176	168	160	7	18	46	4.0	10.7	28.8
3 April 10–16	184	176	160	8	14	10	4.3	8.0	6.3
4 April 17–23	168	160	160	2	21	37	1.2	13.1	23.1
5 April 24–30	168	160	160	27	24	41	16.1	15.0	25.6
6 May 1–7	200	176	160	34	63	35	17.0	35.8	21.9
7 May 8–14	208	192	184	34	45	37	16.3	23.4	20.1
8 May 15–21	192	200	184	22	32	21	11.5	16.0	11.4
9 May 22–28	208	200	184	43	36	19	20.7	18.0	10.3
10 May 29–June 4	192	200	200	15	52	16	7.8	26.0	8.0

(continued)

Table 5.6 Number of CVs Sent, Number of Calls, and Response Rate, by Week and Type of Employment (continued)

Week	Number of CVs sent			Number of calls received			Response rate (%)		
	Professionals	Technicians	Unskilled	Professionals	Technicians	Unskilled	Professionals	Technicians	Unskilled
11 June 5–11	176	192	208	64	34	37	36.4	17.7	17.8
12 June 12–18	208	200	216	24	51	12	11.5	25.5	5.6
13 June 19–25	192	192	200	19	43	28	9.9	22.4	14.0
14 June 26–July 2	216	192	200	35	34	8	16.2	17.7	4.0
15 July 3–9	200	184	200	37	9	17	18.5	4.9	8.5
16 July 10–16	168	184	200	23	39	22	13.7	21.2	11.0
17 July 17–23	176	184	184	26	35	40	14.8	19.0	21.7
18 July 24–30	208	192	200	19	52	22	9.1	27.1	11.0
19 July 31–August 6	192	136	200	5	16	24	2.6	11.8	12.0
20 August 7–13	176	112	200		11	19	0.0	9.8	9.5
Total	3,728	3,536	3,752	452	640	532	12.1	18.1	14.2

Source: Authors' compilation.

Figure 5.2 Number of Days before a Callback

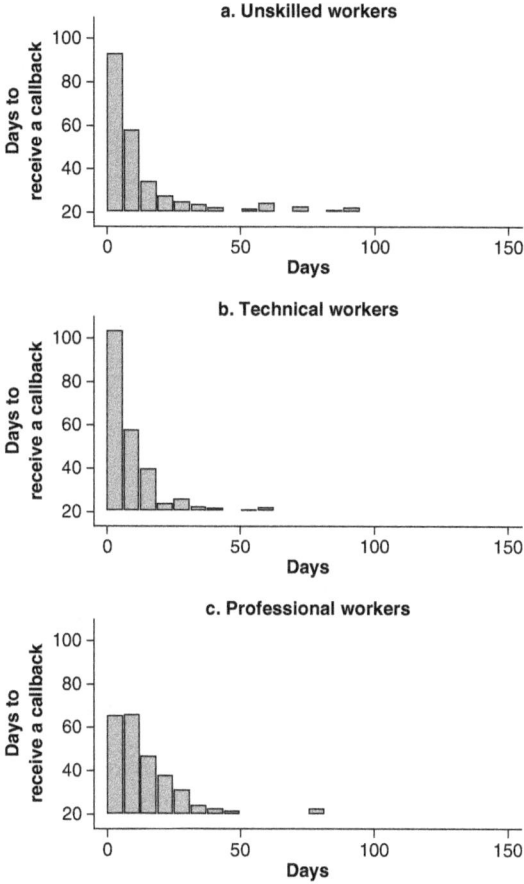

Source: Authors' compilation.

Neighborhood Effects

Table 5.10 presents our results for the analysis of differences in response rates by the socioeconomic classification of place of residence (municipality). The overall response rate of applicants from high-income municipalities is 15.1 percent compared with 14.4 percent for applicants from low-income municipalities.

Table 5.7 Days before Callback, by Type of Job

	Type of job			
	Professionals	Technicians	Unskilled	Total
Average days before callback	14.02	8.69	14.81	12.18
Total calls back	452	640	532	1,624
Total CVs sent	3,728	3,536	3,752	11,016
Response rate (%)	12.12	18.10	14.18	14.74

Source: Authors' compilation.

A more detailed analysis suggests that the observed differences are, on average, smaller than those presented in table 5.10, and most of the differences are not statistically significant (at the 10 percent level).

Social Class Effects

Table 5.11 presents our results for the analysis of discrimination based on social status (as measured by our classification of surnames). The overall response rate observed for fictitious candidates with upper-class surnames is 15.2 percent, whereas the response rate for individuals with lower-class surnames is 14.3 percent. Once again, most of the differences in response rates are not statistically significant. The largest differences occur within the group of women and within the high-income municipalities.

In conclusion, an unexpected finding is the absence of significant gender differences in response rates. In addition, the differences in response rates are lower by municipality or surname than by gender. The analysis of the response rates for professionals generally confirms these findings. All in all, we conclude that there are no significant differences in response rates by gender, municipality, or surname.

Regression Analysis

Table 5.12 undertakes a complementary analysis using linear regression models. The results confirm our previous findings. The dummy variables associated with gender, municipality, or surname are not statistically significant. Therefore, we do not find evidence supporting the presence of discrimination in any of the dimensions investigated in this chapter.

Timing of Callbacks

The results presented until now suggest that there are no differences in callback rates across groups. However, it may be possible to hypothesize

Table 5.8 Days before Callback, by Method of Contact

| | Method for submitting CVs | | | |
	Physical mail	E-mail	Fax	Total
Average days before callback	18.70	8.12	17.00	12.18
Total calls back	621	1,001	2	1,624
Total CVs sent	3,941	7,059	16	11,016
Response rate (%)	15.76	14.18	12.50	14.74

Source: Authors' compilation.

differences favoring some groups in the timing of the callbacks. Since we submitted eight CVs to each job announcement, it may be that employers first called male applicants and, after they did not follow up, proceeded to contact female applicants.

However, this was not the case. Table 5.13 shows the mean number of days it took for applicants to receive a callback after the CV was submitted. None of the differences reported in the number of days to receive a callback across groups is statistically significant.

Left for future research is the estimation of formal statistical models in which the day the person receives a callback is explained by the dimension under consideration—discrimination—and other controls. This analysis will provide more conclusive evidence of whether people who are actually discriminated against are called back later.

Discussion

The findings presented here are certainly surprising, since Latinobarómetro data on discriminatory perception show that Chileans perceive their society as discriminatory. In this section, we present a brief discussion of the possible reasons for these findings.

First, as noted, the findings are only valid for callbacks, which are only the first step when searching for a job. We do not study either interviews or the real assignation of jobs or wages. So we cannot rule out the possibility of some kind of discrimination at those stages.

Likewise, sending CVs to job announcements in the newspaper is not the only way to find a job in Chile. There are Web pages, for instance, that manage banks of CVs. In addition, there is anecdotal evidence that high-skilled workers in Chile use their social networks to search for jobs. In addition, recruiting firms or "head hunters" look for people with special skills and aptitudes. In addition, there is unsubstantiated evidence that recruiters usually look for people who have given surnames, who studied

Table 5.9 Callbacks by Gender, Social Class, and Income

	CVs sent	Men		Women		Differences		Test	
		Calls	Rate (%)	Calls	Rate (%)	Calls	Rate (%)	Z	P value
General									
All	5,508	819	14.9	805	14.6	-14	-0.3	0.376	0.707
Professionals	1,864	232	12.4	220	11.8	-12	-0.6	0.602	0.547
Technicians	1,768	302	17.1	338	19.1	36	2.0	-1.572	0.116
Unskilled	1,876	285	15.2	247	13.2	-38	-2.0	1.778	0.075
High social class									
All	2,754	415	15.1	420	15.3	5	0.2	-0.188	0.851
Professionals	932	115	12.3	120	12.9	5	0.5	-0.349	0.727
Technicians	884	151	17.1	166	18.8	15	1.7	-0.930	0.352
Unskilled	938	149	15.9	134	14.3	-15	-1.6	0.968	0.333
Low social class									
All	2,754	404	14.7	385	14.0	-19	-0.7	0.731	0.465
Professionals	932	117	12.6	100	10.7	-17	-1.8	1.228	0.219
Technicians	884	151	17.1	172	19.5	21	2.4	-1.292	0.196
Unskilled	938	136	14.5	113	12.0	-23	-2.5	1.565	0.118

(continued)

Table 5.9 Callbacks by Gender, Social Class, and Income (continued)

	CVs sent	Men		Women		Differences		Test	
		Calls	Rate (%)	Calls	Rate (%)	Calls	Rate (%)	Z	P value
High-income municipality									
All	2,754	421	15.3	410	14.9	-11	-0.4	0.414	0.679
Professionals	932	116	12.4	116	12.4	0	0.0	0.000	1.000
Technicians	884	159	18.0	167	18.9	8	0.9	-0.491	0.623
Unskilled	938	146	15.6	127	13.5	-19	-2.0	1.244	0.213
Low-income municipality									
All	2,754	398	14.5	395	14.3	-3	-0.1	0.115	0.908
Professionals	932	116	12.4	104	11.2	-12	-1.3	0.861	0.389
Technicians	884	143	16.2	171	19.3	28	3.2	-1.742	0.082
Unskilled	938	139	14.8	120	12.8	-19	-2.0	1.272	0.203

Source: Authors' compilation.

Table 5.10 Callbacks by Municipality, Social Class, and Gender

	CVs sent	High-income municipality		Low-income municipality		Differences		Test	
		Calls	Rate (%)	Calls	Rate (%)	Calls	Rate (%)	Z	P value
General									
All	5,508	831	15.1	793	14.4	−38	−0.7	1.021	0.307
Professionals	1,864	232	12.4	220	11.8	−12	−0.6	0.602	0.547
Technicians	1,768	326	18.4	314	17.8	−12	−0.7	0.524	0.600
Unskilled	1,876	273	14.6	259	13.8	−14	−0.7	0.655	0.512
High social class									
All	2,754	430	15.6	401	14.6	−29	−1.1	1.092	0.275
Professionals	932	117	12.6	118	12.7	1	0.1	−0.070	0.944
Technicians	884	163	18.4	154	17.4	−9	−1.0	0.558	0.577
Unskilled	938	150	16.0	133	14.2	−17	−1.8	1.097	0.273
Low social class									
All	2,754	405	14.7	388	14.1	−17	−0.6	0.652	0.514
Professionals	932	115	12.3	102	10.9	−13	−1.4	0.939	0.348
Technicians	884	163	18.4	160	18.1	−3	−0.3	0.185	0.853
Unskilled	938	123	13.1	126	13.4	3	0.3	−0.204	0.838

(continued)

Table 5.10 Callbacks by Municipality, Social Class, and Gender (continued)

	CVs sent	High-income municipality		Low-income municipality		Differences		Test	
		Calls	Rate (%)	Calls	Rate (%)	Calls	Rate (%)	Z	P value
Men									
All	2,754	421	15.3	398	14.5	−23	−0.8	0.871	0.384
Professionals	932	116	12.4	116	12.4	0	0.0	0.000	1.000
Technicians	884	159	18.0	167	18.9	8	0.9	−0.491	0.623
Unskilled	938	146	15.6	127	13.5	−19	−2.0	1.244	0.213
Women									
All	2,754	410	14.9	395	14.3	−15	−0.5	0.572	0.567
Professionals	932	116	12.4	104	11.2	−12	−1.3	0.861	0.389
Technicians	884	143	16.2	171	19.3	28	3.2	−1.742	0.082
Unskilled	938	139	14.8	120	12.8	−19	−2.0	1.272	0.203

Source: Authors' compilation.

155

Table 5.11 Callbacks by Surname, Income of Municipality, and Gender

	CVs sent	High social class		Low social class		Differences		Test	
		Calls	Rate (%)	Calls	Rate (%)	Calls	Rate (%)	Z	P value
General									
All	5,508	835	15.2	789	14.3	-46	-0.8	1.236	0.216
Professionals	1,864	235	12.6	217	11.6	-18	-1.0	0.903	0.367
Technicians	1,768	317	17.9	323	18.3	6	0.3	-0.262	0.793
Unskilled	1,876	283	15.1	249	13.3	-34	-1.8	1.591	0.112
High-income municipality									
All	2,754	430	15.6	405	14.7	-25	-0.9	0.939	0.348
Professionals	932	117	12.6	118	12.7	1	0.1	-0.070	0.944
Technicians	884	163	18.4	154	17.4	-9	-1.0	0.558	0.577
Unskilled	938	150	16.0	133	14.2	-17	-1.8	1.097	0.273
Low-income municipality									
All	2,754	401	14.6	388	14.1	-13	-0.5	0.500	0.617
Professionals	932	115	12.3	102	10.9	-13	-1.4	0.939	0.348
Technicians	884	163	18.4	160	18.1	-3	-0.3	0.185	0.853
Unskilled	938	123	13.1	126	13.4	3	0.3	-0.204	0.838

(continued)

Table 5.11 Callbacks by Surname, Income of Municipality, and Gender (continued)

| | CVs sent | High social class | | Low social class | | Differences | | Test | |
		Calls	Rate (%)	Calls	Rate (%)	Calls	Rate (%)	Z	P value
Men									
All	2,754	415	15.1	404	14.7	-11	-0.4	0.417	0.677
Professionals	932	115	12.3	117	12.6	2	0.2	-0.140	0.889
Technicians	884	151	17.1	151	17.1	0	0.0	0.000	1.000
Unskilled	938	149	15.9	136	14.5	-13	-1.4	0.836	0.403
Women									
All	2,754	420	15.3	385	14.0	-35	-1.3	1.335	0.182
Professionals	932	120	12.9	100	10.7	-20	-2.1	1.436	0.151
Technicians	884	166	18.8	172	19.5	6	0.7	-0.363	0.717
Unskilled	938	134	14.3	113	12.0	-21	-2.2	1.434	0.152

Source: Authors' compilation.

Table 5.12 Regressions for the Probability of Receiving a Callback

(Dependent variable: Dummy=1 if a callback is received)

Variable	Coeff.	P value	Coeff.	P value	Coeff.	P value	Coeff.	P value
Dummy high-income municipality=1	0.0069	0.304	0.0070	0.301	0.0074	0.392	0.0048	0.736
Dummy men=1	0.0026	0.706	0.0029	0.670	0.0020	0.770	-0.0106	0.389
Dummy high-class surname=1	0.0082	0.222	0.0084	0.210	0.0082	0.226	-0.002	0.863
Dummy professional job ad=1			-0.0217	0.009	-0.0262	0.003	-0.0249	0.004
Dummy technician job ad=1			0.0380	0.000	0.0369	0.000	0.0370	0.000
Dummy studied at private school=1					-0.0030	0.780	-0.0114	0.741
Dummy studied at municipal school=1					-0.0173	0.038	0.0061	0.668
Controls for type of mail sent	No		No		Yes		Yes	
Including interactions	No		No		No		Yes	
Pseudo R^2	0.0003		0.006		0.0189		0.009	
Number of observations	11,016		11,016		11,016		11,016	

Source: Authors' compilation.
Note: Probit regressions. Coefficients are expressed in probability points for discrete changes of dummy variables from 0 to 1 (evaluated at means).

158

Table 5.13 Number of Days to Receive a Callback

	Mean	Median
Gender		
Men	12.8	8
Women	11.6	7
Difference	1.2	1
Municipality		
High income	11.8	7
Low income	12.5	7
Difference	−0.7	0
Surname		
High class	12.3	7
Low class	12.1	7
Difference	0.2	0

Source: Authors' compilation.

in private and exclusive schools, and who possess a large network of contacts. Thus we may be looking at just one part of the labor market, the part that is not discriminating.

Additionally, we use a different experimental design than that used by Bertrand and Mullainathan (2004). We argue, however, that our methodology is more robust. While we constructed equally qualified CVs and then assigned names, those authors took samples of CVs from the real world and assigned them different names using the same share of population groups as in the real world. This difference has two major implications that may raise additional questions. First, constructing fictitious individuals helps us to have real exogenous variations. Second, this fake world may differ from the real world, and, as a consequence, employers could have applied positive discrimination. They could have thought, "If this person, under these circumstances, reaches such a level of education and experience, she or he must be a good applicant."

Yet it is still surprising that, although Bertrand and Mullainathan (2004) find statistically significant differences among surnames associated with African American and white population groups, we do not find similar results in our study. This may mean that discrimination is deeper in the United States than in Chile, which, unlike other Latin American countries such as Bolivia, Brazil, or Peru, does not display a great deal of racial diversity. The country's population is overwhelmingly of European descent, with only a small indigenous population.

Finally, what we consider to be subjective discrimination in the labor market may indeed be related more to historical factors of inequality of opportunities. Following Ferreira and Gignoux (2008), the principle of equality of opportunity is based on three concepts: circumstances, results, and opportunities. On the one hand, circumstances are exogenous factors that people do not choose to have and that are out of their control, such as socioeconomic background of origin, place of birth, gender, or physical and mental disability. On the other hand, results are an individual's achievements, which are obtained after a process of creation, accumulation, and performance, such as educational level, employment, wages, benefits, and others. Opportunities are variables that influence results and determine an individual's performance. Some opportunities are out of the control of the individual, and some, like public policy, are endogenous to society. The principle of equality of opportunity states that, for the results to be fair, all individuals, independent of their circumstances, should have the same opportunities in life. In this context, when we observe that human capital and access to employment (results) differ between groups of the population, this may be due to poor public policies that fail to equalize opportunities of different groups rather than to discrimination in the labor market. Thus results are more related to circumstances.

Conclusions

In this chapter we study the Chilean labor market and analyze the presence of gender discrimination. In order to transcend the limitations of earlier works, we used an experimental strategy, the first of its kind in Chile. This design allowed us to investigate the presence of socioeconomic discrimination associated with social status (name) and place of residence in the Chilean labor market.

The study consisted of sending fictitious curriculum vitae for real job vacancies published weekly in a widely read Chilean newspaper. We submitted a set of strictly equivalent CVs to each job classified, varying only the gender, name, and place of residence, and then analyzed the differences in call response rates across various demographic groups.

We find no statistically significant differences in callbacks for any of the groups we explored: gender, socioeconomic background, or place of residence. The findings are surprising and generate new questions. Several issues may be behind these findings. In particular, we only consider one step in the hiring process, the callback, not the complete behavior of the labor market. We leave for further research the use of formal econometric models to estimate different effects of the timing of the call (see Bravo, Sanhueza, and Urzúa 2009).

Annex

Table 5A.1 CVs Sent in (Unskilled)

Unskilled	Number	Percentage
Administrativo	952	25.37
Aseador	208	5.54
Auxiliar Aseo	48	1.28
Bodeguero	384	10.23
Cajero	328	8.74
Cobrador	96	2.56
Conductor	48	1.28
Digitador	368	9.81
Encuestador	88	2.35
Fotocopiador	8	0.21
Garzon	152	4.06
Guardia	56	1.49
Operario Producción	8	0.21
Operario Tintoreria	8	0.21
Promotor	304	8.10
Recepcionista	16	0.42
Vendedor	624	16.63
Volantero	56	1.49
Total	3,752	100

Source: Authors' compilation.

Table 5A.2 CVs Sent in (Professional)

Professionals	Number	Percentage
Abogado	192	5.14
Constructor Civil	640	17.14
Contador Auditor	912	24.47
Ing. Civil	264	7.06
Ing. Comercial	576	15.44
Ing. Ejecucion	144	3.84
Ing. Informatico	256	6.86

(continued)

Table 5A.2 CVs Sent in (Professional) *(continued)*

Professionals	Number	Percentage
Profesor	720	19.17
Psicologo	16	0.42
Supervisor Educacional	8	0.21
	3,728	100

Source: Authors' compilation.

Table 5A.3 CVs Sent in (Technicians)

Technicians	Number	Percentage
Soporte Computacional	8	0.23
Administrador	16	0.45
Administrador Empresas	8	0.23
Administrador Sistema	8	0.23
Administrador de Botilleria	8	0.23
Administrador de Empresas	8	0.23
Administrador de Local	16	0.45
Administrador de Redes	16	0.45
Administrador de Restaurant	8	0.23
Administrador de Sistemas	16	0.45
Administrador de red	8	0.23
Administrador de redes	8	0.23
Administrativo en Comex	8	0.23
Adquisiciones	8	0.23
Agente de Ventas	16	0.45
Agente de Ventas Intangibles	8	0.23
Analista Computacional	8	0.23
Analista Programador	200	5.66
Analista Sistemas	8	0.23
Analista de Sistema	32	0.90
Analista de Sistemas	24	0.68
Analista o Programador	8	0.23
Asistente Adquisiciones	16	0.45

(continued)

Table 5A.3 CVs Sent in (Technicians) *(continued)*

Technicians	Number	Percentage
Asistente Comercio Exterior	8	0.23
Asistente Contable	40	1.13
Asistente Técnico Hardware	8	0.23
Asistente de Enfermeria	8	0.23
Asistente de Enfermos	16	0.45
Auxiliar Enfermería	8	0.23
Auxiliar Paramedico	16	0.45
Auxiliar Paramédico	32	0.90
Auxiliar Técnico de Laboratorio	8	0.23
Auxiliar de Enfermeria	40	1.13
Auxiliar de Enfermería	40	1.13
Auxiliar de Laboratorio	8	0.23
Auxiliar de enfermería	8	0.23
Auxiliar de laboratorio	8	0.23
Auxiliar de toma de muestra	8	0.23
Ayudante Contable	8	0.23
Ayudante de Contador	40	1.13
Chef	32	0.90
Cheff Ejecutivo	8	0.23
Comercio Exterior	8	0.23
Conocimientos en Computacion	8	0.23
Contador	200	5.66
Contador Administrador	8	0.23
Contador Asistente	16	0.45
Contador General	72	2.04
Contador general	8	0.23
Desarrollador de Web	8	0.23
Dibujante Autocad	48	1.36
Dibujante Estructural	8	0.23
Dibujante Gráfico	8	0.23
Dibujante Mecánico Autocad	8	0.23
Dibujante Proyecticta	8	0.23

(continued)

Table 5A.3 CVs Sent in (Technicians) *(continued)*

Technicians	Number	Percentage
Dibujante Técnico	32	0.90
Dibujante de Arquitectura	8	0.23
Dibujante técnico	24	0.68
Dibujante y Proyectistas	8	0.23
Diseñador Gráfico	128	3.62
Diseñador Industrial	32	0.90
Diseñador Internet	8	0.23
Diseñador Web	16	0.45
Diseñador Web Master	8	0.23
Diseñador de Página web	8	0.23
Diseñador de web	8	0.23
Ejecutivo Comercio Exterior	8	0.23
Ejecutivo Telemarketing	8	0.23
Ejecutivo de Ventas	8	0.23
Encargado de Adquisiciones	16	0.45
Encargado de Adquisisciones	8	0.23
Encargado de Compras	8	0.23
Encargado de Informatica	8	0.23
Encargado de Informática	8	0.23
Encargado de Local	8	0.23
Encargado de Remuneraciones	8	0.23
Encargado de comercio exterior	8	0.23
Encargado de informática	8	0.23
Encargado de remuneraciones	8	0.23
Experto en Computación	8	0.23
Experto en Diseño Página Web	8	0.23
Explotador de Sistemas	8	0.23
Informático	8	0.23
Informático Hardware	8	0.23
Jefe Adquisiciones	8	0.23
Jefe Facturación	8	0.23
Jefe de Abastecimiento	8	0.23

(continued)

Table 5A.3 CVs Sent in (Technicians) *(continued)*

Technicians	Number	Percentage
Jefe de Bodega	8	0.23
Jefe de Local	56	1.58
Jefe de Locales	8	0.23
Jefe de Personal	8	0.23
Jefe de Recursos Humanos	8	0.23
Jefe de Tienda	32	0.90
Jefe de Tiendas	8	0.23
Jefe para cafeteria y pasteleria	8	0.23
Operador Informático	8	0.23
Paramedico	16	0.45
Paramedico RX	8	0.23
Paramedicos	8	0.23
Pedidor Aduanero	8	0.23
Prevencionista Riesgos	8	0.23
Procurador	32	0.90
Programador	544	15.38
Programador Analista	8	0.23
Programador Clipper	8	0.23
Programador Web	80	2.26
Programador Webmaster	8	0.23
Programador o Analista	8	0.23
Programador y Analistas	8	0.23
Proyectista Autocard	8	0.23
Soporte	16	0.45
Soporte Computacional	88	2.49
Soporte Informático	8	0.23
Soporte Tecnico	8	0.23
Soporte Técnico	24	0.68
Soporte en Redes	16	0.45
Supervisor	8	0.23
Supervisor Cobranzas	24	0.68
Supervisor Locales Comerciales	8	0.23

(continued)

Table 5A.3 CVs Sent in (Technicians) *(continued)*

Technicians	Number	Percentage
Supervisor Logístico	16	0.45
Supervisor de Call Center	8	0.23
Supervisor de Facturación y cobranzas	8	0.23
Supervisor de Venta	8	0.23
Técnico Informatico	8	0.23
Técnico Paramedico	8	0.23
Técnico Paramedicos	8	0.23
Técnico Soporte	16	0.45
Técnico en Computación	8	0.23
Técnico en Redes	8	0.23
Técnico paramedico	8	0.23
Técnico Administración de Redes	8	0.23
Técnico Administrador Empresas	8	0.23
Técnico Comercio Exterior	32	0.90
Técnico Computación	16	0.45
Técnico Gastronómico	8	0.23
Técnico Informático	32	0.90
Técnico Instalación Redes	8	0.23
Técnico Jurídico	24	0.68
Técnico Paramédico	88	2.49
Técnico Prevención	8	0.23
Técnico Programador	24	0.68
Técnico Químico	8	0.23
Técnico Soporte Terreno	8	0.23
Técnico Soporte en Linux	8	0.23
Técnico de Comercio Exterior	8	0.23
Técnico en Comercio Exterior	16	0.45
Técnico en Comex	8	0.23
Técnico en Computación	128	3.62
Técnico en Computación y Redes	8	0.23
Técnico en Enfermería	8	0.23
Técnico en Gastronomía	8	0.23

(continued)

Table 5A.3 CVs Sent in (Technicians) *(continued)*

Technicians	Number	Percentage
Técnico en Hardware y Redes	8	0.23
Técnico en Hardware y Software	8	0.23
Técnico en Informática	16	0.45
Técnico en Logística	8	0.23
Técnico en Mantención	8	0.23
Técnico en Programación	8	0.23
Técnico en Redes Computacionales	8	0.23
Técnico en Reparación	8	0.23
Técnico en Soporte	72	2.04
Técnico en Soporte Computacional	8	0.23
Técnico en comex	8	0.23
Técnico paramédico	8	0.23
Técnico pc grafico	8	0.23
Vendedores Isapre	8	0.23
Web Master	8	0.23
Total	3,536	100

Source: Authors' compilation.

Table 5A.4 Number of Days before a Callback, by Type of Job

Days	Type of job			Total
	Professionals	Technicians	Unskilled	
0	10	90	54	154
1	55	92	65	212
2	11	57	45	113
3	10	36	44	90
4	3	19	15	37
5	14	20	7	41
6	26	22	15	63
7	19	58	50	127
8	31	50	21	102
9	26	23	28	77

(continued)

Table 5A.4 Number of Days before a Callback, by Type of Job
(continued)

Days	Type of job			Total
	Professionals	Technicians	Unskilled	
10	17	11	22	50
11	31	5	4	40
12	7	5	2	14
13	11	5	5	21
14	24	28	15	67
15	9	24	11	44
16	12	13	11	36
17	9	7	5	21
18	11	3		14
19	2	2	1	5
20	15		2	17
21	7	4	12	23
22	13	4	7	24
23	5	1	3	9
24	9	5		14
26	1	9	1	11
27	18	4	3	25
28	3	6	5	14
29	1	3	2	6
30	9	1	5	15
31		1		1
32			1	1
33	1	9		10
34			4	4
35	2		1	3
36	7	1	1	9
37	2		5	7
38	3			3
40	2		1	3

(continued)

Table 5A.4 Number of Days before a Callback, by Type of Job
(continued)

Days	Type of job			Total
	Professionals	*Technicians*	*Unskilled*	*Total*
41	2		5	7
42	1	1		2
43		4	1	5
44		2		2
48	2	2		4
49		1	1	2
50	3		2	5
51			4	4
52			1	1
54		4		4
55			1	1
57			4	4
58		1	8	9
59		3	2	5
64		1		1
66		3		3
73			4	4
74			4	4
76			1	1
77	5		2	7
84	3		1	4
85			2	2
86			1	1
90			2	2
91			4	4
93			1	1
95			1	1
98			1	1
105			2	2

(continued)

Table 5A.4 Number of Days before a Callback, by Type of Job
(continued)

	Type of job			
Days	Professionals	Technicians	Unskilled	Total
111			1	1
116			1	1
125			1	1
126			1	1
Average days	14.02	8.69	14.81	12.18
Total calls back	452	640	532	1624
Total CVs sent	3,728	3,536	3,752	11,016
Response rate (%)	12.12	18.10	14.18	14.74

Source: Authors' compilation.
Note: Empty cells = no callback.

Table 5A.5 Number of Days before a Callback, by
CV Submission Method

	CV submission method			
Days	Physical mail	E-mail	Fax	Total
0		154		154
1		212		212
2	4	109		113
3	47	43		90
4	26	11		37
5	16	25		41
6	19	44		63
7	66	61		127
8	54	48		102
9	61	16		77
10	21	29		50
11	19	21		40
12	2	12		14
13	4	17		21
14	27	40		67

(continued)

Table 5A.5 Number of Days before a Callback, by
CV Submission Method *(continued)*

| Days | CV submission method | | | Total |
	Physical mail	E-mail	Fax	
15	29	15		44
16	20	16		36
17	9	10	2	21
18	10	4		14
19	3	2		5
20	10	7		17
21	11	12		23
22	17	7		24
23	5	4		9
24	11	3		14
26	9	2		11
27	6	19		25
28	8	6		14
29	5	1		6
30	14	1		15
31		1		1
32		1		1
33	1	9		10
34	4			4
35		3		3
36	4	5		9
37	7			7
38	2	1		3
40		3		3
41	6	1		7
42	2			2
43		5		5
44	2			2
48	2	2		4

(continued)

Table 5A.5 Number of Days before a Callback, by
CV Submission Method *(continued)*

	CV submission method			
Days	Physical mail	E-mail	Fax	Total
49	2			2
50	2	3		5
51	4			4
52	1			1
54		4		4
55	1			1
57	4			4
58	8	1		9
59	3	2		5
64		1		1
66		3		3
73	4			4
74	4			4
76	1			1
77	7			7
84	3	1		4
85	2			2
86	1			1
90	2			2
91	4			4
93	1			1
95	1			1
98		1		1
105		2		2
111	1			1
116	1			1
125	1			1
126		1		1

(continued)

Table 5A.5 Number of Days before a Callback, by
CV Submission Method *(continued)*

	CV submission method			
Days	*Physical mail*	*E-mail*	*Fax*	*Total*
Average days	18.70	8.12	17.00	12.18
Total call backs	621	1,001	2	1,624
Total CVs sent	3,941	7,059	16	11,016
Response rate (%)	15.76	14.18	12.50	14.74

Source: Authors' compilation.
Note: Empty cells = no callback.

Figure 5A.1 Example of a Scanned Ad

Source: Chilean newspaper.

CURRICULUM VITAE

MICHAEL BAILEY LAVAGNINO

I. DATOS PERSONALES

Fecha de Nacimiento	:	17 de Julio de 1975
Nacionalidad	:	Chilena
Cédula de Identidad	:	12.408.860 – 3
Estado Civil	:	Casado, 1 hijo
Dirección	:	Av. Pocuro 2900, Depto. 304, Providencia
Teléfono	:	08 – 4724260
E-mail	:	Pcs.2541@gmail.com

II. DATOS PERSONALES

Educación Básica y Media	:	Colegio San Ignacio El Bosque, Providencia (1989 – 1992).
Educación Universitaria	:	Construcción Civil, Escuela de Construcción Civil Universidad Católica de Chile (1998).
Educación Post Universitaria (TAC) Mención en Obras Civiles.	:	Postítulo en Tecnologías avanzadas en Construcción, Facultad de Ingeniería, Pontificia Universidad Católica de Chile (2000).

III. IDIOMAS

Inglés, nivel medio, hablado y escrito

IV. EXPERIENCIA LABORAL

- **Constructora Maihue Ltda.**, Asistente en el Estudio de Presupuestos de Obra. (Part Time), 2001 – 2002.
- **Constructora Fernández Wood Ltda.**, Jefe de Oficina Técnica de presupuestos de obras, 2002 – 2004..
- **E.C. Pumpin e Irarrazabal**, Administrador de Obra: Edificio y Caseta Planta Agas Con Con y Profesional de Terreno: Edificio en construcción, 2005 – 2006.

V. OTROS

Manejo de Microsoft Office (Excel, Word, Power Point, Outlook).

VI. PRETENSIONES DE RENTA

$ 1.000.000.

Con disponibilidad para viajar fuera de Santiago.

Santiago, Abril de 2006

CAROLINA HARMSEN BERNAL

Antecedentes Personales

Fecha de nacimiento:	14 de diciembre de 1976
Carnet de identidad:	12.325.974-7
Dirección:	Av. Simon Bolivar 5501- C, La Reina
Estado civil:	Casada, 2 hijos
Teléfono:	08 – 4734992
E-mail:	Profesional2525@gmail.com

Experiencia Laboral Postulante

Ingeniería

Fecha:	01/2005 – 02/2006
Empresa:	Dirección de Obras Sanitarias del MOP
Actividad de la empresa:	Obras sanitarias
Descripción de funciones:	Proyectar, ejecutar y dirigir obras hidráulicas.

Jefe Área

Fecha:	04/2002 – 12/2004
Empresa:	Constructora Sega Ltda.
Actividad de la empresa:	Construcción
Descripción de funciones:	Jefe del departamento de obras civiles.

Ingeniería y Construcción

Fecha:	05/2000 – 01/2001
Empresa:	Delmar Construcciones Ltda.
Actividad de la empresa:	Construcción
Descripción de funciones:	Jefe depto. Obras Civiles, encargado de llevar a cabo las políticas en cuanto a seguridad, eficacia y eficiencia de los sistemas implementados, además de interactuar con proveedores, consultores externos y los departamentos financiero y operativo de la empresa.

Educación

Universitaria Completa

Título:	**Constructor Civil**
Institución:	Pontificia Universidad Católica de Chile
País:	CHILE
Ciudad:	Santiago
Fecha:	1999

Secundaria

Institución:	Colegio Nuestra Señora del Pilar
País:	CHILE - Santiago
Fecha:	1987 – 1993

Cursos de Especialización Completos

Nombre Curso :	**MAGÍSTER EN CIENCIAS DE LA INGENIERÍA M/ INGENIERÍA GEOTÉCNICA.**
Institución:	Universidad de Chile, Facultad de Ciencias Físicas y Matemáticas
País:	CHILE
Ciudad:	Santiago
Fecha:	2001

Cursos de Especialización Completos

Nombre Curso :	Dominio de aplicaciones Microsoft Office e Internet a nivel de usuario (Word, Power Point, Access, Excel
Institución:	Infoland
País:	CHILE
Ciudad:	Santiago
Fecha:	1999
Nombre Curso :	Diplomado, Implantación de la Calidad para la Certificación ISO 9001:2000
Institución:	Pontificia Universidad Católica de Chile
País:	CHILE
Ciudad:	Santiago
Fecha:	2005

Idiomas

Inglés	Nivel Medio
Pretensión de Renta	$ 900.000

Disponible para viajar
   dentro del país.

SANTIAGO, abril de 2006

CURRICULUM VITAE

ANTECEDENTES PERSONALES

NOMBRE COMPLETO   SALOMON DABDUB ARANCIBIA
FECHA DE NACIMIENTO   11 de noviembre de 1971
CEDULA DE IDENTIDAD   10.452.187-4
NACIONALIDAD   Chilena
ESTADO CIVIL   Casado, 1 hijo
DIRECCION PARTICULAR   Combarbalá 4560, La Granja
FONO PARTICULAR   08 – 4716515
E-MAIL   ingenieros001@gmail.com

ESTUDIOS REALIZADOS

Secundarios   Saint Christian College, 1988
Universitarios   Construcción Civil.
                    Pontificia Universidad Católica de Chile - 1994
                    Postítulo en Administración de Empresas
                    Pontificia Universidad Católica de Chile 1996
Postítulo   Administración de Empresas Constructoras
                    mención en desarrollo inmobiliario.
                    Pontificia Universidad Católica de Chile, 2002.

EXPERIENCIA PROFESIONAL

1998 – 2000	Constructora SOCOVESA S.A. Supervisor de planta de hormigones premezclados, con labores operacionales, técnicas y comerciales asesorando empresas en faenas de hormigado.
2001 – 2003	Promet Servicios S.A. Jefe del Departamento de Control de Calidad para faena en Minera Escondida Ltda. correspondiente al Proyecto Expansión Fase IV. Labores de jefe de terreno y subadministrador.
2004 – 2005	Flesan Ingeniería S.A. Jefe del Departamento de Construcción de la empresa, realizando propuestas y ejecución de obras menores.

Idiomas	Inglés nivel Medio

Dominio de Sofware
Aplicaciones de Microsoft Office e Internet a nivel de usuario (Word, Excell, Power Point, y Access).

Pretensión de Renta

$ 1.000.000.
Disponible para viajar a regiones.

Santiago, abril de 2006.

CURRICULUM VITAE

MARCELA ROSS VARGAS

I. DATOS PERSONALES

Fecha de nacimiento	23 de septiembre de 1972
Nacionalidad	Chilena
Cédula de identidad	10.668.374 – 7
Estado civil	Casada, 1 hijo
Dirección	Rolando Petersen 1502, Cerro Navia
Teléfono	08 – 4724283
E-mail	2006profesional@gmail.com

II. EDUCACIÓN

Educación Media	Liceo Isaura Dinator de Guzmán A4 Santiago (1989).
Educación Universitaria	Escuela de Construcción Civil, Universidad Católica de Chile. Construcción Civil (Diciembre de 1995).
Educación Post Universitaria	Post Título en Administración de Empresas Constructoras, Mención en Desarrollo en Obras Civiles. Pontificia Universidad Católica de Chile (1997).

III. IDIOMAS

Inglés (Nivel Medio).

IV. EXPERIENCIA LABORAL

– **EMPRESA CONSULTORA, Consultoría/Asesoría, Asesor** Análisis, Gestión de Control, Evaluación y Programación de proyectos de infraestructura urbana, Vial e Hidráulica, 2002 – 2003.

– **EMPRESA INGEVEC S.A.** Jefa del Área Obras Civiles y como Inspector de Obra en las diferentes sucursales a lo largo del país. 2003 – 2004.

– **EMPRESA CONSTRUCTORA RALUN LTDA.** Inspector de diversas obras. 2005 – 2006.

V. OTROS

Dominio de aplicaciones Microsoft Office e Internet a nivel de usuario (Word, Excel, Power Point, Access).

VI. PRETENSIÓN DE RENTA

$ 1.000.000.

Con disponibilidad para viajar a Regiones.
Santiago, abril de 2006.

Pablo Calfil Gonzalez

Información personal	• Estado civil: Casado, 1 Hijo • Nacionalidad: Chilena • Edad: 33 • María Soledad 670, Las Condes • Rut: 11.051.154-0 • Teléfono 08 – 7621538 • Email: ing.profesional@gmail.com
Educación	• 1990, Colegio Francisco de Asís de Las Condes
Educación Superior	• Construcción Civil, Universidad Católica de Chile. **Constructor Civil** • Postítulo en tecnologías avanzadas en construcción (TAC) mención en obras civiles. Universidad Católica de Chile. • Curso Auditor Interno ISO 9000:2000, IRAM e IQNET • Preparación y Evaluación de Proyecto Inmobiliario, Facultad de Arquitectura de la Universidad de Chile.
Experiencia profesional	• 1999 – 2000, DELVA, Metalmecánica Asesor en métodos constructivos, control de obras (Ms-proyect), rectificación topográfica, administración de obras, contratación personal de obras, presupuestos y análisis de costos. • 2000 – 2003, Enginner Chile, Construcción Asesor, Supervisor y Ejecutor de proyectos como contratista en la empresa. • 2004 – 2005, CINTAC, Materiales de Construcción Supervisor labores de faena, propias del método constructivo METALCON (gestión de calidad).
Software	• Dominio de aplicaciones Microsoft Office e Internet a nivel de usuario (Word, Power Point, Access, Excel).
Idioma	Inglés Medio
Pretensión de Renta	$ 1.000.000.
Disponibilidad	Para viajar fuera de Santiago.
Abril, 2006.	

Analia Socorro Socorro

Constructor Civil

ANTECEDENTES PERSONALES

FECHA DE NACIMIENTO	14 de Julio de 1974
CEDULA DE IDENTIDAD	12.152.187 – 5
NACIONALIDAD	Chilena
ESTADO CIVIL	Casada, 1 hijo
DIRECCIÓN PARTÍCULAR	El Gabino 4340 Dpto. 301, Lo Barnechea
FONO PARTÍCULAR	08 – 7627022
E-MAIL	Amarillo.camino@gmail.com

EDUCACIÓN

SECUNDARIOS	Colegio La Dehesa, 1991.
UNIVERSITARIOS	Construcción Civil Pontificia Universidad Católica de Chile (1997).
EDUCACIÓN POST - UNIVERSITARIA	Postitulo en Administración de Empresas Constructoras, Mención en Desarrollo inmobiliario, Pontificia Universidad Católica de Chile (1999).

EXPERIENCIA PROFESIONAL

2000–2002	Constructora Ecopsa S.A. Catastro de viviendas en garantías. Administración de RRHH. Encargada de las terminaciones de las viviendas de la obra, de un condominio en la comuna de Lo Barnechea.
2003 – 2004	Ingeniería e Inmobiliaria S.A. Evaluación Económica de maquinaria pesada, compra, venta, arriendo y costos de operación.
2004 – 2006	Constructora Propuerto Ltda. Ingeniero de Estudio de Propuestas, creación de precios unitarios, programación de obras y plazos, asignación de recursos, cotizaciones, interpretación de planos y bases técnicas.

IDIOMA

Dominio del Inglés Medio.

OTROS ANTECEDENTES

Dominio de aplicaciones Microsoft Office e Internet a nivel de usuario (Word, Excel, Power Point, Access).

PRETENSIÓN DE RENTA

$ 1.000.000.

Con Disponibilidad para viajar a regiones.
Santiago, abril de 2006.

CURRICULUM VITAE

I. Antecedentes Personales

Nombre	Pablo Ayulef Muñoz
Profesión	Constructor Civil, Universidad de Chile
Fecha de Nacimiento	24 de febrero de 1975
Cédula de Identidad	12.166.357-8
Nacionalidad	Chilena
Estado Civil	Casado, 1 hijo
Dirección	Antonio Machado 1951, El Bosque
Teléfono	(08) 7621526
Correo Electrónico	ingcivil2006@gmail.com

II. Estudios

- Licenciatura Media (1992)
  Centro Educacional Matías Cousiño, El Bosque
- Título Universitario de **Constructor Civil** (1998)
  Universidad Católica de Chile, Santiago.
- Magíster en Ciencias de la Ingeniería área ingeniería y gestión de la Construcción.
  Facultad de Ingeniería Universidad Católica de Chile.
- Curso, Auditor Interno ISO 9001:2000, Fundación Sercal

III. Antecedentes Laborales

2001 – 2003	Inspector Técnico, Profesional de Terreno
	Empresa Constructora Fe Grande, Santiago
	Principales funciones:
	Coordinación de trabajos en estudio y aprobados para ser realizados a la brevedad.
	Redistribución de funciones a ingenieros calculistas y proyectistas.
2004 – 2005	Ingeniero
	Ingeniería y Proyectos IPSA S.A., Santiago
	Principales funciones:
	Miembro del Departamento de Estudios de la empresa en apoyo al control y desarrollo de proyectos de ingeniería, realizando trabajos en la parte técnica y administrativa.
Marzo 2005 a la fecha	Jefe de Departamento de Estudios
	Ingeniería Cocivil Ltda., Santiago.
	Principales funciones:
	Coordinación de los trabajos para su estudio y real factibilidad de desarrollo.

IV. Otros Antecedentes

Dominio de aplicaciones Microsoft Office e Internet a nivel de usuario (Word, Excel, Power Point, Access).
Ingles: Nivel Medio.

VI. Pretensión de Renta

$ 1.000.000.

Disponible para viajar fuera de Santiago.
Abril, 2006

CURRICULUM VITAE

I. Antecedentes Personales

Nombre   **_Johanna Paineman Ojeda_**
Profesión   Constructor Civil
Fecha de Nacimiento 02 de julio de 1976
Cédula de Identidad 12.497.158 – 3
Nacionalidad   Chilena
Estado Civil   Casada, 2 hijos
Dirección   Los Morros 13570, La Pintana
Teléfono   (08) 7627540
Correo Electrónico Viaje.3201@gmail.com

II. Antecedentes Laborales

2002 – 2003
: Inspector de Obras
Bustamante Ltda., Construcción
Principales funciones:
Contratada como profesional de obra, para terminaciones de viviendas, en el sector de "La Reserva", en la comuna de Chicureo.

2004 – 2005
: Inspector Técnico y Asesor en la confección de Morteros y Hormigones, fabricados en obras.
Fernández Word Constructora

2005 a la fecha
: Jefe de Terreno: Proyecto "Mejoramiento de Barrios" la obra consta de 450 soluciones de casetas sanitarias, mandante I. M. de Valparaíso.
Sociedad Constructora Kaner Ltda.

Estudios Secundarios

1993
: Liceo 1 Javiera Carrera, Santiago.

Estudios Superiores

1994 – 1999
: Título Universitario de Constructor Civil
Pontificia Universidad Católica de Chile, Santiago

2000
: Postítulo prevención de riesgos en el sector productivo
Pontificia Universidad Católica de Chile Santiago.

Idioma
: Inglés nivel medio.

III. Otros Antecedentes

Dominio de aplicaciones Windows, Microsoft Office (Excel, Word, PowerPoint).

IV. Cursos de Especialización

Auditor Interno ISO 9001:2000, Universidad Católica de Chile

VI. Pretensión de Renta

$ 1.000.000.
Disponibilidad para viajar fuera de Santiago.
Santiago, Abril 2006.

Notes

1. Authors' calculations using data from the 2003 Survey of Socioeconomic Characteristics of Chile (hereafter, CASEN 2003). After correcting for differences in human capital and occupational choice, this gap falls to approximately 19 percent.
2. Previous studies for Chile are Bravo (2005); Montenegro (2001); Montenegro and Paredes (1999); Paredes and Riveros (1994).
3. Bravo (2005) shows that, taking all employed workers and controlling for years of schooling and occupation, the wage gap was 13.5 percent in 2000. Using the Blinder-Oaxaca decomposition, he concludes that most of this difference was due to "residual discrimination."
4. According to the International Labour Organisation. Contreras and Plaza (2004) show that cultural factors, such as sexism, significantly influence female labor force participation in Chile.
5. Núñez and Gutiérrez (2004) analyze discrimination by social class in Chile controlling for the potential presence of unobserved variables.
6. See Altonji and Blank (1999) and Blank, Dabady, and Citro (2004) for complete surveys of the econometric problems involved in detecting discrimination in the labor market using regression analysis and field experiments.
7. Riach and Rich (2002, 2004) and Anderson, Fryer, and Holt (2006) offer a complete survey of these studies.
8. It really tests the callback decision.
9. Repeat rate refers to the proportion of ads that were repeated from the week before. It is common to publish ads for more than one Sunday.
10. See http://www.laborum.com and http://www.infoempleo.cl.
11. The central element in training the individuals in charge of this process was to ensure that the eight CVs prepared for each vacancy were equivalent with regard to qualifications and human capital.

References

Altonji, Joseph, and Rebecca Blank. 1999. "Race and Gender in the Labor Market." In *Handbook of Labor Economics,* vol. 3, ed. Orley Ashenfelter and David Card. Amsterdam: North Holland.

Anderson, Lisa, Roland Fryer, and Charles Holt. 2006. "Discrimination: Experimental Evidence from Psychology and Economics." In *Handbook on Economics and Discrimination,* ed. William Rogers. Cheltenham: Elgar.

Antonovics, Kate, Peter Arcidiacono, and Randall Walsh. 2004. "Competing against the Opposite Sex." Economics Working Paper Series 2003-08, University of California at San Diego, San Diego.

———. 2005. "Games and Discrimination: Lessons from 'The Weakest Link.'" *Journal of Human Resources* 40 (4): 918–47.

Bertrand, Marianne, and Sendhil Mullainathan. 2004. "Are Emily and Greg More Employable Than Lakisha and Jamal? A Field Experiment on Labor Market Discrimination." *American Economic Review* 94 (4): 991–1013.

Blank, Rebecca, Marilyn Dabady, and Constance Citro. 2004. *Measuring Racial Discrimination: Panel on Methods for Assessing Discrimination.* Washington, DC: National Academies Press.

Blinder, Alan. 1973. "Wage Discrimination: Reduced Form and Structural Estimates." *Journal of Human Resources* 7 (4): 436–55.

Bravo, David. 2005. *Elaboración, validación y difusión de Índice Nacional de Calidad del Empleo Femenino.* Report prepared for the Secretary of Gender (Ministerio Servicio Nacional de la Mujer). Santiago: Universidad de Chile, Centro de Microdatos.

Bravo, David, Claudia Sanhueza, and Sergio Urzúa. 2009. "Using an Experimental Approach to Identify Labor Market Discrimination Based on Gender and Social Class in a Developing Economy." Unpublished mss., Universidad de Chile, Departamento de Economía, Santiago.

Contreras, Dante, and Gonzalo Plaza. 2004. "Participación femenina en el mercado laboral Chileno ¿Cuánto importan los factores culturales?" Universidad de Chile, Departamento de Economía, Santiago.

Ferreira, Francisco, and Jérémie Gignoux. 2008. "The Measurement of Inequality of Opportunity: Theory and an Application to Latin America." Policy Research Working Paper Series 4659, World Bank, Washington, DC.

Goldin, Claudia, and Cecilia Rouse. 2000. "Orchestrating Impartiality: The Impact of 'Blind' Auditions on Female Musicians." *American Economic Review* 90 (4): 715–41.

Heckman, James. 1998. "Detecting Discrimination." *Journal of Economic Perspectives* 12 (2): 101–16.

Heckman, James, and Peter Siegelman. 1993. "The Urban Institute Audit Studies: Their Methods and Findings." In *Clear and Convincing Evidence: Measure of Discrimination in America,* ed. Michael Fix and Raymond Struyk. Washington, DC: Urban Institute Press.

Levitt, Steven. 2004. "Testing Theories of Discrimination. Evidence from 'The Weakest Link.'" *Journal of Law and Economics* 47 (2): 431–52.

Montenegro, Claudio. 2001. "Wage Distribution in Chile: Does Gender Matter? A Quantile Regression Approach." Policy Research Report on Gender and Development, Working Paper 20, World Bank, Washington, DC.

Montenegro, Claudio, and Ricardo Paredes. 1999. "Gender Wage Gap and Discrimination: A Long-Term View Using Quantile Regression." Unpublished mss., Universidad de Chile, Santiago.

Neal, Derek A., and William R. Johnson. 1996. "The Role of Premarket Factors in Black-White Wage Differences." *Journal of Political Economy* 104 (5): 869–95.

Newmark, David, Roy J. Bank, and Kyle D. Van Nort. 1996. "Sex Discrimination in Restaurant Hiring: An Audit Study." *Quarterly Journal of Economics* 111 (3): 915–41.

Núñez, Javier, and Roberto Gutiérrez. 2004. "Classism, Discrimination, and Meritocracy in the Labor Market: The Case of Chile." Documento de Trabajo 208, Universidad de Chile: Departamento de Economía, Santiago.

Oaxaca, Ronald. 1973. "Male-Female Wage Differentials in Urban Labor Markets." *International Economic Review* 14 (3): 693–709.

Paredes, Ricardo, and Luis Riveros. 1994. "Gender Wage Gaps in Chile: A Long-Term View: 1958–1990." *Estudios de Economía* 21 (número especial).

Riach, Peter, and Judith Rich. 2002. "Field Experiments of Discrimination in the Marketplace." *Economic Journal* 112 (483): 480–518.

———. 2004. "Deceptive Field Experiments of Discrimination: Are They Ethical?" *Kyklos* 57 (3): 457–70.

Urzúa, Sergio. 2008. "Racial Labor Market Gaps: The Role of Abilities and Schooling Choices." *Journal of Human Resources* 43 (4): 919–71.

6

Ability, Schooling Choices, and Gender Labor Market Discrimination: Evidence for Chile

David Bravo, Claudia Sanhueza, and Sergio Urzúa

Significant gender differentials in labor market outcomes (labor income and labor force participation, among others) have been extensively studied and well documented (Altonji and Blank 1999). The structural reasons behind these gaps, however, are not fully understood. This chapter contributes to the literature by studying gender differences in a framework in which schooling decisions and labor market outcomes are endogenously determined. Our framework allows individual heterogeneity, not only from the point of view of observable characteristics, but also from that of unobserved variables. We assume that individuals know this additional source of heterogeneity, and they base their schooling and labor market decisions on it. Unobserved heterogeneity therefore plays a crucial role in our approach.

David Bravo is with the Centro de Microdatos, Departamento de Economía, Universidad de Chile; Claudia Sanhueza is with the Instituto Latinoamericano de Doctrina y Estudios Sociales (ILADES), Universidad Alberto Hurtado; and Sergio Urzúa is with the Department of Economics and the Institute for Policy Research, Northwestern University. This study was undertaken as part of the Latin American and Caribbean Research Network Project "Discrimination and Economic Outcomes."

Ours is a challenging task for several reasons. First, a comprehensive analysis of gender differences in a variety of outcomes is subject to the usual and irremediable data limitations. Second, the natural complexities associated with econometric models of multiple, endogenous, and correlated outcomes usually make these models empirically unappealing. Finally, the fact that we allow individuals' decisions to depend on variables unobserved by the researcher but known to the agent represents an additional challenge of our approach.

We deal with each of these difficulties. First, we use a new data set from Chile that contains detailed information on labor market and schooling outcomes at the individual level. Second, following the analysis of Heckman, Stixrud, and Urzúa (2006), we postulate a simple factor structure model based on economic theory that allows us to deal with multiple endogenous variables. Finally, we interpret this factor as unobserved heterogeneity since the researcher does not need to know the individual's factor level (although it is assumed to be known by the individual). We argue that the factor represents a combination of different skills (cognitive and personality skills).

Chile provides an interesting example of an apparently significant gender gap in different dimensions of the labor market. The evidence for Chile usually comes from the estimation of regression models in which the outcome of interest (usually log monthly income or hourly wage) is regressed on a set of observable characteristics, including gender. The coefficient associated with the gender dummy is commonly interpreted as *discrimination* (for example, Contreras and Puentes 2001; Montenegro 1999; Montenegro and Paredes 1999; Núñez and Gutiérrez 2004; Paredes and Riveros 1994). As we explain in this chapter, our empirical approach shares some of the characteristics of these previous studies (for example, functional forms), but it relaxes many of their assumptions, as it presents a more comprehensive model of the Chilean labor market.[1]

The evidence in table 6.1 provides the initial perspective of the gender differences that motivate this chapter. It presents basic information for a variety of schooling and labor market outcomes obtained from a sample of males and females between the ages of 28 and 40 years.[2] A comparison of the schooling outcomes (panel A in table 6.1) leads us to conclude that, on average, (a) females are slightly more educated than males, (b) females are less likely to repeat a grade in both primary and secondary school, and (c) females perform better in school than males (measured by the average grade in secondary school). However, this educational advantage of women over men seems to have no impact on the labor market. The evidence in panel B illustrates this point, showing that males overwhelmingly dominate females in every dimension of the labor market (monthly earnings, employment, and experience). This chapter seeks to identify the factors determining this phenomenon.

The chapter is organized as follows. The first section describes the data, the second presents evidence on the differences in labor market outcomes

Table 6.1 Means of Schooling and Labor Market Outcomes
by Gender from SPS02

Variable (Dummy = 1 if apply)	Females		Males	
	Mean	Standard deviation	Mean	Standard deviation
A. School information				
Maximum schooling level = primary education	0.11	0.32	0.17	0.38
Maximum schooling level = secondary education	0.51	0.50	0.49	0.50
Maximum schooling level = some tertiary education	0.26	0.44	0.24	0.43
Maximum schooling level = complete tertiary education	0.11	0.31	0.10	0.30
Grade retention in primary school	0.22	0.41	0.30	0.46
Grade retention in secondary school	0.20	0.40	0.24	0.43
Average grade in secondary school[a]	0.16	0.98	–0.17	1.00
B. Labor market variables				
Monthly earnings[b]	215,266	214,323	285,140	360,046
Hours worked per week	43.41	11.74	48.17	9.81
Hourly wage[b]	1,292	1,257	1,636	4,649
Working during last month	0.59	0.49	0.82	0.39
Less than 10 years of experience	0.56	0.50	0.25	0.43
Between 10 and 15 years of experience	0.26	0.44	0.34	0.47
More than 15 years of experience	0.18	0.39	0.41	0.49
Number of observations	1,765		1,801	

Source: Authors' compilation.
Note: The numbers presented in this table correspond to the sample of individuals between 28 and 40 years old at the time of the interview.
a. We normalize the mean of average grades to 0, and the loading to 1.
b. Monthly earnings and hourly wages are in Chilean pesos.

between males and females using a conventional approach, the third introduces our model and discusses its empirical implementation, and a fourth discusses our results. A final section concludes.

Data

This chapter uses information from the Chilean Social Protection Survey 2002 (SPS02). This survey was designed to identify and analyze the most important determinants of social security decisions (participation in the social security system) among Chileans. In order to do this, a representative sample of 17,246 participants in the Chilean pension system was interviewed between June 2002 and January 2003. For each individual in the sample, the survey collected information on household composition (age, gender, and level of schooling of household members as well as their relations with the interviewee), current employment status, sources of income, educational variables (maximum schooling attained, average grades in primary and secondary school, characteristics of the primary and secondary schools attended), family history (mother's and father's education, characteristics of the place of residence where the individual grew up, and number of previous relationships), labor history since age 15 or since 1980, depending on the year in which the individual became 15 years old (periods of employment, unemployment, and inactivity), training programs (information on the three most important training programs since 1980), expectations (job, retirement, and life), savings (instruments and amounts), and a set of variables describing the individual's knowledge of the characteristics and performance of the Chilean pension system.

We use the sample of individuals with ages in the range of 28 through 40 years, representing approximately 21 percent of the original sample (3,566 versus 17,246).[3] We restrict the ages of the sample for several reasons. First, since the information on labor history begins only in 1980 (or since age 15), by using individuals 28–40 years old we ensure that the individuals in our sample report complete labor histories beginning at age 18. Second, since schooling is a critical ingredient of our analysis, by excluding individuals 27 years old and younger, we focus our attention on individuals who most likely had reached their final level of schooling at the time of the interview.[4]

Finally, it is worth noting that the current Chilean schooling system was designed only in the early 1980s. Therefore, since our analysis includes information on the characteristics of the primary and secondary schools in which the individual was enrolled, by restricting the analysis to individuals ages 28–40, we ensure that such information is comparable across the individuals in our sample. Table 6.2 presents the summary statistics of the variables used in this chapter.

The Conventional Gender Gap Analysis

The gender differences in labor market outcomes are usually analyzed in the context of linear models in which the variable of interest is regressed

Table 6.2 Descriptive Statistics from SPS02 by Gender

	Females		Males	
Variable (Dummy = 1 if apply)	Mean	Standard deviation	Mean	Standard deviation
Age	33.76	3.76	33.71	3.79
A. School information				
Maximum schooling level = primary education	0.11	0.32	0.17	0.38
Maximum schooling level = secondary education	0.51	0.50	0.49	0.50
Maximum schooling level = some tertiary education	0.26	0.44	0.24	0.43
Maximum schooling level = complete tertiary education	0.11	0.31	0.10	0.30
A.1. Primary school				
Primary school in urban area	0.91	0.29	0.89	0.31
Repeating a grade in primary school	0.22	0.41	0.30	0.46
Was primary school public?	0.77	0.42	0.81	0.39
Was primary school private-subsidized?	0.16	0.37	0.13	0.33
Was primary school managed by a corporation?	0.00	0.05	0.00	0.04
Was primary school private?	0.07	0.25	0.06	0.23
A.2. Secondary school				
Secondary school in urban area	0.98	0.14	0.99	0.12
Repeating a grade in secondary school	0.20	0.40	0.24	0.43

(continued)

Table 6.2 Descriptive Statistics from SPS02 by Gender *(continued)*

	Females		Males	
Variable (Dummy = 1 if apply)	*Mean*	*Standard deviation*	*Mean*	*Standard deviation*
Was secondary school public?	0.70	0.46	0.70	0.46
Was secondary school private-subsidized?	0.23	0.42	0.22	0.42
Was secondary school managed by a corporation?	0.01	0.08	0.02	0.13
Was secondary school private?	0.07	0.25	0.06	0.24
Average grade in secondary school	0.16	0.98	-0.17	1.00
B. Family background				
Mother's employment – salaried	0.56	0.50	0.55	0.50
Father's employment – salaried	0.99	0.07	0.99	0.09
Total number of children	1.64	1.19	1.47	1.22
Mother's education (years of schooling)	7.51	3.77	7.42	3.69
Father's education (years of schooling)	8.14	4.11	7.91	4.00
Growing up under poverty	0.28	0.45	0.35	0.48
Growing up in a broken home	0.96	0.20	0.96	0.20
C. Labor market variables				
Monthly earnings (Chilean pesos)	215,266	214,323	285,140	360,046
Hours worked per week	43.41	11.74	48.17	9.81

(continued)

Table 6.2 Descriptive Statistics from SPS02 by Gender *(continued)*

Variable (Dummy = 1 if apply)	Females		Males	
	Mean	Standard deviation	Standard deviation	Standard deviation
Hourly wage (Chilean pesos)	1,292	1,257	1,636	4,649
Working during last month	0.59	0.49	0.82	0.39
Total work experience since Jan. 1980 (months)	113.43	66.00	165.02	63.52
Less than 10 years of experience	0.56	0.50	0.25	0.43
Between 10 and 15 years of experience	0.26	0.44	0.34	0.47
More than 15 years of experience	0.18	0.39	0.41	0.49
C.1 Type of job				
Salaried	0.81	0.39	0.20	0.40
Domestic service	0.11	0.32	0.00	0.02
Employer or self-worker	0.08	0.27	0.20	0.40
C.2 Type of occupation				
Administrative and managerial workers	0.03	0.17	0.06	0.24
Professionals	0.13	0.34	0.08	0.27
Technicians and associate professionals	0.14	0.35	0.11	0.32
Clerks	0.26	0.44	0.10	0.30
Service workers and shop and market sales workers	0.22	0.42	0.09	0.29

(continued)

Table 6.2 Descriptive Statistics from SPS02 by Gender *(continued)*

Variable *(Dummy = 1 if apply)*	Females		Males	
	Mean	Standard deviation	Mean	Standard deviation
Skilled agricultural and fishery workers	0.01	0.09	0.06	0.23
Craft and related trades workers	0.04	0.19	0.23	0.42
Plant and machine operators and assemblers	0.04	0.19	0.17	0.37
Elementary occupations	0.13	0.34	0.10	0.31
D. Place of residence				
North (regions I to III)	0.13	0.33	0.11	0.32
Central (regions IV to VII)	0.65	0.48	0.62	0.49
South (regions VIII to XII)	0.23	0.42	0.26	0.44
Santiago (region XIII)	0.43	0.49	0.42	0.49
Number of observations	1,765		1,801	

Source: Authors' compilation.
Note: The numbers presented in this table correspond to the sample of individuals between 28 and 40 years old at the time of the interview.

on the gender dummy variable and a set of additional controls.[5] The coefficient associated with the gender dummy is interpreted as the estimated gender gap. Given its popularity, our first attempt to quantify the gender gap closely follows this idea. Table 6.3 presents the results from the following model of (log) hourly wages ($\ln W$):

$$\ln W = \alpha + \varphi \, Male + \beta X + U, \tag{6.1}$$

where *Male* represents the gender dummy (*Male* = 1 if individual is male and 0 if female), X represents the individual's observable characteristics, and U is the error term in the regression. In this simple model, the (conditional) gender gap is simply φ. Each column in table 6.3 represents a different specification of equation 6.1. In particular, column A presents the results of a model in which we include the characteristics of both place of residence and occupation in the vector of controls X. Column B adds a set of variables controlling for the individual's accumulated experience, and column C adds to the controls in column B a set of variables controlling for schooling levels.[6] The results indicate that males make approximately 23 percent more than females in terms of hourly wages. This gender gap is statistically significant regardless of the column analyzed.

The last model in table 6.3 (column D) includes a correction for the fact that the labor market outcome is reported only for individuals who are working (Heckman 1974, 1981). This is particularly important given the gender differences in employment rates reported in table 6.1 (panel B). Thus, the model in column D is

$$\begin{aligned} \ln W &= \alpha + \varphi \, Male + \beta X + U \text{ if wage is observed } (D = 1) \\ D &= 1[\gamma Z + V > 0], \end{aligned} \tag{6.2}$$

where 1[A] is an indicator function that takes a value of 1 if A is true and 0 otherwise, Z is a vector of observables, and V represents the unobservables. $D = 1[\cdot]$ is the censoring rule for wages. In our empirical model, Z includes variables such as number of children, whether the individual grew up in a poor household, and mother's and father's occupational status. The estimated gender gap after correcting for selection is 29 percent, and it is statistically significant. Thus, after controlling for selection, we find not only a significant but also a larger gender gap in wages (compared with the gap estimated without using the correction). This fact illustrates the importance of paying particular attention to an individual's endogenous decisions (in this case, employment decisions) when analyzing the gender gap. We exploit this point in the following section.

The analysis of the gender gap in wages is interesting and important, but it represents only one dimension of many among which males and females can differ. We first extend our analysis to the case of monthly hours worked. We model (log) hours worked using a linear-in-parameter

Table 6.3 The Gender Gap in Hourly Wages from SPS02

Variables	(A)	(B)	(C)	(D)
Male	0.24	0.23	0.23	0.29
	(0.03)	(0.03)	(0.03)	(0.03)
Schooling[a]				
Secondary education			0.29	0.30
			(0.04)	(0.04)
Some tertiary education			0.49	0.50
			(0.04)	(0.05)
Complete tertiary education			0.90	0.92
			(0.06)	(0.06)
Experience[b]				
Between 10 and 15 years of experience		0.04	0.05	0.14
		(0.03)	(0.03)	(0.03)
More than 10 years of experience		0.04	0.10	0.19
		(0.03)	(0.03)	(0.04)
Residence[c]				
Central	−0.15	−0.15	−0.15	−0.15
	(0.04)	(0.04)	(0.04)	(0.04)
South	−0.04	−0.04	−0.05	−0.004
	(0.04)	(0.04)	(0.04)	(0.04)
Santiago	0.22	0.22	0.21	0.24
	(0.03)	(0.03)	(0.03)	(0.03)
Type of job[d]				
Employer or self-worker	−0.13	−0.13	−0.10	−0.11
	(0.03)	(0.03)	(0.03)	(0.03)
Domestic service	−0.08	−0.08	−0.04	−0.06
	(0.07)	(0.07)	(0.07)	(0.07)
Occupations[e]				
Professionals	0.09	0.10	−0.18	−0.17
	(0.07)	(0.07)	(0.07)	(0.07)
Technicians and associate professionals	−0.33	−0.33	−0.27	−0.25
	(0.07)	(0.07)	(0.07)	(0.07)
Clerks	−0.71	−0.72	−0.56	−0.53
	(0.07)	(0.07)	(0.06)	(0.06)
Service workers and shop and market sales workers	−1.08	−1.08	−0.84	−0.83
	(0.07)	(0.07)	(0.07)	(0.07)

(continued)

Table 6.3 The Gender Gap in Hourly Wages from SPS02 *(continued)*

Variables	(A)	(B)	(C)	(D)
Skilled agricultural and fishery workers	−1.35 (0.08)	−1.36 (0.08)	−0.96 (0.08)	−0.93 (0.09)
Craft and related trades workers	−1.05 (0.06)	−1.05 (0.06)	−0.77 (0.06)	−0.74 (0.06)
Plant and machine operators and assemblers	−1.11 (0.07)	−1.11 (0.07)	−0.85 (0.07)	−0.82 (0.07)
Elementary occupations	−1.28 (0.07)	−1.28 (0.07)	−0.94 (0.07)	−0.91 (0.07)
Constant	7.63 (0.07)	7.61 (0.07)	7.04 (0.08)	6.75 (0.10)
Correction for selection	No	No	No	Yes

Source: Authors' compilation.

Note: For each model, schooling corresponds to the declared schooling level for each individual in the sample. Specification (D) includes the same controls as (C) but is estimated including a correction for selection. The variables used in the first stage are number of children, mother's occupational situation, father's occupational situation, and whether the individual grew up in a poor household. Standard errors are presented in parentheses.

a. The baseline category is primary education.

b. The baseline category is less than 10 years of experience.

c. The baseline category is north (regions I to III). Central represents regions IV–VII (including the XIII region), south represents regions VIII–XII.

d. The baseline category is public and private employees.

e. The baseline category is administrative and managerial workers.

model similar to equation 6.1 and the same set of controls as the ones used for wages. Table 6.4 presents the estimated gender gap in monthly hours worked. The structure of this table is identical to the structure of table 6.3. The results from columns A, B, and C suggest that males work approximately 11 percent more hours per month than females. This difference is statistically significant and stable across the three specifications. However, the last column in table 6.4 presents (again) a different story. Unlike the results for wages, the correction for selection significantly reduces the gender gap in hours worked. The estimated gap is only 0.04 percent, and it is not statistically significant.

We also extend our analysis to employment status. In this case, we use a probit model instead of a linear regression model. Table 6.5 presents the results for three different specifications. For each specification, we present both estimated coefficients and estimated marginal effects.[7]

Table 6.4 The Gender Gap in Monthly Hours Worked from
SPS02

Variables	(A)	(B)	(C)	(D)
Male	0.12	0.11	0.11	0.004
	(0.02)	(0.02)	(0.02)	(0.02)
Schooling[a]				
Secondary education			−0.01	−0.04
			(0.02)	(0.02)
Some tertiary education			0.02	−0.03
			(0.03)	(0.02)
Complete tertiary education			−0.03	−0.04
			(0.04)	(0.03)
Experience[b]				
Between 10 and 15 years of experience		0.08	0.08	−0.07
		(0.02)	(0.02)	(0.02)
More than 10 years of experience		0.08	0.08	−0.08
		(0.02)	(0.02)	(0.02)
Residence[c]				
Central	−0.002	−0.005	−0.01	0.02
	(0.03)	(0.03)	(0.03)	(0.03)
South	−0.05	−0.05	−0.05	−0.10
	(0.02)	(0.02)	(0.02)	(0.03)
Santiago	0.02	0.02	0.02	−0.03
	(0.02)	(0.02)	(0.02)	(0.02)
Type of job[d]				
Employer or self-worker	−0.20	−0.20	−0.20	−0.05
	(0.02)	(0.02)	(0.02)	(0.02)
Domestic service	−0.11	−0.12	−0.12	0.01
	(0.04)	(0.04)	(0.04)	(0.03)
Occupations[e]				
Professionals	−0.30	−0.28	−0.27	−0.22
	(0.04)	(0.04)	(0.04)	(0.03)
Technicians and associate professionals	−0.24	−0.24	−0.25	−0.17
	(0.04)	(0.04)	(0.04)	(0.03)
Clerks	−0.18	−0.18	−0.19	−0.16
	(0.04)	(0.04)	(0.04)	(0.03)
Service workers and shop and market sales workers	−0.19	−0.19	−0.19	−0.11
	(0.04)	(0.04)	(0.04)	(0.03)

(continued)

Table 6.4 The Gender Gap in Monthly Hours Worked from SPS02
(continued)

Variables	(A)	(B)	(C)	(D)
Skilled agricultural and fishery workers	−0.18 (0.05)	−0.20 (0.05)	−0.20 (0.05)	−0.16 (0.04)
Craft and related trades workers	−0.16 (0.04)	−0.17 (0.04)	−0.18 (0.04)	−0.13 (0.03)
Plant and machine operators and assemblers	−0.12 (0.04)	−0.13 (0.04)	−0.13 (0.04)	−0.06 (0.03)
Elementary occupations	−0.24 (0.04)	−0.25 (0.04)	−0.25 (0.04)	−0.17 (0.03)
Constant	3.95 (0.04)	3.91 (0.04)	3.92 (0.05)	4.21 (0.04)
Correction for selection	No	No	No	Yes

Source: Authors' compilation.
Note: For each model, schooling corresponds to the declared schooling level for each individual in the sample. Specification (D) includes the same controls as (C) but is estimated including a correction for selection. The variables used in the first stage are number of children, mother's occupational situation, father's occupational situation, and whether the individual grew up in a poor household. Standard errors are presented in parentheses.
a. The baseline category is primary education.
b. The baseline category is less than 10 years of experience.
c. The baseline category is north (regions I to III). Central represents regions IV–VII (including the XIII region); south represents regions VIII–XII.
d. The baseline category is public and private employees.
e. The baseline category is administrative and managerial workers.

The results indicate that males are 22 percentage points more likely to report employment (during the month previous to the date of the interview) than females when schooling and experience are excluded as controls. When schooling or schooling and experience are included as controls, the estimated gap is 14 percentage points. The gap is statistically significant regardless of the specification.

In summary, the results show that men dominate women in all labor market outcomes. Additionally, the results are robust across different specifications; only in the case of hours worked and after controlling for selection do we find neither sizable nor statistically significant gender differences.

Up to this point, we have treated the individual's schooling decisions and accumulated experience as exogenous controls. However, these variables can also be subject to gender differences. Tables 6.6 and 6.7 shed light on this point. The implications of separate analyses of schooling choices and accumulated experience for our previous results are left for

Table 6.5 The Gender Gap in Employment from SPS02

Variables	(A)		(B)		(C)	
	Coefficient	Marginal effect	Coefficient	Marginal effect	Coefficient	Marginal effect
Male	0.67	0.22	0.42	0.14	0.41	0.14
	(0.05)	(0.02)	(0.05)	(0.02)	(0.05)	(0.02)
Background[a]						
Number of children	-0.09	-0.03	-0.08	-0.03	-0.04	-0.01
	(0.02)	(0.01)	(0.02)	(0.01)	(0.02)	(0.01)
Age	0.02	0.01	-0.03	-0.01	-0.04	-0.01
	(0.01)	(0.00)	(0.01)	(0.00)	(0.01)	(0.00)
Mother's occupation	-0.05	-0.02	-0.03	-0.01	-0.06	-0.02
	(0.05)	(0.02)	(0.05)	(0.02)	(0.05)	(0.02)
Father's occupation	-0.27	-0.08	-0.21	-0.07	-0.13	-0.04
	(0.29)	(0.08)	(0.30)	(0.09)	(0.31)	(0.09)
Growing up in poverty	-0.24	-0.08	-0.27	-0.09	-0.14	-0.05
	(0.05)	(0.02)	(0.05)	(0.02)	(0.05)	(0.02)
Schooling[b]						
Secondary education					0.26	0.09
					(0.07)	(0.02)
Some tertiary education					0.59	0.17
					(0.08)	(0.02)

(continued)

Table 6.5 The Gender Gap in Employment from SPS02 *(continued)*

	(A)		(B)		(C)	
Variables	Coefficient	Marginal effect	Coefficient	Marginal effect	Coefficient	Marginal effect
Complete tertiary education					1.22 (0.12)	0.27 (0.01)
Experience[c]						
Between 10 and 15 years of experience			0.66 (0.06)	0.20 (0.02)	0.73 (0.06)	0.21 (0.02)
More than 10 years of experience			0.88 (0.07)	0.26 (0.02)	1.04 (0.08)	0.29 (0.02)
Residence[d]						
Central	-0.08 (0.08)	-0.03 (0.03)	-0.09 (0.08)	-0.03 (0.03)	-0.06 (0.08)	-0.02 (0.03)
South	0.22 (0.08)	0.07 (0.03)	0.24 (0.08)	0.08 (0.03)	0.24 (0.08)	0.08 (0.03)
Santiago	0.24 (0.06)	0.08 (0.02)	0.24 (0.06)	0.08 (0.02)	0.18 (0.06)	0.06 (0.02)
Constant	0.03 (0.37)		1.25 (0.40)		0.91 (0.42)	

Source: Authors' compilation.

Note: Standard errors are presented in parentheses.

a. Mother's and Father's Education are dummy variables that take a value of one if the respective parent worked as a salaried worker and zero otherwise.

b. The baseline category is primary education.

c. The baseline category is less than 10 years of experience.

d. The baseline category is north (I to III regions). Central represents regions IV–VII (including region XIII); south represents regions VIII–XII.

Table 6.6 The Gender Gap in Accumulated Experience from SPS02

| Variables[b] | Less than 10 years[a] | | Between 10 and 15 years[a] | | More than 15 years[a] |
	Coefficient	Marginal effect	Coefficient	Marginal effect	Marginal effect
Male	1.11	−0.40	1.92	0.11	0.29
	(0.07)	(0.02)	(0.09)	(0.02)	(0.02)
Secondary	0.26	−0.04	−0.08	0.09	−0.04
education	(0.11)	(0.03)	(0.12)	(0.03)	(0.02)
Some college	0.08	0.04	−0.61	0.08	−0.13
	(0.13)	(0.04)	(0.14)	(0.03)	(0.02)
College graduate	−0.07	0.11	−1.16	0.07	−0.18
	(0.16)	(0.04)	(0.19)	(0.04)	(0.02)
Mother's years	−0.01	0.002	0.00	−0.002	−0.0003
of schooling	(0.01)	(0.003)	(0.01)	(0.003)	(0.003)
Father's years	−0.02	0.01	−0.04	−0.003	−0.01
of schooling	(0.01)	(0.003)	(0.01)	(0.003)	(0.003)
Growing up in	−0.05	0.003	0.06	−0.02	0.02
poverty	(0.08)	(0.02)	(0.09)	(0.02)	(0.02)
Growing up in	−0.15	0.01	0.16	−0.06	0.05
broken home	(0.17)	(0.05)	(0.21)	(0.04)	(0.03)
Age	0.11	−0.07	0.42	−0.01	0.08
	(0.01)	(0.00)	(0.01)	(0.00)	(0.00)
Constant	−4.10		−15.07		
	(0.40)		(0.55)		

Source: Authors' compilation.

Note: Standard errors are presented in parentheses.

a. The experience levels correspond to the accumulated experience declared during the interview.

b. The schooling level corresponds to the schooling level declared in the sample. Postsecondary education includes technical education (complete and incomplete).

the next section, where they are discussed in the context of a more general framework than the one described here.[8]

We model accumulated experience using a discrete choice approach. Specifically, we assume that the observed level of experience is the result of a decision-making process involving three alternatives: less than 10 years of experience, between 10 and 15 years of experience, and more than 15 years of experience. This decision is assumed to depend on the schooling level of the individual as well as his or her family background (mother's and father's education, broken home, age, and growing up in poverty). Given this setup,

Table 6.7 The Gender Gap in Schooling Decisions from SPS02

Variables	Primary school Marginal effect	Secondary school Coefficient	Secondary school Marginal effect	Some postsecondary education Coefficient	Some postsecondary education Marginal effect	College graduate Coefficient	College graduate Marginal effect
Male	0.04 (0.01)	-0.30 (0.08)	-0.02 (0.02)	-0.33 (0.09)	-0.02 (0.02)	-0.30 (0.10)	-0.004 (0.01)
Mother's years of schooling	-0.02 (0.00)	0.08 (0.02)	-0.01 (0.00)	0.15 (0.02)	0.02 (0.00)	0.17 (0.02)	0.01 (0.002)
Father's years of schooling	-0.01 (0.00)	0.05 (0.01)	-0.02 (0.00)	0.13 (0.01)	0.02 (0.00)	0.16 (0.02)	0.01 (0.002)
Growing up in poverty	0.11 (0.01)	-0.59 (0.08)	0.00 (0.02)	-0.84 (0.09)	-0.08 (0.02)	-0.84 (0.11)	-0.03 (0.01)
Growing up in broken home	-0.09 (0.03)	0.43 (0.17)	0.00 (0.04)	0.83 (0.21)	0.11 (0.03)	0.34 (0.23)	-0.01 (0.03)
Age	0.004 (0.001)	-0.03 (0.01)	-0.002 (0.002)	-0.04 (0.01)	-0.004 (0.002)	-0.01 (0.01)	0.003 (0.001)
Constant		1.07 (0.40)		-0.68 (0.45)		-2.35 (0.52)	

Source: Authors' compilation.
Note: Standard errors are presented in parentheses. The schooling level corresponds to the schooling level declared in the sample. Postsecondary education includes technical education (complete and incomplete).

we compute the gender gap in accumulated experience by estimating a multinomial probit model. Table 6.6 presents the estimated coefficients and marginal effects. The estimates associated with the gender dummy are all significant and suggest that males are considerably more likely to report more experience than females. Specifically, males are 40 percentage points less likely to report less than 10 years of experience and 29 percentage points more likely to report more than 15 years of experience than females.

Table 6.7 sheds light on the existence of a gender gap in schooling decisions. It presents the coefficients and marginal effects obtained from a multinomial model of schooling choice. The model is estimated using the maximum schooling levels reported by individuals in the sample. The schooling levels considered are primary school, secondary school, some postsecondary education, and complete tertiary education (college graduates). The results show that (if anything) females are more likely than males to reach higher levels of schooling.

The advantage of females over males in schooling achievement and attainment (initially suggested in table 6.1) is confirmed in table 6.8. This table presents the estimated gender gap for three variables measuring schooling performance: probability of grade retention during primary school, probability of grade retention during secondary school, and average grades during secondary school. For each variable females consistently outperform males. Males are 7 and 4 percentage points more likely to repeat a grade during primary and secondary school, respectively, and males, on average, have significantly lower grades during high school than females (0.31 points of test's standard deviation).

Therefore, the evidence presented in tables 6.7 and 6.8 leads us to conclude that females should be better prepared than males to enter the labor market. This also implies that, by not including gender differences in schooling variables, our previous results might underestimate the actual unexplained gender gap (or discrimination). We analyze this possibility by introducing a more general model in which schooling decisions, schooling achievement, employment decisions, accumulated experience, hours worked, and hourly wages are modeled jointly.

A Model of Schooling and Labor Market Outcomes under Unobserved Heterogeneity

The model in this section follows the analysis in Heckman, Stixrud, and Urzúa (2006) and Urzúa (2008).[9] These papers estimate economic models with multiple sources of unobserved heterogeneity (unobserved cognitive and noncognitive skills). Conditioned on observables, these unobserved factors account for all of the dependence across choices in the model. The results from these studies confirm that unobserved abilities play a crucial role in explaining a variety of labor market and behavioral outcomes.

Table 6.8 The Gender Gap in Schooling Achievement from SPS02

Variables	Grade retention during primary school		Grade retention during secondary school		Average score during secondary school[a]
	Coefficient	Marginal effect	Coefficient	Marginal effect	Coefficient
Male	0.22 (0.05)	0.07 (0.01)	0.12 (0.05)	0.04 (0.02)	−0.31 (0.04)
Mother's education[b]					
Secondary education	−0.06 (0.06)	−0.02 (0.02)	0.02 (0.06)	0.01 (0.02)	0.05 (0.04)
Some tertiary education	0.14 (0.19)	0.04 (0.06)	−0.06 (0.20)	−0.02 (0.06)	0.11 (0.13)
Complete tertiary education	−0.29 (0.22)	−0.08 (0.06)	−0.13 (0.20)	−0.04 (0.05)	0.35 (0.13)
Father's education[b]					
Secondary education	−0.17 (0.06)	−0.05 (0.02)	−0.05 (0.06)	−0.01 (0.02)	0.14 (0.04)
Some tertiary education	−0.51 (0.16)	−0.13 (0.03)	−0.29 (0.16)	−0.08 (0.04)	0.23 (0.10)
Complete tertiary education	−0.41 (0.16)	−0.11 (0.04)	−0.11 (0.15)	−0.03 (0.04)	0.21 (0.10)

(continued)

Table 6.8 The Gender Gap in Schooling Achievement from SPS02 *(continued)*

Variables	Grade retention during primary school		Grade retention during secondary school		Average score during secondary school[a]
	Coefficient	Marginal effect	Coefficient	Marginal effect	Coefficient
Background					
Growing up in poverty	0.25 (0.05)	0.08 (0.02)	-0.04 (0.06)	-0.01 (0.02)	-0.16 (0.04)
Growing up in broken home	-0.38 (0.11)	-0.13 (0.04)	0.04 (0.13)	0.01 (0.04)	0.10 (0.09)
School characteristics[c]					
Urban primary school	-0.20 (0.08)	-0.07 (0.03)			0.02 (0.08)
Urban secondary school			0.40 (0.24)	0.10 (0.05)	0.22 (0.16)
Private-subsized primary school	-0.10 (0.07)	-0.03 (0.02)			0.07 (0.06)
Corporation – primary school	-0.45 (0.59)	-0.12 (0.12)			0.22 (0.35)
Private primary school	-0.27 (0.12)	-0.08 (0.03)			0.09 (0.09)

(continued)

Table 6.8 The Gender Gap in Schooling Achievement from SPS02 *(continued)*

Variables	Grade retention during primary school		Grade retention during secondary school		Average score during secondary school[a]
	Coefficient	Marginal effect	Coefficient	Marginal effect	Coefficient
Private-subsized secondary school			-0.21 (0.06)	-0.06 (0.02)	0.13 (0.05)
Corporation – secondary school			-0.42 (0.26)	-0.10 (0.05)	0.15 (0.17)
Constant	-0.18		-1.15 0.41	-0.10	-0.33 0.24
Private secondary school	(0.13)		(0.27)		(0.17)

Source: Authors' compilation.
Note: Standard errors are presented in parentheses.
a. The average score is standardized to have mean 0 and variance 1 in the population.
b. The baseline category is primary education.
c. In the case of the dummies controlling for the type of school management the baseline category is public school.

In this chapter we postulate the existence of a single underlying source of unobserved heterogeneity. This is mainly due to data limitations. Specifically, even though the SPS02 contains rich information on variables not previously available, it does not contain enough variables to allow the identification of multiple sources of unobserved heterogeneity.[10] Consequently, we interpret our single source of unobserved heterogeneity as the combination of unobserved cognitive and noncognitive abilities.[11]

Let θ denote the unobserved heterogeneity or latent ability. This ability is unobserved from the point of view of the econometrician, but each individual knows his or her ability level. We assume that this latent ability determines the individual's schooling and labor market outcomes and that there are no intrinsic differences between males and females regarding θ, so that we can work with an overall distribution of θ.[12]

The Model for Schooling

Each agent chooses the level of schooling, among $\bar{S}$ possibilities, such that she maximizes her (net) utility. Let I_s represent the net benefit associated with each schooling level s ($s = \{1, \dots, \bar{S}\}$) and assume the following linear-in-the-parameters model for I_s:

$$I_s = \varphi_s \, Male + \beta_s X_s + \alpha_s \theta + e_s \quad \text{for } s = 1, \dots, \bar{S} \qquad (6.3)$$

where φ_s represents the gender gap associated with schooling level s, X_s is a vector of observed variables determining schooling, β_s is the associated vector of parameters, α_s is the factor loading associated with latent ability, and e_s represents an idiosyncratic component assumed to be independent of θ and X_s. The individual components $\{e_s\}_{s=1}^{\bar{S}}$ are mutually independent. All of the dependence across schooling choices comes through the observable, X_s, and the latent ability θ.

The agent chooses the level of schooling with the highest benefit. Formally,

$$s^* = \underset{s \in \{1, \dots, \bar{S}\}}{\operatorname{argmax}} \{I_s\} \qquad (6.4)$$

where s^* denotes the individual's chosen schooling level. Conditional on X_s (with $s = 1, \dots, \bar{S}$) and θ, equations 6.3 and 6.4 can be interpreted as a standard discrete choice model.

The Model for Accumulated Experience

The model also treats accumulated experience as an endogenous outcome. Specifically, after solving for the optimal schooling level s, the agent is assumed to select her experience level $a(s)$ among $\bar{A}$ different alternatives. Following our schooling model, we assume a linear-in-the-parameters specification for the benefits associated with the experience level a given schooling level s $(I_{a(s)})$:

$$I_{a(s)} = \varphi_{a(s)} \, Male + \beta_{a(s)} X_a + \alpha_{a(s)} \theta + e_{a(s)}$$
$$\text{for } a(s) = 1, \ldots, \overline{A} \text{ and } s = 1, \ldots, \overline{S}, \tag{6.5}$$

where $\varphi_{a(s)}$ is the gender gap, X_a is the vector of observed variables, $\beta_{a(s)}$ is the associated vector of parameters, $\alpha_{a(s)}$ is the factor loading, and $e_{a(s)}$ represents an idiosyncratic component assumed to be independent of θ and X_a. The individual components $\{e_{a(s)}\}_{a=1}^{\overline{A}}$ for any s are mutually independent. Finally, the observed experience level $A^*(s^*)$, where s^* represents the schooling level observed in the data, is obtained as follows:

$$A^*(s^*) = \underset{a(s^*) \in \{1, \ldots, \overline{A}\}}{\mathrm{argmax}} \{I_{a(s)}\}. \tag{6.6}$$

The Model for Hourly Wages and Monthly Hours Worked

For hourly wages and monthly hours worked, we consider schooling-experience specific models. Consider first the model for wages. Denote by s and $a(s)$ the levels of schooling and experience attained by the individual. Wages $(Y_{a(s)})$ are modeled using a linear specification:

$$\ln Y_{a(s)} = \varphi_{Y,a(s)} \, Male + \beta_{Y,a(s)} X_Y + \alpha_{Y,a(s)} \theta + e_{Y,a(s)}$$
$$\text{for } s = 1, \ldots, \overline{S} \text{ and } a(s) = 1, \ldots, \overline{A}, \tag{6.7}$$

where $\varphi_{Y,a(s)}$ is the gender gap, X_Y is a vector of observed controls, $\beta_{Y,a(s)}$ is the vector of coefficients, $\alpha_{Y,a(s)}$ is the coefficient associated with latent ability, and $e_{Y,a(s)}$ represents an idiosyncratic error term such that $e_{Y,a(s)} \perp (\theta, X_Y)$ for any $a(s)(= 1, \ldots, \overline{A})$ and $s(= 1, \ldots, \overline{S})$. This error term is unknown from the point of both the econometrician and the agent.

A parallel strategy is used to model hours worked. Let $H_{a(s)}$ denote the monthly hours worked given schooling level s and experience level $a(s)$. Thus we assume the following:

$$\ln H_{a(s)} = \varphi_{H,a(s)} \, Male + \beta_{H,a(s)} X_H + \alpha_{H,a(s)} \theta + e_{H,a(s)}$$
$$\text{for } s = 1, \ldots, \overline{S} \text{ and } a(s) = 1, \ldots, \overline{A}, \tag{6.8}$$

where $\varphi_{H,a(s)}$ is the gender gap, X_H is a vector of observed controls, $\beta_{H,a(s)}$ is the vector of coefficients associated with X_H, $\alpha_{H,a(s)}$ is the parameter associated with latent ability, and $e_{H,a(s)}$ represents an idiosyncratic error term such that $e_{H,a(s)} \perp (\theta, X_H)$ for any $a(s)(= 1, \ldots, \overline{A})$ and $s(= 1, \ldots, \overline{S})$. As before, the agent and econometrician do not know the error term $e_{H,a(s)}$.

The Model for Employment

Let $I_{E,a(s)}$ denote the net benefit associated with employment (versus the alternatives of unemployment or out of the labor force) given schooling level s and accumulated experience $a(s)$. As in the previous cases, we assume a linear-in-the-parameters specification for $I_{E,a(s)}$:

$$I_{E,a(s)} = \varphi_{E,a(s)}\, Male + \beta_{E,a(s)} X_E + \alpha_{E,a(s)}\theta + e_{E,a(s)}$$
$$\text{for } s = 1, \ldots, \overline{S} \text{ and } a(s) = 1, \ldots, \overline{A}, \tag{6.9}$$

where $\varphi_{E,a(s)}$, $\beta_{E,a(s)}$, X_E, $\alpha_{E,a(s)}$, and $e_{E,a(s)}$ are defined as before. Finally, the error term is such that $e_{E,a(s)} \perp (\theta, X_E)$ for any $a(s) (= 1, \ldots, \overline{A})$ and $s (= 1, \ldots, \overline{S})$.

We use equation 6.9 to model the employment decisions observed in the data. Specifically, if we let $D_{E,a(s)}$ denote a binary variable such that it is equal to 1 if the individual is employed and 0 otherwise, we estimate a binary model assuming that $D_{E,a(s)} = 1[I_{E,a(s)} > 0]$, where $1[\cdot]$ is (again) the indicator function.

Schooling Performance: The Measurement System

The identification of the model can be established using the arguments developed in Carneiro, Hansen, and Heckman (2003) and Hansen, Heckman, and Mullen (2004). The identification strategy assumes the existence of a set of measurements (variables not affected by the endogenous labor market outcomes and schooling choices).

Let T_i ($i = 1, \ldots, n$) denote the ith measure. We distinguish the unobserved ability from the observed ability measure T_i. This is important because T_i is likely to depend on the characteristics of the school as well as on the family background of the individual at the time of the test. Thus if X_T denotes these characteristics, we have the following:

$$T_i = \varphi_{T_i} Male + \beta_{T_i} X_T + \alpha_{T_i}\theta + e_{T_i} \quad \text{for } i = 1, \ldots, n, \tag{6.10}$$

where $e_{T_i} \perp (\theta, X_T)$ and $e_{T_i} \perp e_{T_j}$ for any $i, j \in \{1, \ldots, n\}$ such that $i \neq j$.

Since there are no intrinsic units for latent ability, we need to normalize one of the loadings in the system to unity to set the scale of latent ability. Therefore, for some T_i ($i = 1, \ldots, n$), we set $\alpha_{T_i} = 1$.

Our assumptions imply that, conditional on observables (variables contained in X), the dependence across all measurements, choices, and outcomes comes through the unobserved heterogeneity (θ).

Implementing the Model

In summary, our empirical model with unobserved heterogeneity has the following ingredients: the schooling decision model; the linear models for hourly wages and monthly hours worked, by schooling level s and experience level $a(s)$; the models for employment, by schooling level s and experience level $a(s)$; the model for accumulated experience, by schooling level; and finally, the system of measurements or school achievement. Unobserved heterogeneity θ appears as a determinant of each of these components. In this chapter, we assume that θ is distributed according to a two-component mixture of normals. Formally,

$$\theta \sim pN\left(\mu_1, \sum\nolimits_1^2\right) + (1-p)N\left(\mu_2, \sum\nolimits_2^2\right) \tag{6.11}$$

With this assumption we allow a flexible functional form for the distribution of unobserved heterogeneity.

We estimate the schooling choice model and the experience models using multinomial choice models. Thus we assume that the idiosyncratic shocks in the equations describing the net utilities are normally distributed. The four final schooling levels considered in our analysis are primary school, secondary school (or high school), some postsecondary education, and complete tertiary education (or a college degree). For accumulated experience, we use the following categories: less than 10 years of experience, between 10 and 15 years of experience, and more than 15 years of experience.

In estimating the model, we use the schooling and experience level reported at the time of the interview.[13] For the models of wages and hours worked, we use the information for the month previous to the interview. The same applies in the case of employment status. This is consistent with what we use to estimate the gender gap.

The measurement system uses the following variables: average grade during secondary education, grade retention during primary education (dummy variable), and grade retention during secondary education (dummy variable). We normalize the mean of the factor to 0, and we normalize the loading to be equal to 1 in the equation for the average grade during secondary education.[14]

Table 6.9, panels A and B, display the variables used in the empirical implementation of the model as well as the normalization ensuring the identification of the model. The model is estimated using Markov chain Monte Carlo methods. See Heckman, Stixrud, and Urzúa (2006) and Hansen, Heckman, and Mullen (2004) for a formal exposition of our identification and estimation strategies.[15]

Table 6.9A Variables in the Empirical Implementation of the Model Outcome Equations

Variables	Hourly wage[a]	Monthly hours worked[a]	Employment[a]	Accumulated experience[b]	Educational choice model[c]
Gender dummy	Yes	Yes	Yes	Yes	Yes
Region of residence	Yes	Yes	Yes		
Growing up in broken home					Yes
Mother's education				Yes	Yes
Father's education				Yes	Yes
Growing up in poverty				Yes	Yes
Age			Yes	Yes	Yes
Type of occupation	Yes	Yes			
Type of job	Yes	Yes			
Unobserved ability	Yes	Yes	Yes	Yes	Yes

Source: Authors' compilation.

Note: a. Hourly wages, monthly hours worked, and employment models are estimated for four different schooling categories (primary, secondary, some tertiary, and complete tertiary) and three different levels of accumulated experience (less than 10 years, between 10 and 15 years, and more than 15 years). In each case, the labor market outcome refers to the previous month individual's outcome.

b. Accumulated experience is modeled with a multinomial choice model. The categories considered are less than 10 years, between 10 and 15 years, and more than 15 years. The level of accumulated experience is the total work experience reported at the time of the interview.

c. The educational choice model is estimated considering four different categories: primary, secondary, some tertiary, and complete tertiary.

Table 6.9B Variables in the Empirical Implementation of the
Model Auxiliary Measures

Variables	Average grade in secondary education	Grade retention in primary school	Grade retention in secondary school
Primary school in an urban area (dummy)	Yes	Yes	
Secondary school in an urban area (dummy)	Yes		Yes
Growing up in broken home	Yes	Yes	Yes
Mother's education	Yes	Yes	Yes
Father's education	Yes	Yes	Yes
Growing up in poverty	Yes	Yes	Yes
Primary school system (public, private, etc.)	Yes	Yes	
Secondary school system (public, private, etc.)	Yes		Yes
Unobserved ability	Yes	Yes	1.0

Source: Authors' compilation.

Main Results

Table 6.10 presents the gender gap in hourly wages obtained from the model with unobserved heterogeneity. The estimated gaps are, in general, sizable and statistically significant. We do not observe clear patterns either by schooling or by experience levels, although we consistently estimate the largest gender gap among college graduates (regardless of the level of experience considered). In this group we estimate that males make between 36 and 38 percent more than women. These differences are larger than those presented above. But table 6.10 also presents a range for the gender gap in wages, which goes from –6 percent (nonsignificant) for high school dropouts reporting less than 10 years of experience to 38 percent for college graduates reporting between 10 and 15 years of experience. In only two cases do we estimate a gender gap below 15 percent. Therefore, our evidence indicates the existence of wage differentials that cannot be explained by observed or unobserved characteristics.

Table 6.10 Model with Essential Heterogeneity Gender Gap in Hourly Wages, by Schooling Level and Accumulated Experience[a] from SPS02

Variables	High school dropouts			High school graduates			Some postsecondary education			College graduates		
	Less than 10 years	Between 10 and 15 years	More than 15 years	Less than 10 years	Between 10 and 15 years	More than 15 years	Less than 10 years	Between 10 and 15 years	More than 15 years	Less than 10 years	Between 10 and 15 years	More than 15 years
Male	-0.06 (0.29)	0.30 (0.18)	0.07 (0.14)	0.35 (0.09)	0.15 (0.06)	0.19 (0.05)	0.23 (0.08)	0.35 (0.08)	0.15 (0.10)	0.38 (0.08)	0.38 (0.15)	0.36 (0.20)
Employer or self-worker[b]	-0.41 (0.37)	-0.34 (0.15)	-0.30 (0.10)	0.19 (0.11)	-0.19 (0.08)	-0.23 (0.06)	0.22 (0.12)	0.06 (0.14)	-0.12 (0.14)	0.00 (0.15)	-0.10 (0.20)	0.41 (0.39)
Domestic service[b]	-0.52 (0.37)	0.18 (0.24)	-0.27 (0.20)	-0.11 (0.16)	-0.13 (0.17)	0.16 (0.17)		0.08 (0.28)	-1.44 (0.61)	-0.11 (0.50)		
Professionals[c]				-1.04 (0.63)		-0.52 (0.48)	0.26 (0.22)	0.42 (0.36)	-0.11 (0.29)	-0.21 (0.14)	-0.18 (0.24)	-0.18 (0.30)
Technicians and associate professionals				-0.96 (0.28)	-0.36 (0.20)	-0.40 (0.15)	0.03 (0.18)	0.26 (0.25)	-0.41 (0.23)	-0.11 (0.18)	-0.46 (0.30)	-0.03 (0.35)
Clerks			-0.83	-1.22	-0.48	-0.43	-0.38	-0.11	-0.53	-0.55	-0.79	-0.56
Service workers and shop and market sales workers		-0.57	-0.48	-1.66	-0.61	-0.84	-0.64	-0.46	-0.59	-0.84		

(continued)

Table 6.10 Model with Essential Heterogeneity Gender Gap in Hourly Wages, by Schooling Level and Accumulated Experience[a] from SPS02 (continued)

Variables	High school dropouts			High school graduates			Some postsecondary education			College graduates		
	Less than 10 years	Between 10 and 15 years	More than 15 years	Less than 10 years	Between 10 and 15 years	More than 15 years	Less than 10 years	Between 10 and 15 years	More than 15 years	Less than 10 years	Between 10 and 15 years	More than 15 years
Skilled agricultural and fishery workers	0.39	−0.55	−0.78	−1.75	−0.83	−0.92	−0.44	0.47	−0.81			
Craft and related trades workers	0.25	−0.38	−0.57	−1.44	−0.68	−1.67	−0.57	−0.27	−0.63			1.22
	(0.34)	(0.38)	(0.60)	(0.25)	(0.18)	(0.13)	(0.19)	(0.26)	(0.24)	(0.19)	(0.39)	(0.47)
			(0.28)	(0.26)	(0.17)	(0.12)	(0.22)	(0.26)	(0.25)			(0.85)
Plant and machine operators and assemblers	0.69	−0.36	−0.57	−0.52	−0.72	−0.81	−0.80	−0.52	−1.11		0.59	−1.37
	(0.56)	(0.48)	(0.32)	(0.25)	(0.18)	(0.13)	(0.20)	(0.26)	(0.24)		(0.52)	
		(0.40)	(0.30)	(0.26)	(0.17)	(0.12)	(0.27)	(0.27)	(0.32)		(0.69)	
Elementary occupations	0.35	−0.67	−0.63	−1.66	−0.80	−0.88	−0.91	−0.55	−1.18	−0.97	−1.75	
	(0.57)	(0.40)	(0.29)	(0.37)	(0.24)	(0.16)	(0.63)	(0.46)	(0.38)	(0.38)	(0.50)	
	(0.32)	(0.38)	(0.28)	(0.26)	(0.20)	(0.13)	(0.28)	(0.30)	(0.28)			
Central	0.48	−0.11	−0.13	−0.29	−0.21	−0.15	−0.05	−0.19	0.11	−0.13	0.38	−0.58
	(0.51)	(0.22)	(0.13)	(0.12)	(0.09)	(0.07)	(0.15)	(0.15)	(0.23)	(0.17)	(0.28)	(0.38)

(continued)

Table 6.10 Model with Essential Heterogeneity Gender Gap in Hourly Wages, by Schooling Level and Accumulated Experience[a] from SPS02 (continued)

Variables	High school dropouts			High school graduates			Some postsecondary education			College graduates		
	Less than 10 years	Between 10 and 15 years	More than 15 years	Less than 10 years	Between 10 and 15 years	More than 15 years	Less than 10 years	Between 10 and 15 years	More than 15 years	Less than 10 years	Between 10 and 15 years	More than 15 years
South	0.41 (0.43)	-0.13 (0.21)	-0.03 (0.14)	-0.24 (0.11)	-0.07 (0.09)	0.03 (0.08)	-0.10 (0.13)	-0.13 (0.14)	0.11 (0.23)	0.03 (0.15)	0.42 (0.27)	-0.12 (0.34)
Santiago	-0.25 (0.35)	0.36 (0.16)	0.19 (0.11)	0.22 (0.10)	0.25 (0.07)	0.27 (0.06)	0.08 (0.11)	0.20 (0.10)	0.12 (0.13)	0.35 (0.11)	-0.05 (0.19)	0.39 (0.26)
Intercept	5.56 (0.47)	7.04 (0.51)	7.04 (0.34)	8.10 (0.27)	7.36 (0.19)	7.37 (0.13)	7.28 (0.21)	7.12 (0.30)	7.52 (0.30)	8.07 (0.25)	7.98 (0.43)	8.80 (0.55)
Unobserved heterogeneity	-0.20 (0.13)	0.71 (0.43)	-0.03 (0.07)	0.17 (0.15)	0.13 (0.11)	-0.19 (0.09)	-0.32 (0.15)	-0.30 (0.17)	-0.004 (0.20)	-0.39 (0.22)	-0.50 (0.39)	-0.89 (0.51)

Source: Authors' compilation.

Note: Standard errors are presented in parentheses.

a. The accumulated experience corresponds to the retrospective information reported by the individual at the time of the interview. The schooling level corresponds to the schooling level declared in the sample. Postsecondary education includes technical education (complete and incomplete).

b. For the characteristics of the type of job (employer or self-worker and domestic service), the baseline category is public and private employees.

c. For the set of variables controlling for occupation characteristics (from professionals to elementary occupations in this table) the baseline category is administrative and managerial workers.

As in the case of wages, the results obtained for hours worked show a range of values for the gender gap. These are presented in table 6.11. The point estimates range between –6 percent (high school dropouts with less than 10 years of experience) and 18 percent (high school dropouts with between 10 and 15 years of experience). In this case, however, less than half of the estimates are statistically significant. For example, among high school and college graduates, we do not find significant gender differences. This is consistent with the evidence presented in the section on conventional gender gap analysis, although the numbers in table 6.11 show a broader picture of the gender gap in hours worked.

Table 6.12 presents the results for employment, with two main findings. First, in general we observe a reduction in the estimated gap when we move from low to high levels of experience (the only exception is for high school graduates). Second, the results suggest that schooling also helps to reduce the estimated gaps (there are only two exceptions in table 6.12). In fact, among college graduates, the estimated coefficients are –0.12 and –0.23 for experience levels between 10 and 15 years and more than 15 years, respectively, so the gap favors females in this case. As in the case of hours worked, only a few estimates are statistically significant, and, when significant, they are usually associated with low levels of schooling and experience.[16]

Table 6.13 presents the results obtained for the four multinomial choice models used to study accumulated experience. The evidence in table 6.13 shows how the gender gap diminishes with schooling. Specifically, the significant gender differences estimated for high school dropouts and high school graduates are 100 percent larger than those estimated among individuals with some college. We do not find significant gender differences among college graduates.

Our analysis of the gender gap in variables associated with the labor market leads us to conclude that (a) there are differences between males and females that cannot be explained with observable or unobservable characteristics and that, in general, (b) these differences are larger among individuals reporting low levels of schooling and almost vanish among individuals with more education.[17]

The model also allows us to analyze gender differences in schooling attainment and schooling achievement. It is worth recalling that females outperform males in these two dimensions (tables 6.7 and 6.8). Tables 6.14 and 6.15 repeat the analysis incorporating unobserved heterogeneity (latent ability).

Table 6.14 presents the gender gap in schooling decisions. The results show (again) that females are more likely than males to reach higher schooling levels. Compared with the results in table 6.7, the effects are now larger. Something similar is observed in the case of grade retention during primary school, grade retention during secondary school, and average grades during high school. The results are shown in table 6.15. The evidence in this table suggests that females outperform males, the differences are statistically significant, and they are larger than the ones

Table 6.11 Model with Essential Heterogeneity Gender Gap in Hours Worked, by Schooling Level and Accumulated Experience[a] from SPS02

Variables	High school dropouts			High school graduates			Some postsecondary education			College graduates		
	Less than 10 years	Between 10 and 15 years	More than 15 years	Less than 10 years	Between 10 and 15 years	More than 15 years	Less than 10 years	Between 10 and 15 years	More than 15 years	Less than 10 years	Between 10 and 15 years	More than 15 years
Male	-0.06 (0.15)	0.18 (0.13)	0.14 (0.08)	0.08 (0.07)	0.10 (0.03)	0.07 (0.03)	0.17 (0.05)	0.12 (0.04)	0.10 (0.05)	0.02 (0.06)	0.00 (0.08)	0.08 (0.10)
Employer or self-worker[b]	-0.01 (0.18)	-0.12 (0.11)	-0.17 (0.06)	-0.53 (0.09)	-0.06 (0.04)	-0.16 (0.03)	-0.24 (0.08)	-0.31 (0.07)	-0.22 (0.07)	-0.09 (0.11)	-0.02 (0.10)	-0.07 (0.20)
Domestic service[b]	0.18 (0.19)	-0.09 (0.18)	0.08 (0.11)	-0.25 (0.14)	0.00 (0.08)	-0.18 (0.09)		0.07 (0.14)	-0.75 (0.30)	-0.09 (0.36)		
Professionals[c]				-0.96 (0.55)		-0.08 (0.26)	-0.34 (0.15)	-0.45 (0.18)	-0.33 (0.15)	-0.20 (0.10)	-0.29 (0.13)	-0.15 (0.15)
Technicians and associate professionals				-0.34 (0.24)	-0.05 (0.10)	-0.21 (0.08)	-0.42 (0.12)	-0.38 (0.12)	-0.22 (0.11)	-0.19 (0.13)	-0.19 (0.15)	-0.31 (0.17)
Clerks	(0.17)	(0.28)	0.31 (0.18) (0.34)	-0.21 (0.22) (0.22)	-0.11 (0.08) (0.09)	-0.25 (0.06) (0.07)	-0.27 (0.15) (0.13)	-0.34 (0.13) (0.13)	-0.22 (0.12) (0.12)	-0.02 (0.14) (0.19)	-0.15 (0.19) (0.24)	-0.02 (0.43) (0.24)

(continued)

Table 6.11 Model with Essential Heterogeneity Gender Gap in Hours Worked, by Schooling Level and Accumulated Experience[a] from SPS02 (continued)

Variables	High school dropouts			High school graduates			Some postsecondary education			College graduates		
	Less than 10 years	Between 10 and 15 years	More than 15 years	Less than 10 years	Between 10 and 15 years	More than 15 years	Less than 10 years	Between 10 and 15 years	More than 15 years	Less than 10 years	Between 10 and 15 years	More than 15 years
Service workers and shop and market sales workers	(0.28)	0.36 (0.30) (0.36)	-0.27 (0.20) (0.20)	-0.11 (0.23) (0.21)	-0.11 (0.09) (0.09)	-0.23 (0.06) (0.07)	-0.38 (0.18) (0.13)	-0.31 (0.13) (0.13)	-0.28 (0.16) (0.12)	-0.02 (0.28)	0.00 (0.36) (0.27)	(0.29)
Skilled agricultural and fishery workers	0.01 (0.16) (0.29)	-0.10 (0.28) (0.29)	-0.09 (0.18) (0.19)	-0.31 (0.22) (0.30)	-0.06 (0.10) (0.12)	-0.22 (0.07) (0.09)	0.11 (0.18) (0.41)	-0.29 (0.15) (0.23)	-0.09 (0.14) (0.18)		(0.26)	
Craft and related trades workers	-0.11	0.07	-0.06	-0.23	-0.05	-0.23	-0.27	-0.33	-0.09			0.38
Plant and machine operators and assemblers	0.06	0.03	-0.08	-0.09	-0.02	-0.16	-0.06	-0.25	-0.43		-0.06	0.02
Elementary occupations	-0.16	0.01	-0.09	-0.28	-0.09	-0.27	-0.68	-0.64	-0.05		0.52	

(continued)

Table 6.11 Model with Essential Heterogeneity Gender Gap in Hours Worked, by Schooling Level and Accumulated Experience[a] from SPS02 (continued)

Variables	High school dropouts			High school graduates			Some postsecondary education			College graduates		
	Less than 10 years	Between 10 and 15 years	More than 15 years	Less than 10 years	Between 10 and 15 years	More than 15 years	Less than 10 years	Between 10 and 15 years	More than 15 years	Less than 10 years	Between 10 and 15 years	More than 15 years
Central	0.05 (0.25)	-0.07 (0.16)	0.05 (0.08)	-0.04 (0.10)	-0.02 (0.05)	-0.02 (0.04)	0.13 (0.09)	-0.05 (0.07)	-0.12 (0.12)	-0.07 (0.12)	-0.26 (0.14)	-0.20 (0.20)
South	-0.19 (0.22)	-0.01 (0.16)	-0.15 (0.08)	0.00 (0.09)	0.00 (0.04)	-0.04 (0.04)	0.07 (0.09)	-0.04 (0.07)	-0.07 (0.12)	-0.19 (0.11)	-0.22 (0.14)	-0.31 (0.17)
Santiago	-0.09 (0.17)	-0.02 (0.12)	-0.02 (0.06)	0.07 (0.09)	0.05 (0.04)	0.01 (0.03)	-0.03 (0.07)	0.03 (0.05)	0.09 (0.07)	0.02 (0.08)	0.02 (0.10)	0.03 (0.14)
Intercept	4.35 (0.27)	3.54 (0.37)	4.01 (0.22)	3.91 (0.22)	3.85 (0.09)	4.05 (0.07)	3.92 (0.14)	4.17 (0.14)	4.06 (0.15)	3.90 (0.17)	4.04 (0.21)	4.05 (0.27)
Unobserved heterogeneity	0.40 (0.13)	-0.39 (0.26)	0.23 (0.06)	-0.15 (0.12)	0.01 (0.05)	0.03 (0.05)	0.18 (0.10)	0.06 (0.08)	0.08 (0.10)	0.08 (0.13)	0.17 (0.17)	-0.04 (0.22)

Source: Authors' compilation.

Note: Standard errors are presented in parentheses.

a. The accumulated experience corresponds to the retrospective information reported by the individual at the time of the interview. The schooling level corresponds to the schooling level declared in the sample. Postsecondary education includes technical education (complete and incomplete).

b. For the characteristics of the type of job (employer or self-worker and domestic service), the baseline category is public and private employees.

c. For the set of variables controlling for occupation characteristics (from professionals to elementary occupations in this table) the baseline category is legislators, senior officials, and managers.

Table 6.12 Model with Essential Heterogeneity Gender Gap in Employment Status, by Schooling Level and Accumulated Experience from SPS02

Variables	High school dropouts[a]			High school graduates			Some postsecondary education			College graduates[b]	
	Less than 10 years	Between 10 and 15 years	More than 15 years	Less than 10 years	Between 10 and 15 years	More than 15 years	Less than 10 years	Between 10 and 15 years	More than 15 years	Less than 10 years	Between 10 and 15 years
Male	1.40 (0.54)	0.35 (0.35)	-0.10 (0.35)	0.98 (0.14)	0.30 (0.12)	0.34 (0.13)	0.80 (0.14)	0.36 (0.20)	0.18 (0.24)	-0.12 (0.25)	-0.23 (0.47)
Central				-0.17 (0.17)	-0.09 (0.21)	0.00 (0.22)	0.03 (0.23)	0.42 (0.32)	0.42 (0.48)	-0.39 (0.61)	
South				0.16 (0.17)	0.05 (0.20)	-0.06 (0.22)	0.29 (0.23)	1.17 (0.37)	1.45 (0.62)	-0.36 (0.59)	
Santiago				0.17 (0.14)	0.27 (0.16)	0.10 (0.16)	-0.06 (0.18)	0.20 (0.26)	0.10 (0.33)	-0.19 (0.33)	
Number of children	0.09 (0.10)	0.04 (0.13)	0.11 (0.10)	-0.11 (0.05)	-0.07 (0.05)	-0.07 (0.05)	-0.04 (0.07)	-0.03 (0.09)	0.01 (0.10)	0.14 (0.13)	0.17 (0.21)
Intercept	-2.20 (1.17)	-0.26 (0.54)	0.13 (0.61)	-0.08 (0.17)	0.62 (0.20)	0.79 (0.23)	0.06 (0.21)	0.40 (0.29)	0.38 (0.44)	1.13 (0.72)	3.16 (2.09)
Unobserved heterogeneity	-1.65 (1.35)	-1.63 (1.27)	-1.64 (1.62)	0.37 (0.22)	0.21 (0.27)	0.10 (0.25)	0.07 (0.29)	0.07 (0.44)	0.22 (0.54)	0.59 (0.70)	-1.69 (1.81)

Source: Authors' compilation.

Note: Standard errors are presented in parentheses. The accumulated experience corresponds to the retrospective information reported by the individual at the time of the interview. The schooling level corresponds to the schooling level declared in the sample. Postsecondary education includes technical education (complete and incomplete).

a. Among high school dropouts, the characteristics of the place of residence perfectly predict the labor status, so those variables are excluded in these cases.

b. For the group of individuals reporting more than 15 years of experience and a college degree, the gender dummy perfectly predicts the labor status: the 29 women in these category reported to be working (34 out of 37 males report to be working). Since the gender coefficient is the main interest of this table we do not include this model here.

Table 6.13 Model with Essential Heterogeneity Gender Gap in Accumulated Experience, by Schooling Level from SPS02

Variables	High school dropouts		High school graduates		Some postsecondary		College graduates	
	Between 10 and 15 years	More than 15 years	Between 10 and 15 years	More than 15 years	Between 10 and 15 years	More than 15 years	Between 10 and 15 years	More than 15 years
Male	1.47 (0.23)	2.95 (0.24)	1.48 (0.12)	2.50 (0.15)	0.75 (0.14)	1.02 (0.21)	0.14 (0.28)	0.41 (0.42)
Mother's years of schooling	0.04 (0.05)	-0.02 (0.05)	0.03 (0.02)	0.03 (0.02)	-0.01 (0.02)	0.05 (0.04)	-0.04 (0.06)	-0.11 (0.09)
Father's years of schooling	-0.04 (0.05)	0.00 (0.04)	0.00 (0.02)	-0.02 (0.02)	-0.02 (0.02)	0.00 (0.04)	0.09 (0.06)	-0.06 (0.10)
Growing up in poverty	-0.21 (0.24)	-0.03 (0.22)	-0.16 (0.12)	-0.14 (0.14)	0.02 (0.19)	0.25 (0.26)	-0.30 (0.42)	0.79 (0.69)
Age	-0.05 (0.03)	0.26 (0.03)	0.11 (0.02)	0.46 (0.03)	0.20 (0.03)	0.61 (0.06)	0.39 (0.06)	0.78 (0.11)
Intercept	1.37 (1.29)	-10.45 (1.21)	-4.22 (0.64)	-17.06 (0.97)	-6.98 (1.00)	-22.97 (2.73)	-16.69 (3.54)	-25.84 (4.42)
Unobserved heterogeneity	1.19 (0.74)	-0.20 (0.17)	1.23 (0.28)	1.57 (0.36)	0.53 (0.45)	2.09 (0.96)	2.95 (1.55)	-1.71 (3.10)

Source: Authors' compilation.

Note: Standard errors are presented in parentheses. The accumulated experience corresponds to the retrospective information reported by the individual at the time of the interview. The table presents the results for three multinomial choice models (each for each schooling level). The baseline category is less than 10 years of accumulated experience.

Table 6.14 Model with Essential Heterogeneity Gender Gap in Schooling Decisions from SPS02

Variables	Secondary school	Some postsecondary	College graduates
Male	−0.47	−0.55	−0.61
	(0.11)	(0.13)	(0.30)
Mother's years of schooling	0.13	0.23	0.41
	(0.02)	(0.03)	(0.06)
Father's years of schooling	0.09	0.21	0.44
	(0.02)	(0.02)	(0.07)
Growing up in poverty	−0.03	−0.03	0.08
	(0.01)	(0.02)	(0.04)
Growing up in broken home	0.53	1.02	0.46
	(0.22)	(0.30)	(0.71)
Age	−0.81	−1.25	−2.20
	(0.11)	(0.15)	(0.46)
Intercept	1.10	−1.66	−12.93
	(0.51)	(0.64)	(2.99)
Unobserved heterogeneity	1.90	3.52	10.90
	(0.38)	(0.48)	(1.96)

Source: Authors' compilation.
Note: Standard errors are presented in parentheses. The schooling level corresponds to the schooling level declared in the sample. Postsecondary education includes technical education (complete and incomplete). The baseline category is primary school.

presented in table 6.8. Specifically, when comparing the estimated gender gap across tables, we obtain 18 percent (0.26 versus 0.22) and 41 percent (0.17 versus 0.12) increments in the gender coefficient associated with grade retention during primary school and with grade retention during secondary school, respectively. In the case of average grade during secondary school, we obtain an increment of 6.4 percent in the gender gap (0.33 versus 0.31).

Can Unobserved Heterogeneity Explain the Gender Gap in the Labor Market?

Our results indicate that, after controlling for unobserved heterogeneity, there are nonsignificant gender differences in a variety of labor market variables among educated individuals (for example, hours worked, accumulated experience, employment), but we still find gender differences

Table 6.15 Model with Essential Heterogeneity Gender Gap in Schooling Achievement from SPS02

Variables[a]	Grade retention in primary school	Grade retention in secondary school	Average score during secondary school[b]
Male	0.26 (0.05)	0.17 (0.06)	-0.33 (0.04)
Mother: secondary education	-0.08 (0.07)	-0.04 (0.07)	0.10 (0.04)
Mother: some tertiary education	0.06 (0.21)	-0.20 (0.22)	0.23 (0.12)
Mother: complete tertiary education	-0.30 (0.25)	-0.18 (0.23)	0.38 (0.12)
Father: secondary education	-0.20 (0.06)	-0.12 (0.07)	0.20 (0.04)
Father: some tertiary education	-0.61 (0.18)	-0.44 (0.18)	0.30 (0.10)
Father: complete tertiary education	-0.40 (0.17)	-0.17 (0.17)	0.24 (0.09)
Growing up in poverty	0.28 (0.06)	0.04 (0.07)	-0.23 (0.04)
Growing up in broken home	-0.09 (0.08)	0.45 (0.26)	0.01 (0.08)
Urban primary school	-0.40 (0.12)		0.13 (0.09)

(continued)

Table 6.15 Model with Essential Heterogeneity Gender Gap in Schooling Achievement from SPS02 (continued)

Variables[a]	Grade retention in primary school	Grade retention in secondary school	Average score during secondary school[b]
Urban secondary school		0.01 (0.16)	0.19 (0.14)
Private-subsized primary school	0.00 (0.08)		-0.01 (0.05)
Corporation – primary school	-0.57 (0.68)		0.26 (0.32)
Private primary school	-0.11 (0.13)		-0.06 (0.08)
Private-subsized secondary school		-0.20 (0.07)	0.12 (0.05)
Corporation – secondary school		-0.47 (0.28)	0.16 (0.15)
Private secondary school		-0.28 (0.14)	0.17 (0.09)
Intercept	-0.36 (0.14)	-1.17 (0.30)	-0.40 (0.16)
Unobserved heterogeneity	-0.98 (0.09)	-1.22 (0.12)	1.00

Source: Authors' compilation.

Note: Standard errors are presented in parentheses.

a. In the case of mother's and father's education the baseline category is primary education. In the case of the dummies controlling for the type of management the baseline category is public school.

b. The average score is standardized to have mean 0 and variance 1 in the population.

among the other schooling groups. These differences can, in principle, be interpreted as "pure" discrimination. However, this interpretation requires several qualifications.

First, our empirical strategy assumes that a one-dimensional model of unobserved heterogeneity is sufficient to capture and control for selection (endogeneity) across different decisions. Nevertheless, previous studies have shown the existence of at least two underlying sources of unobserved heterogeneity when explaining labor market outcomes and social behavior.[18] In this context, our one-dimensional model may capture only some of the unobserved heterogeneity in the data. The consequences of incorporating additional sources of essential heterogeneity for our results are hard to predict. In this context, we cannot discard the possibility that what we interpret as "unexplained gaps" can be in fact explained by, for example, heterogeneity in other unobserved traits (self-esteem or locus of control) or preferences (preferences for leisure).[19]

Second, and following up on the previous point, the coefficients associated with what we identify as unobserved heterogeneity are not always significant in our results. The strongest effect of unobserved heterogeneity is obtained for the schooling variables (tables 6.14 and 6.15) and for accumulated experience (table 6.13). Although the effects are sizable for the other outcomes, they are usually not statistically significant. This suggests that our source of unobserved heterogeneity is more closely related to scholastic ability, which apparently is not significantly valued in the Chilean labor market after schooling and experience levels are taken into account. Nevertheless, there might be other sources of unobserved heterogeneity that are indeed priced in the labor market. This again illustrates the potential benefits of extending the model to multiple dimensions of unobserved heterogeneity.

Another consideration regarding the interpretation of our results is whether they are robust to the assumption of a unique distribution of unobserved heterogeneity in the sample. The consequences of allowing gender-specific distributions on our previous results are (again) hard to predict, but we believe that the complications of such an extension would most likely dominate any potential new insights; this is because the identification of gender-specific distribution has additional complications, and it relies on even stronger assumptions than the one already made.[20] Besides, from an intuitive point of view, we do not find *a priori* deep reasons to believe that there are gender differences in the distribution of unobserved heterogeneity. As a result, we leave the estimation of gender-specific distribution for future research.

Conclusions

In this chapter, we present a comprehensive analysis of the gender gap in a variety of labor market outcomes for Chile. The analysis is carried out using two different approaches. The first approach follows the literature by estimating linear and nonlinear models of a variety of variables on different observable controls and the gender dummy. This approach does not pay attention to potential selection problems (endogeneity). The second approach is more general. It allows for the presence of individuals' unobserved heterogeneity that is assumed to be the cause of the endogeneity problems in the conventional approach.

Our main results are robust across the approaches. They suggest the existence of a gender gap in labor market variables that cannot be explained by observable or unobservable characteristics or by underlying selection mechanisms that generate endogeneity. Nevertheless, the findings from the model with unobserved heterogeneity indicate that the gender gap critically depends on individuals' human capital (schooling level). This is particularly important among college graduates. For this group, gender differences are in general not statistically significant.

The evidence also demonstrates that females outperform males in schooling achievement and schooling performance. This is observed regardless of the approach, but we find the stronger effects in the model with unobserved heterogeneity. The gender differences favoring women represent an argument against the conventional idea that labor market differences can be interpreted as the result of gender differences in human capital.

Overall, the estimates in this chapter could lead us to conclude that women are effectively discriminated against in the labor market, with the largest gender gap observed among the less educated groups. However, we prefer to interpret our results cautiously. We believe that the availability of better data and the estimation of even more general models than the one considered here could indeed explain some of the unexplained estimated gender gap.

Notes

1. Chapter 5 in this volume uses an experimental design for the analysis of gender differences in the labor market.
2. The information comes from the Social Protection Survey 2002 of Chile (SPS02), which is the source of information used in this chapter.
3. Our sample is obtained after considering the following exclusions. We first exclude the military sample (57 individuals) and individuals reporting as occupation "family member without salary" (12 individuals). Then we exclude individuals 27 years old or younger and 41 years old or older. This reduces the sample from 17,177 to 5,439. Finally, individuals with missing values in any of the following variables are excluded: years of education, mother's education, father's education, growing up in poverty, and growing up in a single-parent household. This exclusion reduces the sample to the final 3,566 individuals. The final exclusion is required because, for each individual, we need to have valid values for the controls entered in the schooling decision model presented later in the chapter.

4. A more general analysis of schooling decisions would require a dynamic model for schooling choices. The SPS02 does not allow us to carry out such an analysis.

5. The conventional approach is typically based on the analysis in Oaxaca (1973) and Blinder (1973).

6. Our data contain reported labor market experience, as individuals were asked about their labor market history. Therefore, our results use real, not potential, experience.

7. The marginal effects are computed at the mean values of the variables in the model.

8. This is particularly important if we consider that schooling decisions and accumulated experience are probably endogenous variables in the context of the models presented in tables 6.3, 6.4, and 6.5. The model presented in the next section deals with this endogeneity.

9. Our approach also shares some of the features of the empirical model proposed by Bourguignon, Ferreira, and Lustig (1998) and Ferreira and Paes de Barro (1999). However, we relax some of the assumptions imposed by them, such as no selection based on unobserved components and specific assumptions on the distributions of the error terms.

10. See Carneiro, Hansen, and Heckman (2003) for a detailed discussion of identification arguments in the context of models with unobserved heterogeneity.

11. We expect to extend our model to a multifactor model in which we can precisely distinguish between cognitive and noncognitive abilities.

12. The alternative would have been to estimate gender-specific distributions. We consider this an attractive possibility. However, given the data limitations (sample size) and the large number of parameters in the model, we prefer to follow a simple analysis by considering an overall distribution for θ. Future research should consider the potential differences in unobserved heterogeneity between males and females. The agents in our model not only know their own ability level but also know all of the parameters affecting future outcomes. The agents, however, do not have perfect information, since they do not know the idiosyncratic shocks affecting labor market outcomes.

13. In the case of experience, we use the retrospective information provided by the respondent. The labor history is reported from age 15 or since 1980, depending on the year in which the individual turned 15.

14. The variables included in the measurement system are self-reported. A valid concern in this context is the presence of nonclassical measurement. Our approach deals with this statistical problem, since we explicitly allow the unobserved component in the equations for average grade during secondary education and grade retention during primary and secondary education to be determined by unobserved variables correlated with the other components of the model.

15. The estimation is carried out using a Gibbs sampling algorithm. See Robert and Casella (1999) for details.

16. For the group of individuals reporting more than 15 years of experience and a college degree, the gender dummy perfectly predicts labor status: the 29 women in this category reported a job during the week prior to the interview. These coefficients are the point estimates of the parameters associated with the gender dummy variable; they need to be interpreted cautiously since they do not represent the marginal effects.

17. The only exception to this point, and an important one, comes from the analysis of hourly wages.

18. See Heckman, Stixrud, and Urzúa (2006), and Urzúa (2008).

19. The assumption of a single source of unobserved heterogeneity can be relaxed depending on the availability of more comprehensive information at the

individual level. The need for better and more comprehensive information comes from the identification argument of the models. Recall that the source of unobserved heterogeneity in this chapter is identified using the schooling achievement variable. In order to identify additional sources of heterogeneity, we would need additional variables in the measurement system. The availability of information on personality traits, IQ tests, or time preferences could allow the identification and estimation of more general models of unobserved heterogeneity. See Carneiro, Hansen, and Heckman (2003) for details.

20. Specifically, even though we can ensure the identification of gender-specific variance-covariance matrixes, the identification of gender-specific mean differences in the distribution of unobserved heterogeneity would require the existence of at least one discrimination-free variable. The selection and existence of such variable(s) are arguably nontrivial as well. See Urzúa (2008) for details.

References

Altonji, Joseph, and Rebecca Blank. 1999. "Race and Gender in the Labor Market." In *Handbook of Labor Economics,* vol. 3C, ed. Orley Ashenfelter and David Card, 3143–259. Amsterdam: Elsevier Science, North-Holland.

Blinder, Alan. 1973. "Wage Discrimination: Reduced Form and Structural Estimates." *Journal of Human Resources* 7 (4): 436–55.

Bourguignon, François, Francisco Ferreira, and Nora Lustig. 1998. "The Microeconomics of Income Distribution Dynamics in East Asia and Latin America." World Bank research proposal (April), World Bank, Washington, DC.

Carneiro, Pedro, Karsten Hansen, and James Heckman. 2003. "Estimating Distributions of Treatment Effects with an Application to the Returns to Schooling and Measurement of the Effects of Uncertainty on College Choice." *International Economic Review* 44 (2): 361–422.

Contreras, Dante, and Esteban Puentes. 2001. "Is Gender Wage Discrimination Decreasing in Chile? Thirty Years of 'Robust' Evidence." Universidad de Chile, Departamento de Economía, Santiago.

Ferreira, Francisco, and Ricardo Paes de Barro. 1999. "The Slippery Slope: Explaining the Increase in Extreme Poverty in Urban Brazil, 1976–96." Policy Research Working Paper 2210, World Bank, Washington, DC.

Hansen, Karsten, James Heckman, and Kathleen Mullen. 2004. "The Effect of Schooling and Ability on Achievement Test Scores." *Journal of Econometrics* 121 (1-2): 39–98.

Heckman, James. 1974. "Shadow Prices, Market Wages, and Labor Supply." *Econometrica* 42 (4): 679–94.

———. 1981. "Statistical Models for Discrete Panel Data." In *Structural Analysis of Discrete Data with Econometric Applications,* ed. Charles Manski and Daniel McFadden. Cambridge, MA: MIT Press.

Heckman, James, Jora Stixrud, and Sergio Urzúa. 2006. "The Effects of Cognitive and Noncognitive Abilities on Labor Market Outcomes and Social Behavior." *Journal of Labor Economics* 24 (3): 411–82.

Montenegro, Claudio. 1999. "Wage Distribution in Chile: Does Gender Matter? A Quantile Regression Approach." Unpublished mss., Universidad de Chile, Santiago.

Montenegro, Claudio, and Ricardo Paredes. 1999. "Gender Wage Gap and Discrimination: A Long-Term View Using Quantile Regression." Unpublished mss., Universidad de Chile, Santiago.

Núñez, Javier, and Roberto Gutiérrez. 2004. "Classism, Discrimination, and Meritocracy in the Labor Market: The Case of Chile." Documento de Trabajo 208, Universidad de Chile, Departamento de Economía, Santiago.

Oaxaca, Ronald. 1973. "Male-Female Wage Differentials in Urban Labor Markets." *International Economic Review* 14 (3): 693–709.

Paredes, Ricardo, and Luis Riveros. 1994. "Gender Wage Gaps in Chile: A Long-Term View: 1958–1990." *Estudios de Economía* 21 (número especial).

Robert, Christian, and George Casella. 1999. *Monte Carlo Statistical Methods.* New York: Springer-Verlag.

Urzúa, Sergio. 2008. "Racial Labor Market Gaps: The Role of Abilities and Schooling Choices." *Journal of Human Resources* 43 (4): 919–71.

7

What Emigration Leaves Behind: The Situation of Emigrants and Their Families in Ecuador

*Ximena Soruco, Giorgina Piani,
and Máximo Rossi*

This chapter seeks to identify, analyze, and measure discrimination against international emigrants and their families in southern Ecuador (specifically, the city of Cuenca and the rural canton of San Fernando). Up to now, the literature has focused primarily on analyzing the migrants' situation in the receiving countries (mainly the United States and Spain); less effort has been made to produce scientific knowledge on the effects of the phenomenon in the migrants' home country. Moreover, studies addressing the local effects of international emigration have emphasized its causes, development, and consequences for the national economy; discrimination against emigrants' families who are residing in their home country is largely absent from the academic and public discussion.

Since 1999 the diaspora has constituted Ecuador's second most important source of income, after oil, and yet emigrants and their families are frequently discriminated against. The recently coined term "resident" refers to the sons, daughters, and parents of emigrants. They are often portrayed as "problematic people," likely to be engaged in criminal activities, with a low educational profile, and an unlikely future within the country.

This chapter seeks to open up the discussion on discrimination against emigrants and their families in Ecuador and to devise a social and cultural

Ximena Soruco is with the Fundación Sur (Cuenca, Ecuador), and Giorgina Piani and Máximo Rossi are with the Departamento de Economía, Universidad de la República Oriental del Uruguay.

approach to understanding discrimination. It is organized as follows. The first section presents the context for international migration from Ecuador, the second presents the theoretical framework, and the third describes the methodology. This is followed by sections on the qualitative and quantitative results. A final section concludes.

The Context

The Ecuadorian people have a long history of spatial displacement, brought about by economic need and political crisis. During the nineteenth and twentieth centuries, Ecuador experienced internal migration, both temporary and permanent, such as the migration from Cuenca's valley to Guayaquil (the country's main port and most industrial city) and to Quito, Ecuador's capital city. International migration is a relatively new phenomenon, starting in the 1970s in the south, the region addressed in this chapter. Since then, social networks have been created between Cuenca and the United States as well as between Cuenca and Spain, as Ecuadorian emigration has accelerated. Only in 1999 did emigration become a nationwide phenomenon and a subject of public opinion, increasing 250 percent. Between 2000 and 2005 more than a million people left the country, and an estimated 3 million Ecuadorians are now living and working abroad (Acosta 2005). The main cause of this rise is the financial crisis that culminated in 2000 in the bankruptcy of the banking system and the dollarization of the national economy (Acosta 2005, 3; Ramírez and Ramírez 2005, 70).

As international emigration has skyrocketed, Ecuador's public social investment has grown slowly. In 1991 remittances totaled US$109 million, while social spending reached US$513 million. By 2001 these figures had moved in opposite directions: remittances soared to US$1.4 billion, while social spending grew slightly to US$685 million (Ramírez and Ramírez 2005, 77). In 2001 remittances were more than double the amount of social spending, nearly 10 times the amount of economic aid, and 5 times the International Monetary Fund's credit for that year. According to an Inter-American Development Bank communication, "The most efficient means to combat poverty in Latin America does not come from governments or international cooperation but from emigrants' remittances" (Ramírez and Ramírez 2005, translated by the authors).

Most rural emigrants enter the host country illegally. Those wishing to enter the United States pay a *coyote* between US$10,000 and US$14,000 to organize the illegal entrance. If the individual succeeds in entering the host country, he will work at least two years just to pay back the debt and release the mortgage on the family's land. Once this amount has been paid, the emigrant will begin to save money to send to the family. Thus for at least two years the new head of the household (usually the wife and mother) will have to support the family. The emigrant will not be able to return to Ecuador until his legal status has been regularized.

Theoretical Framework

At times of profound world market integration, postcolonial societies inten-
sify their colonial forms of distinction (mainly race) to avoid becoming
meritocratic, fully modern societies in which individual merit serves as the
basis for social mobility. As Balibar and Wallerstein (1992) point out, race
and gender are central categories in the world division of labor. Discrimination against international emigrants, as in Ecuador, must be contextualized
in the current geopolitical division of labor (Quijano 2000).

This chapter analyzes discrimination as a social and cultural construction that encompasses visible, measurable behaviors (face-to-face
or institutional discrimination) that affect the society as a whole. Areas
of particular importance include social hierarchy, channels of mobility,
collective social imagery, individual and group identities, and long-
term expectations. In practical terms, discrimination encompasses
social investment (for example, education, health, and rural and agricultural development) and incentives for certain types of production
(for example, agroindustrial business instead of small-scale subsistence
production).

We understand discrimination as a "social construction," meaning a
product of human practices. Developed by the school of sociological phe-
nomenology (Berger and Luckmann 2001), this approach privileges "common sense." Perception is the first constitutive moment of reality and of
the social. This common sense becomes materialized or institutionalized
over time, acquiring a structure independent of individual perceptions.
Social constructions are not only subjective perceptions but also objective
social conditions, cultural values, or concrete historical contexts. By this
we mean "social dispositions" that are internalized and therefore conditioned practices, such as discrimination.

This does not mean that social dispositions determine individual behaviors; the social is not a world of fixed and immutable laws, but a space of
interactions between subjects, the specific situation of the action, and the
subjects' context (structures, social representations, history). As Bourdieu
(1999) states, there is a "conditioned freedom."

Social interactions, conducted in a setting of social dispositions and
individual freedom, are also based on power relationships. This point of
view allows us to consider conflict at the level of face-to-face interactions.
According to Foucault (1994, 125–26; authors' translation),

In human relationships, being whatever they might be—verbal
communication, loving, institutional, economic relationships—
power is always present. I mean, any relationship where one tries
to direct somebody else's behavior. . . . These power relationships
are mobile, they can be modified, they are not determined once
and for all.

Thus discrimination is a social interaction that depends on an individual's perceptions. These perceptions are not "transparent" or natural. Instead, they are conditioned by what the individual has learned (internalized structure) about emigrants and how this new category ("resident," illegal) is related to old meanings (indigenous, uneducated, rural). These dispositions condition, but do not determine, the (discriminatory) interaction. Individual freedom and the specificity of the situation (where it takes places, between whom, in which power balance, and for what purpose) materialize the interaction.

These subjective and objective aspects configure the discriminatory interaction. To analyze discrimination as a matter of individual choice, guided by rational actions, denies its social and cultural dimensions or at least reduces it to a homogeneous, universal social scenario.

Liberal economics presupposes that human behavior is guided by rational intentions. By nature, humans are seen as acting according to a rational calculus of means and ends. Human actions are thus defined as the result of rational decisions based on the knowledge and resources available and on selfish or altruistic motivations. As the accumulation of internalized representations in the individual and in the context of the interaction (power relationships, intersubjectivity, social meanings), history is excluded from the analysis, and with it the possibility of understanding social settings that promote or restrain discriminatory behaviors. Thus the liberal economic framework tends to homogenize the social or cultural realm. "Homo economicus," the individual acting on means-ends rationality, is not a natural entity, but rather the product of the specific historical context of modernity and capitalism.

The disciplines of anthropology and history have shown that, in other cultural settings, human beings act according to other rationalities (social prestige, symbolic interchange, the community over the individual). To understand discrimination in Latin America, we need to consider that modernity and capitalism are not completed processes.

We therefore seek to complement the approach taken by mainstream economists. Phenomena such as "statistical discrimination" (defined as a result of an information problem on the basis of appearance), discrimination based only on individuals' preferences (taste), and self-exclusion (self-imposed discrimination), although manifested by individual behaviors, preferences, and rationalities, are socially and culturally conditioned.

Methodology

To address the questions posed in this chapter, we crafted a methodology of qualitative and quantitative design. Specifically, we sought to obtain quantitative and qualitative information to identify, characterize, and measure discrimination against emigrants. We conducted 20 in-depth interviews in San Fernando (a rural area) and collected pertinent news from the most important newspapers, one local and one national. We also conducted two surveys, one in Cuenca and one in San Fernando, to measure perceptions and behaviors toward international emigrants. The annex to this chapter presents details of the methodology. The rest of the chapter describes and analyzes the main results of this research.

Qualitative Results and Analysis

Qualitative methods consist of in-depth interviews and secondary sources of information as well as the analysis of media content. We deal with each in turn.

In-Depth Interviews and Secondary Sources of Information

We conducted 20 in-depth interviews in the rural town of San Fernando. According to the last census, 434 people (305 men and 129 women) had emigrated from San Fernando at the date of the interview, most of them between the ages of 17 and 27 years (INEE 2001). This means that 11 percent of the population of San Fernando left their hometown in search of better conditions in other cities of the country or abroad.

In the last decade, San Fernando's main productive activity has shifted from agriculture to animal husbandry, which requires fewer workers than traditional agriculture and offers daily income to peasants who sell milk to local traders. Emigration, remittances, and new cultural patterns, along with stockbreeding activity, have tended to individualize the peasant community. This shift is reflected in, among other things, the preference for paid employment and commerce over traditional communal activities.

According to a study by Bendicen and Associates (2003), Ecuadorian emigrants working abroad send home about US$1.5 billion monthly, or approximately to US$176 per household. According to our research in San Fernando, 46 percent of those who receive remittances do so on a monthly basis, and another 27 percent receive remittance income every two or three months. When asked about the destination of this money, 61 percent of the respondents said they use it to pay for living expenses, 17 percent use it for some kind of luxury good or activity, 8 percent use it to invest in business, 8 percent use it for savings, 4 percent use it to invest in real estate, and 2 percent use it to pay educational expenses. Interviewees said that the local economy improved significantly following the economic crisis of 2000 and the change in currency from sucres to dollars.

Figure 7.1 Percent of Households That Receive Remittances, by Monthly Income

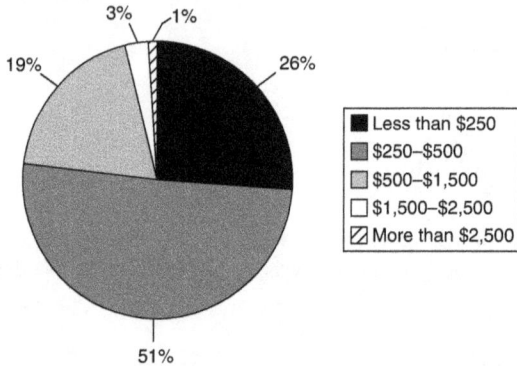

Source: Bendicen and Associates 2003, 13.

Perception of the economic situation. When discussing San Fernando's economic situation, interviewees frequently mentioned the dollarization of the economy in 2000 and international emigration.

After dollarization, real estate prices rose significantly, while prices of cattle and farm products decreased. Some interviewees said that, before dollarization, it was possible to buy a ranch with the money obtained from selling a few head of cattle. They could also sell small animals (chickens, pigs, guinea pigs) to buy daily supplies like food and clothing.

Before dollarization, remittances allowed recipients to increase their purchasing power by exchanging incoming dollars for sucres. Emigrants could quickly pay their debts to local moneylenders (*chulqueros*) as well as buy lands and build new dwellings for their family. Nowadays, the number of families who lose their lands because they are not able to pay the loans to moneylenders is growing rapidly. As one interviewee stated, "When I was single, I had quite a lot of cattle, thanks to my parents' inheritance. After I got married, I also had enough cattle, but my children grew up, and they decided to emigrate; that was when I lost everything I had to the *chulqueros*."[1]

In 1990 San Fernando, formerly a parish, became a canton; since then, the town's infrastructure development has been remarkable. The national government is responsible for much of this improvement, but emigrants' contributions have been critical as well. In fact, it is common practice for emigrants to donate money to build or repair churches and sporting facilities and to pay for community religious celebrations.

At the same time, emigration has produced a new socioeconomic hierarchy. Although almost everyone in San Fernando has at least one relative who is an emigrant, noticeable differences exist between households that directly receive remittances (immediate relatives) and those that do not. Consequently, having an emigrant parent, sibling, or child places a household in a favorable socioeconomic situation relative to others. The amount of time since emigration and legal status in the receiving country are also important variables to be considered.

People who emigrated more than five years ago usually enjoy resident status in their host country or at least are able to pay their travel debts; many have built a house in San Fernando or Cuenca. After these two expenses are covered, the emigrant's family is free to invest in land, cattle, and other economic activities (public transportation, grocery stores, clothing stores, restaurants, moneylending); sometimes they also invest in the emigration of another family member. If the emigrant has legal status in the host country, he or she can also visit the family in Ecuador and use his or her accumulated "cultural capital" to open a business or move the family to the nearest big city (Cuenca).

People who emigrated less than two years ago constitute a second group. Their families are not only in less favorable conditions than families in the first group, but they also are more vulnerable than families with no emigrants. In order to undertake the "migratory adventure," the individual asks the family for support. According to interviewees, once contacts are made, the potential emigrant will need between US$10,000 and US$14,000, an amount that is increasing due to additional border controls and tougher immigration regulations in the United States and Europe. To obtain that sum of money, the families ask moneylenders for loans, mortgaging their land and paying interest of approximately 6.5 percent a month.

Once the emigrant obtains a loan, he or she begins the trip, which if successful, could take up to two months. But many emigrants are caught and then deported; they still need to pay half of the loan to the moneylenders and *coyotes*, leaving the family to pay the debt and interest generated by the unsuccessful adventure.

When the emigrant reaches his or her final destination (sometimes after one or more unsuccessful attempts), he or she will save for one or two years in order to pay the mortgage on the family's lands. Once this step has been completed, residents will start to receive remittance income.

With many households receiving remittances, San Fernando's inhabitants evaluate their local economy in a positive way. Interviewees made statements such as "Everybody has enough money; because relatives send money from abroad. There is almost no poverty here. Everybody has lands, cattle, and a place to sow. We are all more or less well off," or "Many people have become rich because of emigration."

Families who do not receive money from emigrants offered a contrasting point of view: "Here, people believe that because some have emigrated to the United States, we all are wealthy. That is why local traders and merchants ask the highest prices, but we do not have money [and we buy in Cuenca]."

According to our interviews and quantitative data (INEE 1997, 2001; Municipio de San Fernando 2005), San Fernando is far from wealthy. Nonetheless, remittances have served to (a) alleviate poverty by supporting families' expenses for food, housing, health, and education and to (b) deepen the social hierarchy, as only the families of emigrants are able to accumulate capital, buy land, and expand their cattle or farming business.

Investment of remittances. After paying their debts, "residents" of San Fernando generally use their remittances to pay for housing and daily goods, productive investment, the migration of other family members, and education.

The first investment is generally to build a new dwelling. When planning to construct a new house, emigrants usually send a picture of an American or European house they would like to have reproduced. These pictures are then mixed with local architectural elements to give birth to a new style, the product of this blending. Cuenca's elite deem these buildings to be "irrational," arguing that, because no one lives in them, they represent an irrational investment that dulls productive investments. Moreover, they are concerned that the once-idyllic rural landscape (the place of their *haciendas*, or estates, and *huasipungos*, or peasant servants) is taking on urban characteristics (Ordóñez 2005). These so-called ghost dwellings are not only criticized by the elites in Cuenca, but also by the peasants in San Fernando: "Emigrants invest in cars, lands, cattle, and they build enormous and luxurious houses that are always abandoned. They want to show their economic power and compete with the rest to gain prestige."

This new construction serves to keep alive the hope of returning home (the "utopia of return"). Such construction also serves practical purposes; since emigrants usually leave their family behind (wife, husband, children, or parents), building a house for them constitutes a show of support. As one interviewee stated, "The canton of San Fernando and its surrounding area have gotten better compared to some years ago. Before, there were no people or houses, but currently the number of inhabitants has increased and people have good houses."

If a new social stratum is being established, then the conspicuous consumption of perishable and nonperishable goods and investment in luxury items would be rational. Such consumption and investment would reflect an economic strategy to become part of the local dominant class and from there to obtain privileges such as favorable treatment by the municipal government.

At the same time, this new spending should be considered as part of the new cultural values that the emigrants have assimilated in their new setting. Most emigrants have settled in a consumer society, and they seek the same level of consumption for their relatives back home. One can easily see signs of this "transculturation"[2] in San Fernando: for example, groceries with canned food, stores with urban-style clothing and electronic goods, and restaurants. According to one interviewee, "Some emigrants come with money, they also return with a business, a car, for example [a public transportation business]. My son came back, bought cattle, land, and now he has a clothing store downtown."

We turn now to the investment in production. Unfortunately, we were unable to find information about San Fernando's dairy production, number of head of cattle, or any land register that would allow us to compare changes in the last years. The 2005 land property register (*catastro*) is the only known source of information (Municipio de San Fernando 2005). For example, San Fernando's average ranch is considerably smaller (2.89 hectares) than the national (8.39 hectares) or the provincial (Azuay, 6.14 hectares) average. How is it possible to talk about emigrants' economic accumulation with ranches that are smaller than average?

The Andean system of landownership is characterized by the possession of small pieces of land in different ecological areas. In San Fernando, landowners tend to own many small pieces rather than a single large ranch. Table 7.1 illustrates a typical case in which different family members (identified by the common last name and mother's maiden name) have multiple properties.

With the exception of Rosendo's single holding of 1 hectare, the table shows that even when these siblings own more than one piece of land, each piece is approximately 0.46 hectare (4,600 cubic meters), conspicuously below San Fernando's average of 2.89 hectares. Analyzed individually, these siblings appear to be poor because they cannot feed even a

Table 7.1 Typical Case of Multiple Land Property, Chumblín, San Fernando 2005

Name	No. of properties	Size (hectares)
Adolfo	5	2.40
José María	3	2.00
Manuel Adolfo	4	2.00
Mariana	6	1.81
Mercedes	8	3.20
Rosendo	1	1.00
Total	27	12.41

Source: Authors' calculations based on Catastro Rural de San Fernando (2005).

single head of cattle, which requires 1 hectare in the valley. However, knowledge of traditional family arrangements and networks suggests that family members have access to all 12.41 hectares. In addition, in the San Fernando area, it is common practice to own two very different size pieces of land, such as one of 0.5 hectare and another of 35 hectares.

Regardless of the size of landholding, some successful "residents" have become landowners and cattle farming businessmen. These families are starting to compete for privileges with Cuenca's upper class, which still owns lands in San Fernando. According to an interviewee, "[Emigrants invest in] buying lands, houses, cattle, and in improving grain crops. They also can compete with the estates, getting more profits with cattle farming."

Successful "residents" (defined by ranch size) have had a considerable impact on the local economy (in trade in goods, real estate, and construction) and on the social hierarchy. "Residents" and their emigrant family members have imposed new values on the community, including individualism, consumerism, and changes in traditional diet, clothing, and music. These new practices affect the youngest generations most and offer an important role model, which constitutes a third kind of investment in the region.

After the first emigrant family member has become established in the host country, and after he or she has repaid travel debts and built a new dwelling, the next step is often to finance a new emigrant, usually a spouse or child. Unlike the first trip, subsequent expenses are paid by the emigrant rather than a moneylender.

In addition, "residents" who have accumulated a decent sum (more than US$10,000) can also lend money to more distant relatives, perhaps charging them a lower interest rate than a moneylender. Lending to distant relatives, though, is the first step toward becoming a *chulquero* (the Ecuadorian term for moneylender).

The term *chulquero* is a sensitive topic in San Fernando. It has negative connotations of both usury and illegality. In the words of one interviewee, "Here in San Fernando is the reign of a network of corruption among the City Hall, the property registry, the city court, and *chulqueros*. Part of my land, obtained by inheritance, was stolen by a *chulquero*. This *chulquero* is my own brother, and today he is San Fernando's richest man. Everything began when his offspring emigrated and started sending money. This money was invested in high-interest loans to the rest of the people who wanted to emigrate. In San Fernando, there are other well-know *chulqueros* who live in Cuenca, but do their business here."

The third step is to investment in education. There are three elementary schools in San Fernando, two public and one private, and only one high school. Some parents send their teenagers to the high school in the nearby canton of Girón, which they believe offers a better curriculum and allows students to acquire a more urbanized cultural background that will provide them a sense of urban belonging and better prospects. The town of Girón has greater economic activity due to its strategic connection to the coastal region. However, sending children to study in Girón significantly increases the cost of education. In addition to the direct expense of bus transportation, families also experience a significant opportunity cost in students' reduced time and ability to help their families in farm or other work.

There is no university in either San Fernando or Girón. Students who complete high school may also obtain a technical certificate in agronomy or veterinary studies, but pursuing a university degree means moving to Cuenca. Once university students settle in Cuenca, however, they are unlikely to return to San Fernando after obtaining a degree; working and living conditions are generally considered better in Cuenca, Ecuador's third largest city. Under these circumstances, as shown in table 7.2, only 15 percent of San Fernando's population over the age of five years has completed a high school education, while 71 percent of the population has only an elementary school education. Moreover, San Fernando's urban population has, on average, 5.1 years of formal education, while the rural population has, on average, only 4.6 years, less than the 6 years needed to complete elementary school.

Education carries high opportunity costs in peasant families, where children's work is needed in the fields and at home. In the words of one interviewee, "As parents, we must send our children to elementary school,

Table 7.2 Percentage of the Population, Aged Five Years and Older, by Highest Level of Education Attained and Urban/Rural Area

Education level reached	Urban		Rural		Total	
	Number	*Percent*	*Number*	*Percent*	*Number*	*Percent*
Total	1,255	100.00	2,275	100.00	3,530	100.00
None	69	5.50	194	8.53	263	7.45
Adults literacy instruction	8	0.64	4	0.18	12	0.34
Elementary school	761	60.64	1,733	76.18	2,494	70.65
High school	289	23.03	229	10.07	518	14.67
Post high school	6	0.48	1	0.04	7	0.20
Undergraduate	47	3.75	15	0.66	62	1.76
Graduate	0	0.00	0	0.00	0	0.00
Not stated	75	5.98	99	4.35	174	4.93

Source: Authors' calculations based on *VI Censo Nacional*, 2001.

but then they have to help us in the fields." Another person noted, "Education is very important for our children. Unfortunately, money scarcity did not allow us to send our children to high school or maybe to study in another region. That is why in these *recintos* [outlying areas] there are no professionals, and because there is neither work nor land to produce, [many] have decided to emigrate. But our main responsibility is to send our children to elementary school. Later they make their future."

San Fernando additionally suffers from a shortage of jobs for educated persons. This may further explain why parents do not make a greater effort to send children to high school. The following statements are representative: "Many students complete high school, but there are no jobs, and they end up being farmers. How does studying help them then?" and "High school education is for people with money, not for poor ones" and "Going to high school or university takes a long time. I prefer to work."

Nonetheless, there are signs that the educational situation has begun to change, at least for some. San Fernando's first and only private school opened very recently (in 2006), and teachers acknowledge that their students are primarily the children of emigrants. As one noted, "Emigrants' children study here, then they go to the university in Cuenca."

However, emigration can have negative as well as positive effects on education. According to one high school principal in San Fernando, emigration is the most common cause of school dropout: "Many teenagers drop out of high school because they are planning to make the trip to the U.S. or Spain. If they do not leave immediately, they drop out of school because they want to work to save some money for the trip. . . . They also think education will not make any difference when they work abroad."

Thus remittances seem to have a positive impact on elementary school education, but a negative effect on high school and university education. Since the offspring of many emigrants hope to join their parent(s) abroad and accept that they will be working in unskilled positions, they find no apparent utility in investing in middle and higher education.

Perception of the emigration phenomenon and discrimination in San Fernando. As we have seen, the migratory phenomenon embodies opposing situations: emigrants who can accumulate enough capital to become the local *nouveau riche* and deepen social differences, at one extreme, and, at the other, suffering, bankruptcy, and even death for those who have tried to emigrate in recent years. Emigration improves access to elementary education but increases high school dropout rates and reproduces low skill levels.

San Fernando's inhabitants acknowledge this complexity. They believe that poverty has diminished because of emigration and that many people have been able to buy land and cattle, fertilize their fodder farms, and build new houses, all of which is bringing prosperity. They also know that emigration is a big risk because of the increasing difficulty of entering the

United States or Europe. The inhabitants of San Fernando have also seen how neighbors and relatives have lost their lands because of loans from *chulqueros*.

Putting these negative individual consequences aside, none of our interviewees considered emigration to be a negative, except one statement that requires further analysis. According to a taxi driver who works in Cuenca, "Emigration brings regrettable things to emigrants' children. They stay with their uncles or grandparents, but they suffer because they do not have the love of their parents. Unaffectionate grandparents mistreat children, although there are laws against it. Unfortunately, there are not authorities who can punish this situation. Children are psychologically ill-treated and battered." Of the 20 interviews conducted, this is the only individual to make such a strong argument against emigration.

Summary. Our qualitative data have been useful in identifying San Fernando's perceptions of emigration, which suggest that emigration is not a discriminatory category, although it creates differences between emigrant and non-emigrant families in regard to economic income, access to education and health care, and cultural capital (goods, music, food). We now turn to the media analysis, which shows how emigration has become a category of discrimination against rural emigrants and their families in Cuenca.

Analysis of Media Content

During a six-month period from September 2005 to February 2006, we monitored two newspapers: *Mercurio*, the newspaper with the highest readership in Cuenca, and *El Comercio*, the leading national newspaper. Our team identified, coded, and analyzed all news discussing any issue related to international emigration. In total, we collected 424 articles, of which 70 percent appeared in *Mercurio* and the remaining 30 percent appeared in *El Comercio*. All news dealing with emigration was coded using the 11 categories displayed in figure 7.2. We now turn to an analysis of the news in each category.

Coyotes and chulqueros. In this category, we found 45 news items, representing 10.6 percent of the stories on emigration. *Coyotes* are said to receive about US$14,000 per illegal immigrant crossing the U.S. border, and *chulqueros* are the local moneylenders who lend the money to potential emigrants. Stories dealing with these critical figures narrate experiences of people who failed to cross the border and, if fortunate, were sent back home, where they had to face the loss of their properties because they were not able to pay their debts. These stories include various complaints about mistreatment by *coyotes* and *chulqueros*, as well as the dangers of the migratory journey, which frequently include fatalities. We found no

Figure 7.2 News on Emigration by Theme/Issue Typology

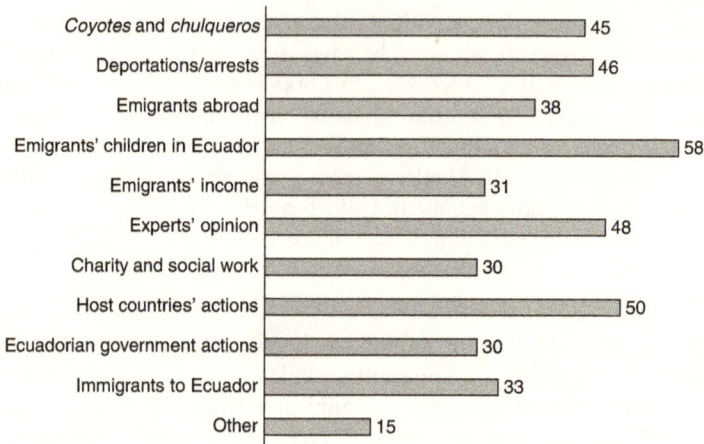

Coyotes and *chulqueros* — 45
Deportations/arrests — 46
Emigrants abroad — 38
Emigrants' children in Ecuador — 58
Emigrants' income — 31
Experts' opinion — 48
Charity and social work — 30
Host countries' actions — 50
Ecuadorian government actions — 30
Immigrants to Ecuador — 33
Other — 15

Source: Authors' calculations based on media content analysis, September 2005–February 2006.

stories of successful border crossings in which emigrants found a job in the recipient country and sent money first to pay their *chulquero* debt and then to help their family.

Arrest and deportation. In this category, we found 46 news items, representing 10.9 percent of the stories on emigration. Detailed descriptions of deportation and arrests complement the stories related to *coyotes* and *chulqueros.* In these accounts, unsuccessful emigrants narrate the violence they suffered when they were captured by immigration authorities, placed under arrest, and deported. These emotionally charged testimonies aim to discourage the Ecuadorian population from even considering emigration as a possible endeavor.

The life of emigrants. In this category, we found 38 news items, representing 9 percent of the stories on emigration. This general category includes stories about the life that awaits emigrants abroad. Here we found news about emigrants' social networks, job markets in host countries, the discrimination that they face in the host countries, and the process of constructing a new identity in the new context, such as articles dealing with religious pilgrimages organized by Ecuadorian emigrants.

Also covered is the cultural transformation that accompanies emigration. With the suggestive title "A Dichotomy of Evolution," one expert's comment reads, "Ecuadorian women [living in Spain] are apparently trapped in a dichotomy of evolution, between a Western society related to an image of liberty and the Ecuadorian culture, associated with tradition. Therefore, they live on a thin line between modernity's liberties and the threat of libertinage" (*Mercurio*, Thursday, October 20, 2005).

Two components of discrimination are evident, gender discrimination and discrimination against emigrants, and they appear to reinforce one another.

The articles dealing with cultural change appear to acknowledge the abandonment of Ecuadorian traditional culture and the embrace of the values of the new culture. Elements of this discourse of "acculturation" are also present in the media's approach to the life of emigrants' children, which is discussed next.

Emigrants' children in Ecuador. In this category, we found 58 news items, representing 13.7 percent of the stories on emigration. This category of analysis involves the most negative consequences of emigration as identified by the media and emigration "experts." Stated in many ways, the articles ask, What will happen to your children if you decide to emigrate?

There are two approaches to this topic. One is to let the experts talk by quoting professionals in the social sciences, such as social work and psychology, and representatives of the Catholic Church, both clergy and laity. The second, sometimes used in combination with the first, is to present the voices of emigrants' children as testimonies. Their voices are heard in various seminars and workshops organized by nongovernmental organizations, the Catholic Church, and local authorities.

In short, articles on the lives of emigrants' children suggest that emigration represents abandonment of children. Emigrants are portrayed as irresponsible parents who abandon their children, causing them psychological damage, low self-esteem, poor educational performance, and social and cultural problems such as gang involvement, drug use, and suicide.

Some journalists refer to emigrants' children as a "social problem," and an emigrant expert who runs a program for youth in Cuenca calls them "marginal": "Marginality does not only refer to poverty: there are many emigrants' children who have money but are isolated. Schools have closed their doors to them because they do not live with their parents; that is marginalization, and that generates low self-esteem" (*Mercurio*, Thursday, September 1, 2005, 6B).

Thus "marginal" is seen as involving "isolation" and "low self-esteem" rather than economic position. In this discourse, emigrants' children are seen as isolated from their parents and not supported by their schools. This statement, though, is contradicted by our preliminary findings that emigrants' families in San Fernando invest in education comparatively more than their counterparts; various private schools in Cuenca and San Fernando specifically target this "new market."

Even when there are reactions against this discrimination and "marginalization" of emigrants' children, those reactions are filtered through the dominant discourse. "I don't think we are a problem, but society has stigmatized us like that" (*Mercurio*, Thursday, November 17, 2005, 6B). "I think they want to have their houses, but they also hurt their families. They [emigrants] think it is all about money, but no money can buy happiness" (*Mercurio*, Thursday, December 8, 2005, 6B). In the words of a child, "Some schoolmates fight against each other, they do not get along well. They are rejected because their parents are poor or rich and because they come from a different social class" (*Mercurio*, Thursday, December 8, 2005, 6B). Thus emigrants' children are discriminated against by their classmates, who say, "Although they have money, they are not the same class as the rest."

According to an article in *Mercurio* (Thursday, November 17, 2005, 6B), "In this testimony we see how they [emigrants' children] assume roles that do not correspond to their ages. He [an emigrant's child] was forced to grow up, he was left on his own very young, and he had to become an adult. His father left when he was 9, and his mother also left when he was 13. He has a hard life." A Catholic priest said, "Emigration is and will be a problem for all of our rural towns and regions . . . Fathers who live far away in different realities, mothers who face new circumstances feel alone and unprotected because their husbands have forgotten about them. Children without their parents' love, who grow up without [moral] values. Now many young people meet to drink, have sex, and use drugs. This is caused by parents who thought emigration was going to resolve their economic problems, but I think their absence is much worse" (*Mercurio*, Thursday, November 24, 2005).

None of these perspectives arose in the in-depth interviews conducted in San Fernando. Marginalization, perversion, and criminal behavior were not among their concerns. They did mention that it is hard for grandparents to take complete responsibility for a child, an opinion that grew out of their own experience of being raised by their grandparents. Emigration is not a new phenomenon in Cuenca's rural areas, but an old survival strategy. In addition, in the countryside, it is a common practice to send children to live with relatives so that they can continue their education after elementary school.

The image of emigrants' children as marginalized appears to be an urban creation, displacing the rural image of emigrants as role models. The popularity of successful emigrants in rural areas (their "reciprocity" in religious celebrations and public works) is inverted in the urban context: "They are no longer the 'best' godfathers a child can have [because of the loans or networks for a migratory endeavor] . . . but loveless, irresponsible, and ambitious parents, who can impact negatively Ecuadorian society as a whole."

This kind of discourse is also evident in well-intentioned social workers and religious people, who have a vertical, racist, and paternalist conception of the phenomenon. An urban elite exists who see their spatial hegemony as being threatened by emigrants and their families. These "residents" can, for the first time, pay for their children to attend the same private schools as the children of the elite and become their neighbors and probably their partners in business. Therefore, members of the elite feel the need to differentiate themselves from this group, creating a new conceptualization of the indigenous peasant: they are still rural, primitive, and irresponsible, and they let their children be marginalized.

Emigrants' income. In this category, we found 31 news items, representing 7.3 percent of the stories on emigration. Another negative stereotype concerns the investments of emigrants. Despite the role of remittances in the alleviation of poverty, many emigration experts and journalists refer to those incomes as "unproductive." According to an article in *Mercurio* (Wednesday, September 21, 2005), "'Migradollars' do not reduce poverty. Those who receive that money consume them all, and what is worse, they end up being dependent on them . . . Migratory incomes are invested in everything except for productive projects. That money is spent as soon as it comes." And in *El Comercio* (Tuesday, November 11, 2005), "Este dinero no tiene que caer en saco roto [This income should not be misspent]."

The media acknowledge the importance of the area's growing real estate sector, but they also refer to these new buildings as "ugly," "inappropriate for the rural context," and "dysfunctional." The following comment refers to a peasant family who has an emigrant son: "They have a house with a dancing hall and garage, but because the road does not get to the house, they have to keep the car in their neighbor's garage. But they buy electronic supplies for the house and the latest technological stuff" (*El Comercio*, Monday, December 19, 2005).

"Residents" are seen not only as irresponsible and careless of their offspring, but also as unproductive, superficial, wasteful, and dysfunctional. Only in some cases does this kind of attribution coexist with data on the contribution of emigrants' income to the national economy. Even then, there is no recognition of emigrants' support for the national economy.

Experts' opinion. In this category, we found 48 news items, representing 11.3 percent of the stories on emigration. Many seminars, conferences, and meetings are held to discuss emigration, in which Ecuadorian and international experts deliberate about its consequences and characteristics. Despite the participation of international researchers and policy makers, these events (usually carried out in Cuenca) tend to portray emigration with the same characteristics discussed in the media. In this sense, the Catholic Church plays a critical role in articulating the national discourse on migration.

Charity and social work. In this category, we found 30 news items, representing 7.1 percent of the stories on emigration. There is a high level of similarity between the opinions of local experts and charitable organization officials, as these groups largely overlap. The Catholic Church and many nongovernmental organizations also conduct social campaigns on behalf of deported emigrants and families cheated by *coyotes* and *chulqueros*.

Host countries and government actions. We found 50 news items on host countries and 30 news items on government actions, representing 11.8 and 7.1 percent of the stories on emigration, respectively. These news items tend to deal with international and national regulations regarding illegal migration, the living situation of migrants in the host countries (primarily Spain and the United States), and public policies that can help the emigrant population. The official voice tends to be bureaucratic and informative, and we found no discriminatory element in these articles.

Immigration in Ecuador. In this category, we found 30 news items, representing 7.8 percent of the stories on emigration. These stories discuss the illegal migration of Peruvians and Colombians to Ecuador. This subject is discussed both in Cuenca and throughout Ecuador, not only in the urban context, but also in rural areas such as San Fernando. The topics covered include illegality, *coyotes*, deportation, and violence. In contrast to the discussion of Ecuadorian emigrants, the media do not devote space to the everyday life of immigrants in Ecuador.

Quantitative Results and Analysis

We conducted two population surveys (one in the city of Cuenca and the other one in the rural area of San Fernando) in June and August 2006 to quantify some of the qualitative findings. This section presents the main results of the surveys. The survey results confirm that migration is an important issue in respondents' everyday lives. "Migration" is listed as one of the most important problems currently facing their city by 21.3 percent of respondents in Cuenca and 21.6 percent of respondents in San Fernando (see table 7.3).

Migration: Some Attitudes

The second set of questions sought to gain insight on the respondent's attitudes and opinions on migration from three perspectives: overall, for migrants themselves, and for their family members who stay in Ecuador.

Tables 7.3 through 7.6 present data on attitudes toward migration in Cuenca and San Fernando. The population of Cuenca appears more critical of migration (53 percent said it is a "bad thing for Cuenca") than the population of San Fernando (40 percent). The same difference is found when respondents were asked about their opinions on migration from the migrant's perspective: 51 percent of the population of Cuenca said that

Table 7.3 What Do You Think Are the Two Main Problems Currently Facing the Population of [Cuenca/San Fernando]?

	Cuenca (%)	San Fernando (%)
Poverty	36.5	50.8
Education	9.2	6.5
Health care/insurance	3.1	9.7
Migration	21.3	21.6
Lack of jobs	16.0	3.2
Delinquency	13.1	2.2
Corruption	0.8	0.5
Don't know/no answer	0.0	5.4
Total	100 (n = 480)	100 (n = 185)

Source: Authors' compilation.

Table 7.4 Overall, Do You Think That International Migration Is . . .

	Cuenca (%)	San Fernando (%)
A good thing for [Cuenca/ San Fernando]	37.5	47.0
A bad thing for [Cuenca/San Fernando]	52.7	40.0
It depends	9.0	11.9
No answer	0.8	1.1
Total	100 (n = 480)	100 (n = 185)

Source: Authors' compilation.

Table 7.5 And for the Migrants Themselves, Do You Think That International Migration Is . . .

	Cuenca (%)	San Fernando (%)
A good thing for migrants	40.2	48.1
A bad thing for migrants	51.0	40.0
It depends	7.1	7.6
No answer	1.7	4.3
Total	100 (n = 480)	100 (n = 185)

Source: Authors' compilation.

Table 7.6 And for Their Immediate Family Members Who Stay
in Ecuador, Do You Think That International Migration Is . . .

	Cuenca (%)	San Fernando (%)
A good thing for (Cuenca/ San Fernando)	14.8	25.4
A bad thing for (Cuenca/San Fernando)	77.9	63.8
It depends	5.6	8.6
No answer	1.7	2.2
Total	100 (n = 480)	100 (n = 185)

Source: Authors' compilation.

migration is negative for the migrants themselves, while 48 percent of the
population of San Fernando said that it is positive. Finally, when asked
their opinion on migration from the point of view of migrants' family
members, respondents in Cuenca and San Fernando said that it is a "bad
thing" for them (78 and 64 percent, respectively).

As shown in table 7.7, 83 percent of respondents in Cuenca and 71
percent of respondents in San Fernando said that a child of an emigrant
will "do worse in school than a child of a non-emigrant."

Migration: Some Facts

The vast majority of the persons interviewed in Cuenca and San Fernando
have at least one family member living and working in a foreign country
(76 percent in Cuenca and 80 percent in San Fernando; see table 7.8).
Almost a quarter of the population in San Fernando has at least one son
outside the country (see table 7.9). San Fernando's migration figures sur-
pass Cuenca's in all categories of family members, except for mothers.

In our sample, 44 percent of respondents in San Fernando and 28 percent
in Cuenca said that they receive remittances from relatives living in a foreign
country (see table 7.10).

Given the importance of remittances, we sought to understand who
receives the money, how often money is received, and how that money is
spent. As shown in table 7.11, most recipients said that they obtain remittances on a monthly basis, while a small percentage said that they receive
remittances less than once a year. Table 7.12 shows how respondents think
that emigrants' families spend the money they receive from abroad, and
table 7.13 shows how these families actually spend their remittances.

Despite the perception that emigrants' families misuse the money
they receive, 20.5 percent of San Fernando's respondents said that these
families spend their remittances buying land. Moreover, as shown in

Table 7.7 Do You Think a Child of an Emigrant Will Have the Same Performance at School as a Child of a Non-Migrant, a Poorer Performance, or a Better Performance?

	Cuenca (%)	San Fernando (%)
Same performance	4.8	6.5
Poorer performance	83.3	71.4
Better performance	1.5	2.2
Depends	8.8	14.6
Don't know/no answer	1.7	5.4
Total	100 (n = 480)	100 (n = 185)

Source: Authors' compilation.

Table 7.8 Is Any Member of Your Family Currently Living and Working in a Foreign Country?

	Cuenca (%)	San Fernando (%)
Yes	76.0	79.5
No	23.5	20.5
No answer	0.4	0.0
Total	100 (n = 480)	100 (n = 185)

Source: Authors' compilation.

Table 7.9 Is Your [Family Member] Currently Living and Working Abroad?

	Cuenca (% Yes)	San Fernando (% Yes)
Father	3.5	3.8
Mother	3.3	0.5
Son	7.5	24.9
Daughter	2.9	8.1
Grandson	1.5	3.2
Granddaughter	0.8	1.1
Sister/brother	28.5	30.8
Brother-in-law/son-in-law	10.4	11.9
Sister-in-law/daughter-in-law	5.0	8.1
Another family member (grandparent/ uncle/aunt/nephew/niece)	36.9	30.8
Total	(n = 480)	(n = 185)

Source: Authors' compilation.

Table 7.10 Do You (or Other Family Members) Receive
Remittances from Relatives Who Live in a Foreign Country?

	Cuenca (%)	San Fernando (%)
Yes	27.7	44.3
No	48.1	35.1
Don't know/no answer	0.2	0.0
Does not apply	24.0	20.5
Total	100 (n = 480)	100 (n = 185)

Source: Authors' compilation.

Table 7.11 How Frequently Do You (or Other Family Members)
Receive Remittances?

	Cuenca (%)	San Fernando (%)
Once a month	13.5	19.5
Every 2 to 3 months	4.6	5.9
Every 4 to 6 months	4.6	9.7
Once a year	4.0	8.6
Less than once a year	1.0	0.5
Don't know/no answer	0.0	0.0
Does not apply	72.3	55.7
Total	100 (n = 480)	100 (n = 185)

Source: Authors' compilation.

Table 7.12 How Do You Think Migrants' Family Members
Spend the Money They Receive from Abroad?

	Cuenca (%)	San Fernando (%)
Open businesses	1.5	0.0
Build or buy a house	45.0	38.9
Buy luxury products	17.9	11.4
Daily consumption products	2.5	1.1
Buy lands	5.8	20.5
Education for their children	2.9	2.2
Savings	1.0	1.1
Don't know/no answer	22.5	24.9
Total	100 (n = 480)	100 (n = 185)

Source: Authors' compilation.

Table 7.13 How Is the Money Spent?

	Cuenca (%)	San Fernando (%)
Regular expenditures (daily goods and clothing)	19.4	34.1
Business investments	0.4	0.5
Savings	0.4	1.6
Building/buying house/properties	0.6	0.0
Education	5.2	3.2
Buying luxury goods	0.4	0.0
Paying debts	1.3	4.9
Does not apply	72.3	55.7
Total	100 (n = 480)	100 (n = 185)

Source: Authors' compilation.

table 7.13, of those that receive remittances, respondents in both Cuenca and San Fernando reported that they spend the money first on living expenses and then on education.

As Bendicen and Associates (2003) indicate, remittances in Ecuador are not primarily a means of improving a family's economic status, but a matter of economic survival. In our survey, a significant percentage of respondents (19 percent in Cuenca and 34 percent in San Fernando) indicated that remittances pay for basic expenditures such as food, rent, and utilities.

In the qualitative study, we learned that rural and urban areas evaluate migration differently. More than a third of the respondents in Cuenca said that there is "a lot" and "some" discrimination against family members of migrants (35 percent), a figure that drops to 15 percent in San Fernando (see table 7.14). More analytical work is needed to understand this difference in perception. Tables 7.15 and 7.16 present figures on perceptions about emigrants and their children.

Using questions from the survey, we estimated three blocks of probit models. First, we evaluated the perception of discrimination against emigrants' relatives. Second, we evaluated the degree of social integration of those relatives. Finally, we used the question about contentment or satisfaction with life to model the impact on happiness of having relatives who have emigrated from the city. Those models were estimated separately, if necessary, for Cuenca and San Fernando.

Four models were estimated within the first block, taking as dependent variables:

1. *Discrimination1*: a binary variable that takes the value of 1 when the respondent perceives that there is much discrimination and the

Table 7.14 How Much Discrimination Is There against Family
Members of People from [Cuenca/San Fernando] Who Go to
Live and Work in Another Country? Would You Say There Is a
Lot of Discrimination, Some, Only a Little, or None at All?

	Cuenca (%)	San Fernando (%)
A lot	19.6	5.9
Some	15.5	9.2
Only a little	30.4	18.9
No discrimination at all	33.5	62.2
Don't know	0.6	3.8
Total	100 (n = 480)	100 (n = 185)

Source: Authors' compilation.

Table 7.15 What Is a Migrant's Child Most Likely to Do as an
Adult?

	Cuenca (%)	San Fernando (%)
Finish university	10.8	12.4
Work as an employee	3.3	11.9
Join a gang	24.2	15.1
Open his/her own business	4.8	6.5
Migrate (leave the country)	50.2	43.2
Don't know/no answer	6.7	10.8
Total	100 (n = 480)	100 (n = 185)

Source: Authors' compilation.

Table 7.16 Agreement with the Following Statements

	Cuenca (%)	San Fernando (%)
"People who leave their children behind to migrate are irresponsible"	54.2	43.2
"Migrants' children are not good students"	60.2	38.9
"Migrants' children are frequently involved in illicit activities"	45.6	28.6
"Migrants' children spend their money on luxury products"	91.4	82.7
"Migrants' children are losing their cultural identity"	89.6	77.8

Source: Authors' compilation.

value of 0 when he or she perceives that there is some discrimination, little discrimination, or no discrimination at all against
migrants' family members.

2. *Discrimination2*: a binary variable that takes the value of 1 when
the respondent thinks of emigration as something positive or beneficial for the city and takes the value of 0 when he or she thinks of
emigration as negative for the city.

3. *Califica*: a binary variable that takes the value of 1 when the
respondent thinks that the sons and daughters of emigrants would
get lower grades than those with non-emigrant parents and a
value of 0 when the respondent thinks that the sons and daughters
of emigrants would get equal or higher grades than those of non-
emigrant parents.

4. *Emigrate*: a binary variable that takes the value of 1 when the
respondent thinks that emigrating is the most probable thing that an
emigrant's son or daughter would do and the value of 0 when the
respondent chooses any other option.

The dependent variables chosen for the social integration block were
the following:

1. *No participation*: a binary variable that takes the value of 1 when
the respondent answers that he or she would never take part in any
form of political demonstration and the value of 0 when the respondent chooses any other provided option.

2. *Social participation*: a binary variable that takes the value of 1 when
the respondent belongs to a political party or labor union; professional, commercial, sport, or cultural association; or any kind of
voluntary organization.

For the last block, the dependent variable was *happy*: a binary variable
that takes the value of 1 when the respondent answers that he or she is
satisfied or very satisfied with his or her life and a value of 0 when the
respondent chooses any other option.

The following independent variables were taken into account: age, sex,
marital status, education, race, having relatives abroad, religion, number
of family members, job characteristics, whether the respondent receives
money from relatives abroad (remittances), household income, and level
of deprivation.

Table 7.17 (panels A and B) shows the models of discrimination in
Cuenca and the marginal effects, Table 7.18 presents the models of social
integration and the marginal effects, and table 7.19 shows the happiness
model and the marginal effects for the same population.

Table 7.17A Models of Discrimination in Cuenca

	Discri1	*Discri2*	*Califica*	*Emigrar*
Male	−0.355**	0.490***	−0.501***	0.182
	(0.157)	(0.138)	(0.163)	(0.135)
Age	−0.009*	−0.007	0.011**	−0.002
	(0.005)	(0.005)	(0.005)	(0.004)
Married	0.318*	0.029	−0.215	0.158
	(0.182)	(0.159)	(0.197)	(0.153)
Divorced	0.418	0.131	−0.487*	0.086
	(0.275)	(0.245)	(0.295)	(0.235)
Secondary education	−0.199	−0.360**	0.115	0.328**
	(0.171)	(0.152)	(0.181)	(0.150)
Tertiary education	−0.464**	−0.306	0.598**	0.325*
	(0.221)	(0.192)	(0.243)	(0.189)
Mestizo	−0.025	0.134	0.322*	0.323**
	(0.168)	(0.154)	(0.165)	(0.151)
Relatives abroad	0.164	0.243	0.025	0.048
	(0.159)	(0.149)	(0.174)	(0.145)
Household size	−0.012	−0.021	−0.043	0.022
	(0.046)	(0.042)	(0.049)	(0.041)
Religious	−0.092	0.072	0.16	−0.075
	(0.220)	(0.187)	(0.239)	(0.188)
Full-time	0.148	−0.286*	0.420**	0.126
	(0.157)	(0.146)	(0.172)	(0.143)
Part-time	−0.036	0.02	0.312	0.181
	(0.203)	(0.172)	(0.215)	(0.174)
Public worker	−0.254	0.117	0.299	−0.16
	(0.268)	(0.220)	(0.329)	(0.221)
Political party	0.144	−0.008	0.713***	−0.164
	(0.180)	(0.165)	(0.241)	(0.167)
Remittances	0.001*	0.001	0	0
	(0.000)	(0.000)	(0.000)	(0.000)
Unmes	−0.422*	−0.221	−0.323	0.15
	(0.248)	(0.208)	(0.239)	(0.208)
Household income	0.000***	0	0	0
	(0.000)	(0.000)	(0.000)	(0.000)
Level of Deprivation	0	−0.174	0.144	−0.277**
	(0.151)	(0.136)	(0.154)	(0.133)

(continued)

Table 7.17A Models of Discrimination in Cuenca *(continued)*

	Discri1	Discri2	Califica	Emigrar
Constant	−0.805 (0.631)	0.292 (0.559)	−0.03 (0.648)	−0.026 (0.548)
Observations	476	476	476	476
Pseudo R-squared	0.06	0.04	0.1	0.05

Source: Authors' compilation.
Note: Robust standard errors in parentheses.
* Significant at 10%.
** Significant at 5%.
*** Significant at 1%.

Table 7.17B Marginal Effects of Discrimination in Cuenca (only significant variables)

	Discri1	Discri2	Califica	Emigrar
Total	0.1823	0.3707	0.8668	0.4970
Male	−0.0895	0.1871	−0.1163	
Age	−0.0023		0.0024	
Married	0.0810			
Divorced			−0.1261	
Secondary education		−0.1334		0.1302
Tertiary education	−0.1113		0.1110	0.1289
Mestizo			0.0766	0.1278
Relatives abroad				
Household size				
Religious				
Full-time		−0.1072	0.0881	
Part-time				
Public worker				
Political party			0.1161	
Remittances	0.0002			
Unmes	−0.0962			
Household income	0.0001			
Level of Deprivation				−0.1106

Source: Authors' compilation.

Table 7.18A Models of Social Integration in Cuenca

	(1) No participation	(2) Social participation
Male	−0.275* (0.141)	0.504*** (0.141)
Age	0.020*** (0.005)	−0.014*** (0.005)
Married	0.187 (0.162)	0.167 (0.162)
Divorced	−0.147 (0.239)	0.432* (0.240)
Secondary education	−0.089 (0.153)	0.299* (0.167)
Tertiary education	−0.125 (0.200)	0.321 (0.203)
Mestizo	0.065 (0.153)	−0.143 (0.164)
Relatives abroad	−0.23 (0.149)	0.340** (0.160)
Household size	0.044 (0.042)	−0.033 (0.045)
Religious	0.058 (0.186)	0.102 (0.201)
Full-time	−0.04 (0.146)	0.478*** (0.158)
Part-time	0.114 (0.178)	0.433** (0.186)
Public worker	−0.252 (0.229)	0.35 (0.224)
Political party	−0.324* (0.176)	
Remittances	0 (0.000)	0 (0.000)
Unmes	−0.034 (0.224)	0.203 (0.219)
Household income	0 (0.000)	0 (0.000)
Level of Deprivation	0.344** (0.134)	−0.323** (0.145)

(continued)

Table 7.18A Models of Social Integration in Cuenca *(continued)*

	(1) No participation	(2) Social participation
Constant	−1.932*** (0.561)	−0.213 (0.573)
Observations	476	476
Pseudo R-squared	0.09	0.12

Source: Authors' compilation.
Note: Robust standard errors in parentheses.
* Significant at 10%.
** Significant at 5%.
*** Significant at 1%.

Table 7.18B Marginal Effects of Social Integration in Cuenca (only significant variables)

	(1) No participation	(2) Social participation
Total	0.3639	0.2763
Male	−0.1013	0.1739
Age	0.0075	−0.0047
Married		
Divorced		0.1559
Secondary education		0.1016
Tertiary education		
Mestizo		
Relatives abroad		0.1071
Household size		
Religious		
Full-time		0.1615
Part-time		0.1548
Public worker		
Political party	−0.1162	
Remittances		
Unmes		
Household income		
Level of Deprivation	0.1292	−0.1080

Source: Authors' compilation.

Table 7.19A Model of Happiness in Cuenca

	Happy
Male	0.061
	(0.144)
Age	−0.008*
	(0.005)
Married	0.086
	(0.168)
Divorced	0.238
	(0.259)
Secondary education	0
	(0.155)
Tertiary education	0.394*
	(0.203)
Mestizo	0.478**
	(0.210)
White	0.766**
	(0.300)
Relatives abroad	−0.375**
	(0.162)
Religious	0.363*
	(0.211)
Household size	0.007
	(0.045)
Full-time	0.207
	(0.150)
Part-time	0.328*
	(0.184)
Public worker	0.276
	(0.289)
Remittances	−0.001
	(0.000)
Unmes	0.115
	(0.211)
Household income	0.000**
	(0.000)
Level of Deprivation	−0.367***
	(0.141)

(continued)

Table 7.19A Model of Happiness in Cuenca *(continued)*

	Happy
Constant	0.935
	(0.589)
Observations	475
Pseudo R-squared	0.12

Source: Authors' compilation.
Note: Robust standard errors in parentheses.
* Significant at 10%.
** Significant at 5%.
*** Significant at 1%.

Table 7.19B Marginal Effects of Happiness in Cuenca (only significant variables)

	Happy
Male	
Age	–0.0028
Married	
Divorced	
Secondary education	
Tertiary education	0.1283
Mestizo	0.1745
White	0.2117
Relatives abroad	–0.1213
Religious	0.1143
Household size	
Full-time	
Part-time	0.1057
Public worker	
Remittances	
Unmes	
Household income	0.0001
Level of Deprivation	–0.1261

Source: Authors' compilation.

Perception of Discrimination in Cuenca

The signs of the significant variables show that women, older citizens, the more educated, and individuals who receive remittances from abroad on a monthly basis said that they perceive lower (higher) discrimination. The level of discrimination perceived is lower for married individuals than for unmarried individuals, and the perception of discrimination lessens as the amount of the remittances received rises as a percentage of household income. The most important marginal effects correspond to women (−), married (+), individuals with university studies (−), and receipt of a monthly remittance (−).

Women and men in Cuenca have different perceptions of the impact of emigration. For men, emigration is beneficial, and the marginal effect is of 19 percentage points. Individuals with high school education and full-time jobs have a negative perception of emigration.

Women and individuals who are divorced disagree with the statement that the children of emigrants do worse in school than other children. Meanwhile, persons who are older, have a university education, and self-identify as being of mixed race, full-time employees, and individuals not affiliated with a political party agree with the statement. The most important marginal effects are sex (−), divorced (−), university (+), and political party (+).

Regarding the perception of emigration as being the most probable activity for an emigrant's son or daughter, the marginal effects are positive and important for individuals with higher levels of education (high school and university) and of mixed race. Not having the goods that the survey took into account has a negative impact.

Women in Cuenca perceive higher levels of discrimination toward emigrants but consider emigration beneficial for the city; they do not consider the school grades of the children of emigrants to be a problem. Respondents with university studies do not find high levels of discrimination, but they do think that the children of emigrants have problems with school grades and that emigrating is their most probable outcome. Among individuals who identify themselves as mestizos, there is a strong perception that children of emigrants have problems with school grades and that they are likely to emigrate. With respect to income, the perception of a high level of discrimination rises with the amount of the remittances received from abroad and with home income, but diminishes among those who receive remittances once a month.

Table 7.18 shows the results of the model and the marginal effects of the models related to social integration in Cuenca: *nopart* and *partsoci*.

Women and persons not currently involved in a political party disagree with the statement, "I would never take part in a political demonstration." Meanwhile, agreeing with the statement rises with age, meaning that older people are more reluctant to take part in this kind of activity, as are persons who report deprivation.

Individuals who take part in community institutions are more likely to be women, divorced, people with a high school education, people with relatives abroad, and individuals with full- or part-time jobs. More deprived and older individuals tend not to participate. Women in Cuenca tend to be more active in community activities and to have a greater awareness of social issues. People who have relatives abroad (10 percentage points marginal effect) and those who are more deprived do not appear to participate or to be interested in community institutions.

Finally, happiness levels rise with having a university education, with being mestizo or white (in comparison with other racial or ethnic identifications), with being religious, with having a part-time job, and with level of family income (see table 7.19). These results coincide in general terms with the literature on these topics. In contrast, having relatives abroad, being deprived, and being older have a negative effect on happiness.

Perception of Discrimination in San Fernando

Respondents in San Fernando do not perceive high levels of discrimination, so the model with *discrimination1* as the dependent variable was not estimated. In this case, *depriva* is the only significant variable with a positive sign, meaning that more-deprived people find higher levels of discrimination.

The results for the variable mestizo and for relatives abroad are significant. People who identify themselves as mestizo think that emigration is beneficial for San Fernando, while people with relatives abroad have the opposite opinion. The marginal effects are important for both variables: +19 percentage points for being mestizo and –24 percentage points for having relatives abroad. For the first group, emigration represents an opportunity, while for others it represents a high cost for society.

Variables corresponding to sex and the amount of the remittance have a negative sign, meaning that the respondents do not agree with the statement, "Emigrants' sons and daughters have lower school achievement." At the same time, they are affirmative for mestizo and political party. The marginal effects of being mestizo are the greatest (25 percentage points) in agreeing with the statement.

In the model for perception of emigration as the most probable future for the son or daughter of an emigrant, three significant variables have large marginal effects. Married persons, individuals with a high school education, and public sector workers tend to agree with the statement that emigration is the most probable future for an emigrant's son or daughter (marginal effects of +20, +24, and +31 percentage points, respectively).

Table 7.20 presents the marginal effects of the discrimination models for the population of San Fernando. While the mestizo population does not consider emigration as negative for the population as a whole, this group perceives emigrants' sons and daughters as having lower grades.

Table 7.20A Models of Discrimination in San Fernando

	Discri1	Discri2	Califica	Emigrar
Male	0.416	−0.036	−0.569**	0.34
	(0.374)	(0.221)	(0.238)	(0.227)
Age	−0.008	0.004	−0.014*	−0.005
	(0.014)	(0.007)	(0.007)	(0.007)
Married	−0.452	0.301	0.236	0.545**
	(0.456)	(0.270)	(0.313)	(0.276)
Divorced	0.162	0.277	−0.288	0.481
	(0.601)	(0.350)	(0.375)	(0.352)
Mestizo	−0.337	0.493*	0.715***	0.059
	(0.387)	(0.254)	(0.263)	(0.253)
Household size	0.07	0	−0.003	−0.072
	(0.111)	(0.062)	(0.068)	(0.063)
Religious	0.913	0.056	0.875	−0.797
	(0.699)	(0.455)	(0.641)	(0.612)
Full-time	−0.149	0.182	0.189	−0.306
	(0.410)	(0.261)	(0.285)	(0.257)
Part-time	0.322	0.161	−0.057	−0.163
	(0.418)	(0.270)	(0.279)	(0.265)
Political party	0.096	0.15	0.679**	−0.772**
	(0.466)	(0.282)	(0.331)	(0.305)
Remittances	0	0.001	−0.002***	−0.001
	(0.001)	(0.001)	(0.001)	(0.001)
Unmes	−0.356	0.368	0.13	−0.009
	(0.578)	(0.308)	(0.333)	(0.317)
Household income	0	0	0	0
	(0.000)	(0.000)	(0.000)	(0.000)
No insurance	−1.388***			
	(0.522)			
Level of Deprivation	1.072***	0.065	0.01	−0.263
	(0.384)	(0.250)	(0.261)	(0.241)
Secondary education		−0.315	0.191	0.618**
		(0.273)	(0.326)	(0.286)
Tertiary education		−0.321	0.55	0.419
		(0.448)	(0.552)	(0.478)
Relatives abroad		−0.609**	0.138	0.071
		(0.263)	(0.286)	(0.262)

(continued)

Table 7.20A Models of Discrimination in San Fernando *(continued)*

	Discri1	Discri2	Califica	Emigrar
Public worker		−0.384	0.062	0.806*
		(0.365)	(0.535)	(0.433)
Constant	−2.765*	−0.762	0.559	0.581
	(1.559)	(0.971)	(1.061)	(0.965)
Observations	113	185	185	185
Pseudo R-squared	0.17	0.07	0.17	0.12

Source: Authors' compilation.
Note: Robust standard errors in parentheses.
* Significant at 10%.
** Significant at 5%.
*** Significant at 1%.

Table 7.20B Marginal Effects of Discrimination in San Fernando (only significant variables)

	Discri1	Discri2	Califica	Emigrar
Male			−0.1213	
Age			−0.0045	
Married				0.2084
Divorced				
Mestizo		0.1899	0.2506	
Household size				
Religious				
Full-time				
Part-time				
Political party			0.1774	−0.2704
Remittances			−0.0005	
Unmes				
Household income				
No insurance				
Level of Deprivation				
Secondary education				0.2426
Tertiary education				
Relatives abroad		−0.2382		
Public worker				0.3101

Source: Authors' compilation.

People with relatives abroad view emigration as having a negative effect on the city.

Table 7.21A presents the results of the models related to social integration in San Fernando: *nopart* and *partsoci*. Marginal effects (table 7.21B) show that women, persons of mixed race, public sector workers, and those not actively involved in a political party would take part in a demonstration or political meeting. Older people and religiously observant people would not take part in a political meeting, and the effect is especially high (+46 percent) for the religious. In contrast, women are very active in the community.

The closer the respondent is to the dominant culture, the more probable it is that he or she will have a discriminatory perception about emigrants (as shown in table 7.22). This is true for all variables except gender. In Cuenca, women have more discriminatory perceptions about emigrants than men.

Table 7.21A Models of Social Integration in San Fernando

	No participation	Social participation
Male	−0.548*	0.515**
	(0.301)	(0.249)
Age	0.016**	−0.006
	(0.008)	(0.007)
Married	−0.016	−0.018
	(0.311)	(0.291)
Divorced	−0.056	−0.077
	(0.366)	(0.389)
Secondary education	−0.159	0.617**
	(0.315)	(0.290)
Mestizo	−0.548**	0.428
	(0.274)	(0.312)
Relatives abroad	−0.455	0.333
	(0.289)	(0.296)
Household income	−0.096	−0.049
	(0.069)	(0.072)
Religious	1.234***	
	(0.404)	
Full-time	0.319	0.301
	(0.324)	(0.293)

(continued)

Table 7.21A Models of Social Integration in San Fernando (*continued*)

	No participation	Social participation
Part-time	0.237	0.325
	(0.310)	(0.318)
Public worker	−1.255**	0.344
	(0.628)	(0.415)
Political party	−1.468***	
	(0.421)	
Remittances	−0.001	0
	(0.001)	(0.001)
Unmes	0.24	0.259
	(0.357)	(0.312)
Household income	0	0
	(0.000)	(0.000)
Level of Deprivation	0.079	−0.098
	(0.316)	(0.274)
Tertiary education		0.724
		(0.470)
Constant	−0.216	−1.254
	(1.261)	(1.065)
Observations	171	176
Pseudo R-squared	0.24	0.17

Source: Authors' compilation.
Note: Robust standard errors in parentheses.
* Significant at 10%.
** Significant at 5%.
*** Significant at 1%.

Table 7.21B Marginal Effects of Social Integration in San Fernando (only significant variables)

	No participation	Social participation
Male	−0.1642	0.1750
Age	0.0053	
Married		
Divorced		

(continued)

Table 7.21B Marginal Effects of Social Integration in San
Fernando *(continued)*

	No participation	Social participation
Secondary education		0.2181
Mestizo	–0.1915	
Relatives abroad		
Household size		
Religious	0.4614	
Full-time		
Part-time		
Public worker	–0.2489	
Political party	–0.3958	
Remittances		
Unmes		
Household income		
Level of Deprivation		
Tertiary education		

Source: Authors' compilation.

Table 7.22 Pattern of Discrimination against Emigrants

Variables	Discrimination + Dominant pole (more integrated)	Discrimination − Subaltern pole (less integrated)
Residence	Urban	Rural
Gender	Male	Female
Civil status	Married	Single, divorced
Age	Adult	Young, elderly
Ethnicity	Mestizo	Indigenous/peasant
Employment	Full-time job	Unemployed
Wage	High	Low
Remittances	None	High/monthly
Education	University	Basic

Source: Authors' compilation.

Conclusions and Recommendations

The use of a mixed methodology has furthered our understanding of the emigration phenomenon in Cuenca and San Fernando. This chapter finds evidence of the existence of discrimination against "residents," the families of emigrants. Moreover, the in-depth interviews confirm that discrimination is deeper in the city of Cuenca than in the rural area of San Fernando.

Public discourse about emigrants (in the media, migration policies, and social relief interventions) is similar to the perceptions in Cuenca about international emigration:

- Emigration is perceived as a problem and as "bad for the region" (Cuenca and the nation), for emigrants themselves, and especially for their families.
- Emigrants are seen as "irrational" and their families as not using their remittances in productive and sustainable activities; they are not seen as contributing to the national economy.
- Emigrants are portrayed as "irresponsible" because they have abandoned their families in search of better living conditions.
- Emigrants' children are perceived as doing worse in school than other children. They are seen as "not integrated into society," and there is a general idea that they will eventually (try to) leave the country.

This social representation of emigrants has its logical conclusion in the idea that emigrants do not contribute to national development and threaten the country's symbolic unity (the discourse of the national family).

However, there are significant differences between the urban and rural context in Ecuador. San Fernando's inhabitants perceive emigration as being negative for the town, but they also see emigrants as successful because they can support their family both within Ecuador and abroad.

The inhabitants of Cuenca see emigrants as irresponsible and unproductive and their offspring as likely to become marginalized and prone to join a gang, drop out of school, or become an illegal emigrant. The perception of emigrants in the local newspaper (*Mercurio*) and in national newspapers such as *El Comercio* coincides with the perception held in Cuenca.

The quantitative results confirm the existence of discrimination against emigrants. The closer the person surveyed is to the dominant culture (being urban, male, married, adult, or mestizo; having a full-time job, a high wage, and education; and not receiving remittances), the more likely it is that he or she will have a negative view of emigrants. This model functions for all of the variables studied except gender. In Cuenca, women have more discriminatory perceptions about emigrants than men.

What are the implications of this pattern of discrimination? Ecuador's national project is based on the idea of an egalitarian (modern) society in which inhabitants are recognized as citizens with the same political (democratic), economic (meritocratic model, income, and education), and cultural (*mestizaje*) rights. However, the country's actual social hierarchy articulates modern categories of status (income, education, cultural capital) with race. The richest and more educated are usually mestizos, while the poorest are indigenous and peasants.

Emigration threatens Cuenca's traditional social hierarchy because of the incomes and cultural capital it offers to "residents." Discrimination against emigrants is a social mechanism that controls this "disturbance" in two ways. First, discrimination reduces the social mobility of "residents." Second, it affects emigrants' incomes and investment in the economic sphere (commerce, service, real estate), which is controlled by the upper class.

What are the costs of discrimination? Discrimination against "residents" could encourage school dropout or weaken the educational performance of the children of emigrants; it undoubtedly reduces their social mobility and integration into society. Finally, public discourse on emigrants as economically irrational justifies the government's lack of rural development policies and agricultural production incentives.

Annex: Methodological Approach

The first stage of the project conducted historical and archival research, in-depth interviews, media analysis, and participant observation. The second tested and quantified some of the qualitative findings, using two population surveys.

Historical, Archival Research

Secondary sources of information (published documents, newspapers, magazines, written records, and previous studies) were used to analyze public opinion regarding emigration in Ecuador. Data from the sixth population census of Ecuador (INEE 2001) helped us to gain a better understanding of specific demographic characteristics of the population of Ecuador and San Fernando.

In-Depth Interviews

We conducted 20 in-depth interviews of a sample of the population of San Fernando. In-depth interviews were conducted one-on-one and lasted between 30 and 60 minutes. The format was flexible, yielding rich information on personal opinions, beliefs, and values. The questionnaire was semistructured, starting with general questions intended to establish rapport and then proceeding to more purposive questions.

Media Analysis

In modern societies, values are formed and transmitted primarily by the available means of communication. In recent decades, the role of mass media has become so relevant that some observers have proposed that social problems are not an entity themselves but are instead defined by what people think and say about them. They see the emergence of social problems through a process of public definitions (Blumer 1951; Kitsuse and Spencer 1973). In this approach, the media are considered to be both a "product" of the society and a technology to produce social images and stereotypes.

For example, Becker (1966) indicates that a situation becomes a social problem when some person or group perceives it as a potential threat to their values. Widespread concern develops gradually after that person or group points out the condition to others and convinces them that it is a problem. When enough people become concerned with this condition or characteristic, institutions are established and charged with the responsibility of monitoring, controlling, and eradicating the problem. These institutions generate cases, information, and data to support their claims; a process of validation and public definition of the problem is established (Hubbard, DeFleur, and DeFleur 1975).

The signs and symbols are the unit of analysis, rather than the intentions or aim of the communicators or the effects produced in the interpreter. It has been argued that the mass media may reinforce certain beliefs of specific groups in society. In this sense, we sought to study "what was said" in the printed press about migrants and their families in order to understand the stereotypes and fantasies associated with that condition in San Fernando and Cuenca.

In general, we analyzed the qualitative data using content analysis. This technique does not aim to quantify the media content, but rather to approach it as a "text" or discourse, a dominant imagery that constitutes stereotypes about residents and the migratory phenomenon in society (the upper and middle classes as well as the families of emigrants, who impose discriminatory criteria on themselves). This technique, developed in the humanities, complements quantitative data by focusing on the hegemonic discourse and cultural features on which discriminatory practices are based.

Population Survey

Once the qualitative stage was finalized, we proceeded to the quantitative method. We implemented two population surveys (Cuenca and San Fernando) in June and August 2006 to test the statistical significance of the qualitative findings. The survey was designed to optimize costs and time constraints and to maximize response rates and data quality.

The population surveys gathered quantitative data that were used to estimate ordered probit models and to analyze the effect of the dependent variables on the levels of discrimination or on the attitudes and opinions regarding discrimination and exclusion. The models sought to determine how individual characteristics affect the formation of favorable opinions or attitudes toward migrants and their families or opinions about the existence of discrimination. This analysis was critical to identifying the key variables related to discrimination.

Qualitative Methods

In March 2006 we conducted 20 in-depth interviews with peasants living in the rural area of San Fernando. Interviewees had to be more than 20 years old and living in the rural area of San Fernando. We conducted another four interviews with "key informants" in the urban area of San Fernando: San Fernando's mayor, a member of the city council, a teacher at the local secondary school, and the vice principal of San Fernando's only high school.

An open-ended questionnaire allowed the questions to be tailored to different interviewees' profiles. The interviews were recorded (with prior consent by the interviewee) and then transcribed and analyzed by members of the team.

The two city newspapers with the highest readership were monitored during a six-month period from September 2005 to February 2006: *Mercurio*, the newspaper with the highest readership in Cuenca, and *El Comercio*, the leading national newspaper. Our team identified, coded, and analyzed all news discussing any issue related to international emigration. In total, 424 articles were collected, of which 70 percent appeared in *Mercurio* and 30 percent appeared in *El Comercio*.

Quantitative Methods

The sample design used for the Migration Household Survey was a random sample of the urban populations of Cuenca and San Fernando. The first stage of selection was the census block,[3] the second was the dwelling, and the third was the respondent member of the household. This sample design was self-weighted, meaning that all of the households had the same probability of being selected for the interview.

The frame of reference was based on the list of blocks produced by the 2001 census of population and dwellings (INEE 2001). This list contains information about the geographic identification of each block and the number of dwellings occupied at the time of the census. Each block is identified with its province, canton, census zone, census sector, and census block.

The canton is the second-largest administrative and political division (after the province) of the national territory of Ecuador. Census zones are subdivisions of the cantons and correspond to the legal sections existing in Ecuador. Census tracts are an intermediate geographic unit, a subdivision of the census zone; in urban areas, sectors consist of a group of blocks. The census block is the smallest geographic unit. In urban areas, this is a city block, and in rural areas it is a clearly defined area of land that can be covered by a single enumerator during the population census.

Once blocks were selected, the interviewer randomly selected dwellings according to the following procedure. Once the interviewer arrived at the selected block, he or she made a list of the private and occupied dwellings and then drew four titular and two alternate dwellings.

The sample sizes presented in table 7A.1 were determined to guarantee a (plus or minus) 5 percent true value of the parameters to be estimated, with a 95 percent confidence level.

The urban area of the canton of San Fernando has only one census zone, four sectors, and 73 blocks. For this reason, the survey was applied in at least three households per selected block. In Cuenca, the random sample drew the census sectors indicated in table 7A.2. The urban area of Cuenca has 53 census zones and 552 census sectors. For this reason, the survey questionnaire was applied to 60 census sectors with eight surveys each.

Once the interviewer had selected the target dwelling, he or she made the first attempt to contact the household and to obtain a list of household members by name and date of birth. In order to select a random

Table 7A.1 Sample Design, Size

	Cuenca	San Fernando
Target population size (occupied dwellings)	67,709	361
Confidence interval (%)	95	95
Confidence level (%)	5	5
Sample size (respondents)	480	185

Source: Authors' compilation.

Table 7A.2 Sample Design, Selection in Cuenca

Number	Zone	Parish	Sector
1	1	San Sebastián	6
2	1	San Sebastián	7
3	3	San Sebastián	1
4	3	San Sebastián	9
5	5	Bellavista	3
6	6	El Vecino	2
7	8	Hno. Miguel	8
8	9	Hno. Miguel	2
9	10	Machángara	7
10	10	Machángara	9
11	11	Machángara	2
12	12	Machángara	1
13	14	El Vecino	7
14	14	El Vecino	8
15	16	El Vecino	2
16	16	El Vecino	11
17	18	Bellavista	7
18	19	Bellavista	4
19	20	Bellavista	7
20	21	San Sebastián	11
21	22	El Batán	7
22	23	El Batán	5
23	23	El Batán	11

(continued)

Table 7A.2 Sample Design, Selection in Cuenca *(continued)*

Number	Zone	Parish	Sector
24	24	El Batán	1
25	24	El Batán	3
26	24	El Batán	5
27	26	Sucre	1
28	26	Sucre	3
29	26	Sucre	9
30	26	Sucre	11
31	28	Gil Ramirez Dávalos	1
32	28	Gil Ramirez Dávalos	10
33	29	El Sagrario	2
34	29	El Sagrario	6
35	29	El Sagrario	10
36	29	El Sagrario	12
37	30	San Blas	9
38	31	Totoracocha	1
39	31	Totoracocha	4
40	33	Totoracocha	3
41	34	Monay	2
42	34	Monay	6
43	37	Cañaribamba	7
44	38	Cañaribamba	12
45	39	San Blas	1
46	39	San Blas	10
47	40	El Sagrario	1
48	40	El Sagrario	3
49	41	Gil Ramirez Dávalos	6
50	41	Gil Ramirez Dávalos	9
51	43	Sucre	1
52	43	Sucre	5
53	44	Yanuncay	6
54	44	Yanuncay	9

(continued)

Table 7A.2 Sample Design, Selection in Cuenca *(continued)*

Number	Zone	Parish	Sector
55	48	Yanuncay	4
56	48	Yanuncay	5
57	48	Yanuncay	10
58	48	Yanuncay	11
59	53	Huayna Capac	8
60	53	Huayna Capac	9

Source: Authors' compilation.

respondent, the interviewers applied the "next birthday" selection method, which consists of selecting the individual who is closest to an upcoming birthday. The survey was conducted in June and August 2006.

The survey instrument was applied using a face-to-face, paper-and-pencil mode. The survey took an average of 25 minutes in Cuenca and 30 minutes in San Fernando. The questionnaire contained six thematic parts:

1. *Introduction.* General questions to "break the ice" and solicit information on likes and dislikes in regard to living in the city and main problems of the city
2. *Migration.* Questions regarding attitudes and opinions about the migration phenomenon
3. *Discrimination.* Questions to identify any possible discriminatory behavior in relation to the migration phenomenon
4. *Satisfaction with life.* Questions to measure happiness and model the social and economic costs of discrimination against migrants' families in Cuenca and San Fernando
5. *Citizenship.* Questions to measure the level of civic participation and community action and to model the costs of discrimination
6. *Sociodemographic characteristics.* Questions regarding standard characteristics of the respondents.

Notes

1. The following quotations come from 20 in-depth interviews in San Fernando, conducted in March 2006. Names have been omitted to preserve interviewees' privacy.

2. We use "transculturation" instead of the more common term "acculturation" to avoid one-sided approaches to cultural change. Acculturation reflects only one-way change, from one culture to the other. Transculturation implies that cultural changes are two-way transformations; a person mixes her own culture with the new one and does not abandon her culture (Ortiz 1999).

3. A census block is the smallest geographic unit used by the U.S. Census Bureau for tabulation of 100 percent data (data collected from all houses rather than a sample of houses). Several blocks make up block groups, which again make up census tracts. There are, on average, about 39 blocks per block group, with variations. Blocks are typically bounded by streets, roads, or creeks. In cities a census block may correspond to a city block, but in rural areas, where roads are fewer, blocks may be limited by other features.

References

Acosta, Alberto. 2005. "El aporte de las remesas para la familia ecuatoriana." Paper presented at the "Expert Group Meeting on International Migration and Development in Latin America and the Caribbean," United Nations Secretariat, Mexico.

Balibar, Etienne, and Immanuel Wallerstein. 1992. *Race, Nation, Class: Ambiguous Identities*. London: Verso.

Becker, Howard S. 1966. *Outsiders: Studies in Sociology of Deviance*. New York: Free Press.

Bendicen and Associates. 2003. *Receptores de remesas en el Ecuador: Una investigación de mercado*. Quito: Inter-American Development Bank.

Berger, Peter, and Thomas Luckmann. 2001. *La construcción social de la realidad*. Buenos Aires: Amorrortu.

Blumer, Herbert. 1951. "Collective Behavior." In *New Outline of the Principles of Sociology*, ed. Alfred M. Lee. New York: Barnes and Noble.

Bourdieu, Pierre. 1999. *Meditaciones pascalianas*. Barcelona: Anagrama.

Foucault, Michel. 1994. *Hermeneútica del sujeto*. Madrid: La Piqueta.

Hubbard, Jeffrey C., Melvin L. DeFleur, and Lois B. DeFleur. 1975. "Mass Media Influences on Public Conceptions of Social Problems." *Social Problems* 23 (1): 22–34.

INEE (Instituto Nacional de Estadística del Ecuador). 1997. *III censo nacional agropecuario*. Quito: INEE.

———. 2001. *VI censo nacional y V de vivienda*. Quito: INEE.

Kitsuse, John I., and Malcolm Spencer. 1973. "Toward a Sociology of Social Problems: Social Conditions, Value Judgments, and Social Problems." *Social Problems* 20 (4): 407–19.

Municipio de San Fernando. 2005. *Catastro rural*. San Fernando, Ecuador: Municipio de San Fernando.

Ordóñez, Santiago. 2005. "Ciudades de blancos y diásporas cholas: El caso contemporáneo de Cuenca, Ecuador." Paper presented at the Society of Latin American Studies, Amsterdam.

Ortiz, Fernando. 1999. *Contrapunteo cubano del tabaco y el azúcar*. Madrid: Letras Hispánicas.

Quijano, Anibal. 2000. *Colonialidad del poder, eurocentrismo y América Latina*. Buenos Aires: Argentina.

Ramírez, Franklin, and Jacques Paul Ramírez. 2005. *La estampida migratoria ecuatoriana: Crisis, redes transnacionales y repertorios de acción migratoria*. Quito: Centro de Investigaciones Ciudad.

8

Gender Differentials in Judicial Proceedings: Evidence from Housing-Related Cases in Uruguay

Eduardo Gandelman, Néstor Gandelman, and Julie Rothschild

The efficiency of the legal system is an important determinant of the development of the housing market. The easier it is to have a person evicted or a mortgaged property executed, the lower the probability of facing a breach by a debtor. Therefore, the available legal remedies facilitate or hamper the development of mortgage markets and have an impact on national homeownership ratios. Within a country, if it is more costly to take over the collateral of women debtors, the market might be less willing to provide women with the required long-term financing to acquire a house.

In this chapter we present evidence that the presence of a woman grants the defendant party judicial benefits that translate into extensions and longer proceedings, and we do so by using micro data to test whether courts are indeed more lenient toward women than men. This chapter finds evidence of favorable treatment of women in the judiciary system, and this is

Eduardo Gandelman, Néstor Gandelman, and Julie Rothschild are with the Universidad ORT Uruguay. This study was undertaken as part of the Latin American and Caribbean Research Network Project "Discrimination and Economic Outcomes." The authors wish to thank Alexis Avcharian, María del Lujan Riaño, Mariana Irazoqui, Rossana Aramendi, Virginia Cutinella, Carolina Pamparato, and María Laura Otegui for their research assistance. This chapter benefited from comments from Marina Andreas Moro, Hugo Ñopo, and Claudia Piras.

a case of positive discrimination in favor of women that is rarely found in the literature dealing with discrimination.

Gender differences in court outcomes have been explained by, among others, paternalism, court chivalry, differences in male and female criminality, and the practical problems of jailing women with children (see, for instance, Curran 1983; Simon 1975; Steffensmeier 1980). Remaining agnostic about the true cause of gender disparities does not prevent us from concluding that the existence of legal or judicial differentiation in favor of women may induce creditors to offer women worse financing conditions since transactions with them could involve higher costs in case of a breach of the obligations assumed. If so, this may induce worse housing outcomes for females and female-headed families. Thus, in addition to providing insights into the efficiency of the judicial system, this chapter is relevant for housing and poverty alleviation policies.

There is a sizable literature on disparities in judicial decision making, but most of it has focused on the socioeconomic characteristics of the judges or on the gender and ethnic origin of the defendants. Peresie (2005) finds that the gender composition of the bench affects federal appellate court outcomes in sexual harassment and sex discrimination cases. In contrast, Schanzenbach (2005) concludes that judges' race and sex have little influence on prison sentences in general but do affect racial and sex disparities. Manning, Carroll, and Carp (2004) report that younger judges are less inclined to accept allegations of age discrimination. Mustard (2001) finds that blacks, males, and offenders with low education and income levels receive longer sentences in federal courts.

This chapter forms part of this tradition but departs from it in at least three dimensions. First, most of the research conducted so far reflects the situation in developed countries, especially the United States. The efficiency of institutions in general and legal institutions in particular, however, is generally considered to be much worse in less-developed countries, which makes Uruguay an interesting case. Second, our study focuses on housing market–related cases, an area that has been neglected both by the literature on judicial disparities and by the literature on housing discrimination, which has focused on access to mortgage credit (see, for instance, Ladd 1998). Finally, our study focuses on disparities produced by the gender of the defendant in proceedings that are not related to sex issues (for example, sexual harassment).

We find that, all else remaining equal, the presence of women is associated with foreclosure proceedings that take two to three months longer than similar cases against male defendants. This represents a delay of more than 10 percent of the time taken by the average case. Also, in comparison with all-male defendants, the presence of women in the defendant party increases by 25 percent the probability of being granted an extension in eviction cases.

Gandelman (2008) presents evidence of lower probabilities of homeownership for female-headed households in Latin American countries. Although not specifically tested, the evidence presented in this study may explain that result. Favorable legal treatment of women is a partial equilibrium result that may seem "positive" for women. This favorable treatment is likely to be transparent for all actors in the market, and therefore one could expect a general equilibrium result in which the market internalizes the court's favorable treatment in the form of harsher conditions in the housing market.

Methodology and Legal Background

Before 2002, no laws in Uruguay were intended to address explicitly the situation of women in housing market–related issues. With passage of Law 17.495 in 2002, this changed. The law now addresses one specific situation: women who are pregnant during the wintertime.

This law complements an older one (Law 13.405) authorizing judges to extend the time for eviction up to 120 days in cases of *force majeure* (circumstances beyond our control). This new law requires judges to take into account whether a pregnant woman, a child under 14 years old, or a person above 70 years old lives in the house when granting an extension of terms during the wintertime. The law establishes that the presence of a pregnant woman in the house has to be considered as a case of *force majeure*. Commenting on this law, parliamentarians have stated that all of these cases involve especially vulnerable people.

Although no other laws explicitly protect women, it is widely accepted that women are treated more favorably than men in housing market–related cases. It is a matter more of judicial practice than of law: judges seem to take gender differentials into consideration, for example, when granting extensions of the terms to evict or dispossess.

In that sense, establishing the specific determinants of differential treatment in judicial practice seems to be a necessary starting point. In other words, we need to start by determining what favorable treatment of women means with regard to judicial practice.

One possible approach would be to search for gender patterns in judges' final decisions, as in the literature cited in the introduction. However, this approach is not applicable to the cases studied in this chapter because of the type of proceedings considered. The cited literature studies criminal cases where the content of the final decision can vary with the circumstances (the judge can find the defendant either innocent or guilty). In contrast, the content of the final decision in the cases studied for this chapter (taking for the final decision the one that orders dispossession, eviction, or the auction sale of the mortgaged property) is always the same.

The relevant variable is the time (forgone income) that it takes for the claimant to achieve that decision. Therefore, instead of a *consequentialist* approach, we take a *procedural* approach to determine the differential treatment in the judicial practice.

One of the most important determinants is the duration of the proceedings, that is, the time that elapses from the moment a case is submitted to the court until the end of the proceedings. For this reason, we have analyzed, case by case, the duration of the proceedings and differentiated between those with female defendants and those with male defendants.

Five types of judicial proceedings are related to the housing market and are therefore part of this investigation:

- The *mortgage foreclosure process* is the legal action to force the sale of mortgaged property in order to obtain payment for the outstanding balance of a loan, a debt generated on the purchase of said property, or a debt generated by condominium expenses. This action ends with the auction sale of the mortgaged property to a new owner.
- The *annulment of promissory purchase agreement* and the *annulment of purchase agreement* are the proceedings initiated on the breach of the obligation to pay the installments of a purchase or a promissory purchase agreement. These proceedings seek to have the agreement annulled and the property restituted. The action is concluded when the court orders the annulment of the agreement.
- *Eviction* is a legal proceeding that the owner has to initiate for the dispossession of an occupied property. For instance, when a person simply enters into a house without the owner's permission and there is no rental agreement, either verbal or written, an eviction process has to be initiated. This is concluded only when a court orders the occupiers to evict.
- If the former debtor occupies a property that has been auctioned, an *action in rem* needs to be initiated for the dispossession of the property. The new owner has to initiate this legal proceeding in order to access the property. The same happens when the debtor of a purchase agreement that has been annulled occupies the property. This action is concluded when the court orders the dispossession of the property.

Before filing any of these claims, plaintiffs are required to submit certain basic information before the Caseflow Coordination Office (Oficina Distribuidora de Turnos). This office assigns the court that will be in charge of the case and the term and provides a case number that will accompany the file through the process. Once the information is submitted, there is no chance to change the court that was assigned, not even by resubmitting information, since this case will always appear as a "precedent," and all related cases will be sent to the same court.

Data

With the support of the Supreme Court of Justice of Uruguay, we obtained access to the database of the Caseflow Coordination Office. The universe of cases for this investigation was defined on our review of the following database: 1,337 foreclosure proceedings, 66 annulments of purchase agreements, 388 actions in rem, 56 annulments of promissory purchase agreements, and 590 evictions that were submitted to the Caseflow Coordination Office in 2002. Therefore, there is a potential set of 2,437 judicial proceedings.[1]

Once we identified all of the case numbers, we went to the court offices involved to investigate the files, the Supreme Court of Justice having sent letters to each one of the offices requesting that the files be made available for our review. While reviewing the files, we found that 154 actions were related not to real estate but to other issues such as vehicles. Other files were not available for our review. Reasons for this included files were on a judge's desk (ongoing cases) or were "lost" at the office (most of those were not ongoing cases); 215 files were unavailable. We also realized that, even though some cases appeared in the Caseflow Office's database, they had never been submitted to the court. A possible explanation is that agreements were achieved in the time that elapsed between the submission to the Caseflow Office and the filing of the claim; 56 cases were in that situation. Many private transactions occur when legal proceedings have already begun. In fact, 19.5 percent of the investigated cases were closed because the parties entered into private transactions. For all of these reasons, 2,012 cases were included in our database. Finally, due to inconsistencies in the judicial files, we ended up with a database of 1,973 cases.[2]

The creation of the database with all of the relevant information for this investigation was the most time-consuming stage of the research, since courts in Uruguay keep hard, not electronic, copies of the files. Each file has many pages, with copious handwritten notes, which make it difficult to process.

Two types of courts were involved in our investigation: the Juzgados de Paz Departamentales de la Capital and the Juzgados Letrados de Primera Instancia en lo Civil. The former are in charge of the eviction processes and other types of legal actions involving small amounts of money. Cases involving larger amounts are assigned to the latter courts, which are specialized by subject and where judges have more experience because they are more advanced in their careers. Since there is one office per term, we reviewed files in 38 offices of the Juzgados de Paz and 20 offices of the Juzgados Letrados Civiles:

- 829 of the cases investigated were submitted to the Juzgados de Paz. A female judge was in charge of about 90 percent of these cases.
- 1,144 cases were submitted to the Juzgados Letrados. A female judge was in charge of about 70 percent of these cases.

With respect to the presence of women defendants, in 24 percent of the cases investigated (450 cases), all of the defendant party were men, while in 30 percent of the cases (562 cases), all of the defendant party were women. In the rest of the cases, the defendants included both men and women.

Although the cases investigated were submitted to the court during 2002, not all of them were closed. In fact, 18.8 percent of total cases were still ongoing when the data were gathered:[3] three evictions, 14 actions in rem, 347 foreclosures (246 ongoing and 101 in which the property had already been auctioned, but the title deed was still pending), and seven annulments. Only 26 percent of cases had completed all of the legal stages of the judicial proceedings.

Table 8.1 describes the ongoing and closed cases and the reason for the closure. While some plaintiffs obtained the desired result by completing all of the legal steps required, others entered into a private transaction with the defendant. The table shows that private transactions were more common in the foreclosure process than in other proceedings, representing 27 percent of foreclosure cases. Only 11 percent of the foreclosure proceedings completed all of the legal stages leading to the transfer of title deeds, but 9 percent of cases reached the auction stage.

In some cases, the plaintiff simply decided not to continue with the proceeding and gave notice of that decision to the court (2 percent of cases). In other instances, the plaintiff did not communicate with the court but failed to continue with the proceeding (for example, by not submitting the required briefs). Files found to be inactive for a long time are sent to the court's archives, and such cases are considered closed unless the plaintiff files a brief requesting that the case be continued; 18 percent of the cases investigated were in that situation.

Basic Results

As noted, one of the most important determinants of differential treatment in judicial practice is the duration of proceedings. Table 8.2 corroborates that the duration of the proceedings varies in some cases when women are defendants. From the beginning of the foreclosure proceedings until the auction sale of the properties, when there is a female in the defendant party, proceedings last from 50 to 70 more days than in cases with all-male defendants (the variation depends on whether the comparison is made with mixed male and female or with all-females cases). With respect to evictions and actions in rem, we consider the time that elapses from the beginning of the litigation until the case comes to an end with the court's order to evict or dispossess the property. Again looking at the means, there seems to be a positive correlation between the duration of eviction cases and the presence of female defendants. Cases against all-female defendants take longer than cases with both male and female defendants, which, in

Table 8.1 Basic Statistics, by Status of Case

Case	Eviction	Action in rem	Foreclosure	Annulment of Purchase agreement	Annulment of Promised purchase agreement	Total
Ongoing cases	3	14	246	1	6	270
Between auction and title deeds	0	0	101	0	0	101
Cases closed (completed all stages)	224	144	123	6	23	520
Cases closed because of transaction	46	21	298	4	9	379
Cases closed because plaintiff desisted	25	2	14	1	2	44
Cases closed because of inactivity of plaintiff	177	44	129	1	1	352
Cases closed for other reasons	69	38	190	3	7	307
Total	544	263	1,101	16	48	1,972

Source: Authors' compilation.

turn, take longer than cases against all-male defendants. In any case, the average differences reported are small, and a *t* test of mean difference cannot reject the null hypothesis of equal means.

Another important determinant is the extension of deadlines for eviction or dispossession. In cases of both evictions and actions in rem, defendants are allowed to request more than one extension of the deadline for being evicted or dispossessed, and the judge decides whether to grant such extensions and, if so, for how many days. (This is the typical case of the previously mentioned Law 17.495.) If judges take into consideration the presence of women, either when they make the decision to grant an extension or when they decide the length of the extension, then women

Table 8.2 Basic Statistics by the Presence of Women

		Foreclosures	Evictions	Actions in rem
		Time from beginning of case until		
		Auction	Eviction	Dispossession
Only males	Mean	571	299	346
	Standard deviation	335	205	281
	Cases	62	99	25
Males and females	Mean	642	306	372
	Standard deviation	321	218	260
	Cases	205	43	80
Only females	Mean	618	309	381
	Standard deviation	332	226	335
	Cases	85	76	39
Total	Mean	624	304	370
	Standard deviation	326	214	284
	Cases	352	218	144

Source: Authors' compilation.

are indeed treated more favorably than men and the proceedings where women are involved will probably last longer than the merits of the case would have predicted.

Table 8.3 therefore reports that, in evictions and actions in rem, there were extensions of terms in 268 cases, and in 72 percent of those cases (194 cases) the defendant party included a woman (either by herself or with a man). In 36 percent of cases (97 cases) where an extension occurred, defendant parties were made up only of women, and in 28 percent of cases (74 cases) the defendant party was made up only of men. That is to say, of the 252 evictions and actions in rem against all-male defendants, the judge granted an extension in 74 cases (29 percent). In the 265 cases involving all-female defendants, the judge granted an extension in 97 cases (37 percent).

When women are defendants, the amount of days granted for an extension increases. Table 8.4 shows that the average extension in cases with all-female defendants is 15 days, which is three days longer than in cases with all-male defendants. These averages include many cases in which the

Table 8.3 Extensions of Terms by the Presence of Women

	Frequencies			Percentages		
	No	Yes	Total	No	Yes	Total
Only males	178	74	252	35	28	32
Males and females	162	97	259	32	36	33
Only females	168	97	265	33	36	34
Total	508	268	776	100	100	100

Source: Authors' compilation.

Table 8.4 Amount of Days of Extension by the Presence of Women

	Average	Standard deviation	Cases
Only males	12.3	27.9	252
Males and females	13.9	28.9	257
Only females	15.0	30.3	265
Total	13.8	29.1	774

Source: Authors' compilation.

extensions were not granted (either because the defendant never requested them or because the court denied them). Only considering those cases where extensions were granted, the average extension time is 40 days.

Econometric Results

The evidence presented so far is unable to control for joint interactions of relevant variables. In order to do so, we ran several multivariate regressions, and in order to check the robustness of our results we consider three subsets of the sample. The results with respect to gender are summarized in table 8.5. The first row refers to the whole database, the second row is restricted to cases located in Montevideo, and the third row considers only cases of all-male or all-female defendants (that is, the cases of both male and female defendants are dropped). The annex presents a more detailed report of the regressions.

With respect to foreclosures, in column A of table 8.5, we consider the time elapsed from the beginning of the case until the auction takes place. As for evictions and actions in rem, in columns B and C, respectively, we consider the total amount of time from the beginning of the litigation until the case ends with a court order to evict or dispossess, respectively. In these two types of cases, it is possible and relatively common to ask for

Table 8.5 Summary Regression Results

	Foreclosures	Evictions	Actions in rem	Evictions and actions in rem		All cases	
	Time from beginning of case until						
	Auction	*Eviction*	*Dispossession*	*Probability of extension*	*Total extended time*	*Total case duration*	*Probability case is still ongoing*
	A	*B*	*C*	*D*	*E*	*F*	*G*
Estimation method	OLS	OLS	OLS	Probit[a]	Tobit	OLS	Probit[a]
Complete database							
Female	69.3	23.8	27.1	8.9%	16.16	55.0	29.2%
	(35.3)*	(34.9)	(38.6)	(0.03)***	(7.60)**	(25.3)**	(0.04)***
Only houses located in Montevideo							
Female	81.2	19.8	26.1	8.6%	16.80	59.7	19.7%
	(40.8)*	(32.9)	(45.6)	(0.03)***	(7.67)**	(26.7)**	(0.04)***
Only cases against all males and all females							
Female	95.7	23.5	8.4	6.8%	12.69	49.8*	0.0%
	(52.2)*	(42.1)	(54.9)	(0.03)*	(8.65)*	(30.9)	(0.25)

Source: Authors' compilation.
Note: OLS = Ordinary least squares. Cluster standard errors in parentheses.
a. Marginal effects.
* Significant at 15%.
** Significant at 10%.
*** Significant at 5%.

one or more extensions. Therefore, in column D, using a probit model, we estimate the probability of such an event. To estimate the determinants of the total extended time, we need to consider that this variable is truncated at 0, and therefore we estimate a Tobit model in column E. Finally, we consider all types of cases together. Column F reports the determinants of the total time elapsed from the beginning until the end of the case, and column G reports the probability that the case was still ongoing when the field stage of this study was implemented (taking more than four years).

This chapter focuses on gender-based differential treatment. Our perception is that the mere presence of a female in the defendant party (either solely or together with a male defendant, as opposed to proceedings against all-male defendants) changes the duration of the proceedings. Therefore, we define a dummy variable *Female* that takes the value of 1 if at least one of the defendants is female. Exploding the information available in our database, we define several control variables. *Female Judge* is a dummy variable taking the value of 1 if the judge in charge is female and 0 if the judge in charge is male (79 percent of all cases are under a female judge). As noted, the Juzgados Letrados deal with more complex cases than the Juzgados de Paz. We therefore define a dummy *Type of court* that takes the value of 1 for the Juzgados de Paz (42 percent of cases) to control for this complexity. The type of lawyer hired by the defendant may also affect the outcome. *Private defense* takes a value of 1 when the defendant hires a private lawyer (18 percent of all cases).

Although we consider only cases in courts in the capital city, the property in question may not necessarily be located in Montevideo. For cases involving property located in Montevideo, we use the address of the house in dispute to locate the neighborhood. Using information from the Household Survey conducted by the National Institute of Statistics, we then divide the sample according to the implied socioeconomic level of the neighborhood in which the property is located: low, middle-low, middle-high, and high (9, 27, 41, and 22 percent, respectively, of the 1,616 properties located in the capital city).

Using this same strategy, we also infer average household income and average home value. Uruguay has a population of about 3.3 million people divided in approximately equal shares between Montevideo, the capital city, and the rest of the country. The household survey divides Montevideo into 62 neighborhoods and all other urban areas into 37 zones. In our database, we have cases corresponding to 61 of Montevideo's neighborhoods and 30 zones for the rest of the country. Using this division, we calculate the average household income, the average rent, and a comfort index, taking values from 1 to 9 depending on the number of appliances available at the household, and merge them with our database. We find the three measures to be very highly correlated, and therefore we use only one (*Household Income* measured in U.S. dollars) in our estimation to avoid collinearity problems.

In foreclosure proceedings, we control for the size of the debt leading to the legal dispute; in foreclosure cases, the value of the original mortgage is available as well. Even though it is probable that the credits related to the cases in our database are not mortgages, creditors are nonetheless willing to lend more to individuals with larger collateral. Therefore, the original mortgage can be used as a proxy for the value of the house in the foreclosure regressions.

For the proceedings in which we do not have a proxy for the value of the house, we use our data on foreclosures to estimate a proxy. Using the 1,101 foreclosure cases, we calculate the average house value (mortgage) by neighborhoods in Montevideo and by zones in the rest of the country and impute this average to annulments of promissory purchase agreements, annulments of purchase agreements, evictions, and actions in rem.

Finally, in order to avoid spurious results, we adjust the standard errors of all regressions for the cluster structure of the income and house value variables.[4] We find that, after controlling for other variables, the presence of women is associated with longer foreclosure proceedings. In particular, when women are present it takes between 70 and 95 extra days (column A of table 8.5) to reach the actual auction. Considering the average time to get to an auction, according to our estimates using the whole sample, this represents an 11 percent increase in time. When the sample is restricted to Montevideo, the duration of judicial proceedings increases by 13 percent. Finally, when restricting the comparison to cases with all-male and all-female defendants, cases against women take 16 percent longer than cases against men.

Although the point estimates suggest that evicting female defendants or recovering property from a female through an action in rem takes about 20 extra days (column B of table 8.5), these estimates are not statistically different from 0. But, when all eviction and action in rem cases are considered together, we find that the presence of women is associated with a greater probability of being granted an extension (column D). The unconditional probability of obtaining an extension is 33 percent, and the marginal effect of *Female* is 9 percent, according to the estimation using the whole sample or restricting it to Montevideo. The marginal effect when comparing all-female and all-male defendants is 7 percent. Thus the average defendant party with a female presence has an approximately 25 percent greater likelihood of obtaining an extension than an all-male defendant party. According to column E, using the whole sample, female defendants are granted 16 extra days of extension with respect to male defendants. This result is robust in the database restricted to Montevideo but is only significant at the 15 percent level using all-male and all-female defendants.

Finally, columns F and G use information for all cases. The result on the extension of the proceeding in the *Female* row of column F can be seen as a weighted average of columns A, B, and C, whereby female presence translates into proceedings that take between 50 and 60 more days. Finally, column G reports that female presence is associated with a greater probability that the case is still not finished, but with differences between types of judicial proceedings. If these ongoing cases were to finish today, we would have to include in our estimation many proceedings that have been in court for four years. Therefore, the estimations of columns A, B, C, and G should be taken as the minimum effect of female presence.

The rest of the variables included in the regressions present reasonable results (see the annex to this chapter). The lower the income of the household and the lower the value of the house, the longer it takes to auction the property in foreclosure proceedings. In the same regard, our results suggest that the lower the value of the house, the longer it takes to evict someone from it. As for dispossessions and extensions of time, we find no statistically significant evidence of an effect for household income or the value of the property.[5] The result in foreclosure proceedings is in line with the perception that paternalistic judges benefit women and lower-income households.

Likewise, the larger the debt, the longer the extension of the foreclosure proceedings. The dummies for debt quartiles suggest that the relation is nonlinear. Although we find no statistically significant effect for the second and third debt quartiles, the proceedings corresponding to the largest debts (fourth quartile) last about 40 percent longer (from 260 to 300 extra days).

More complex cases in which the defendant hires a private lawyer to defend him take longer for all types of proceedings and increase the probability that an extension will be granted. The extension of time (valued at the mean duration) is on the order of 25 percent in foreclosure proceedings, about 40 percent in evictions, and about 60 percent in dispossessions.

Conclusions

Before 2002, Uruguay had no laws intended to address explicitly the situation of women in housing market–related issues. As of today, only one law specifically takes the situation of women into consideration. This chapter confirms the perception that, even though there is no legal tradition of explicitly addressing the situation of women, in practice courts do treat women more leniently than men. In that context, this study presents field evidence from judicial proceedings that the gender of the defendant affects the duration of the case. All else equal, proceedings against female defendants take longer and women are more likely to be granted extensions than men. Given that female-headed households have a lower probability of attaining homeownership in Uruguay, our results suggest a possible explanation for the poor female outcomes in the housing market.

The favorable treatment of women by the courts is a partial equilibrium result that may seem "positive" for women in the sense that, even when they do not have the right to stay there, they manage to remain in their current homes longer than men.

A necessary condition for development of the housing market (for example, mortgage financing) is the efficiency of the available legal remedies for dealing with a breach by a debtor. If it is more difficult to take over the collateral of women debtors, the market might impose stricter contract conditions on women than on men.

In this sense, it is possible to conjecture that the general equilibrium result of the court's favorable treatment of women may be to create more difficult access for women to long-term financing for acquiring a house and ultimately a lower probability of attaining homeownership. Similarly, if females and female-headed families are more likely to be granted extensions in eviction cases, landlords may reasonably request harsher guaranties in order to rent their properties to them.

Annex: Regression Results

Table 8A.1 Regression Analysis

	Foreclosures	Evictions	Actions in rem	Evictions and actions in rem		All cases	
	Time from beginning of case until						
	Auction	Eviction	Dispossession	Probability of extension	Total extended time	Total case duration	Probability case is still ongoing
	A	B	C	D	E	F	G
Estimation method	OLS	OLS	OLS	Probit	Tobit	OLS	Probit
Female	69.3 (35.3)*	23.8 (34.9)	27.1 (38.6)	0.25 (0.09)***	16.16 (7.60)**	55.0 (25.3)**	4.08 (0.37)***
Female* (promissory purchase agreement)							-3.78 (0.52)***
Female* (purchase agreement)							1.48 (0.35)***
Female* (foreclosure)							-4.04 (0.41)***
Female* (action in rem)							-4.05 (0.26)***
Household income	-0.2 (0.1)***	-0.0 (0.1)	-0.0 (0.2)	-0.00 (0.00)	-0.00 (0.02)	-0.0 (0.0)	-0.00 (0.00)***
House value	-0.6 (0.2)***	-0.5 (0.2)**	0.9 (1.3)	0.00 (0.00)	0.01 (0.14)	-0.2 (0.2)	0.00 (0.00)
Debt (2nd quartile)	66.3 (44.8)						

(continued)

Table 8A.1 Regression Analysis (continued)

	Foreclosures	Evictions	Actions in rem	Evictions and actions in rem		All cases	
	Time from beginning of case until			Probability of extension	Total extended time	Total case duration	Probability case is still ongoing
	Auction	Eviction	Dispossession				
	A	B	C	D	E	F	G
Debt (3rd quartile)	7.0 (41.6)						
Debt (4th quartile)	264.9 (46.8)***						
Female judge	-110.0 (40.2)***	28.1 (47.7)	-15.2 (39.6)	0.12 (0.11)	5.71 (10.83)	-85.7 (27.6)***	0.12 (0.08)
Private defense	160.2 (51.1)***	123.8 (30.5)***	221.4 (60.8)***	0.43 (0.09)***	27.81 (7.60)***	119.1 (28.2)***	0.46 (0.11)***
Type of court (de Paz)	180.8 (76.9)**	138.8 (66.7)**	6.7 (63.4)	-0.20 (0.13)	11.22 (8.36)	-200.2 (25.2)***	-0.76 (0.11)***
Control for type of case included							
Constant	617.6 (55.6)***	113.5 (89.8)	261.3 (104.7)**	-0.67 (0.19)***	-77.32 (16.08)***	573.7 (40.3)***	-5.67 (0.27)***
Observations	364	222	146	789	787	731	1,912
R-squared	0.22	0.08	0.13		0.13	0.13	
Mean dependent variable	621.9	305.2	364.2	0.336	13.5	474.9	0.188

Source: Authors' compilation.
Note: OLS = Ordinary least squares. Cluster standard errors in parentheses.
* Significant at 15%.
** Significant at 10%.
*** Significant at 5%.

Table 8A.2 Regression Analysis (Montevideo)

	Foreclosures	*Evictions*	*Actions in rem*	*Evictions and actions in rem*		*All cases*	
	Time from beginning of case until						
	Auction	*Eviction*	*Dispossession*	*Probability of extension*	*Total extended time*	*Total case duration*	*Probability case is still ongoing*
	A	B	C	D	E	F	G
Estimation method	OLS	OLS	OLS	Probit (coeff.)	Tobit	OLS	Probit (coeff.)
Female	81.2 (40.8)*	19.8 (32.9)	26.1 (45.6)	0.24 (0.09)***	16.80 (7.67)**	59.7 (26.7)**	4.00 (0.43)***
Female* (promissory purchase agreement)							–3.31 (0.68)***
Female* (purchase agreement)							
Female* (foreclosure)							–3.95 (0.49)***
Female* (action in rem)							–4.13 (0.40)***
Household income	–0.1 (0.1)**	–0.0 (0.1)	–0.1 (0.2)	–0.00 (0.00)	–0.01 (0.02)	0.0 (0.1)	–0.00 (0.00)***
House value	–0.8 (0.3)***	–0.4 (0.2)*	1.8 (1.1)	0.00 (0.00)	0.02 (0.14)	–0.3 (0.2)	0.00 (0.00)
Debt (2nd quartile)	113.3 (50.6)**						
Debt (3rd quartile)	21.2 (49.2)						

(continued)

Table 8A.2 Regression Analysis (Montevideo) (continued)

	Foreclosures	Evictions	Actions in rem	Evictions and actions in rem		All cases	
	Time from beginning of case until						
	Auction	Eviction	Dispossession	Probability of extension	Total extended time	Total case duration	Probability case is still ongoing
	A	B	C	D	E	F	G
Debt (4th quartile)	301.5 (59.2)***						
Woman judge	-142.8 (49.4)***	22.3 (46.7)	-26.6 (41.5)	0.12 (0.12)	4.74 (10.93)	-103.1 (29.9)***	0.05 (0.11)
Private defense	173.1 (54.4)***	131.2 (28.5)***	233.8 (65.4)***	0.39 (0.09)***	26.28 (7.63)***	132.2 (28.9)***	0.50 (0.14)***
Type of court (de Paz)	185.9 (84.1)**	43.5 (24.2)*	-0.5 (72.3)	-0.21 (0.13)	9.48 (8.54)	-176.8 (26.1)***	-0.65 (0.11)***
Control for type of case included							
Constant	589.7 (54.6)***	203.9 (72.8)***	285.8 (112.5)**	-0.61 (0.19)***	-72.43 (16.22)***	527.2 (44.3)***	-5.79 (0.31)***
Observations	256	218	137	764	762	610	1,578
R-squared	0.28	0.08	0.14	0.340		0.14	
Mean dependent variable	605.9	300.9	374.7		13.8	445.8	0.155

Source: Authors' compilation.
Note: OLS = Ordinary least squares. Cluster standard errors in parentheses.
* Significant at 15%.
** Significant at 10%.
*** Significant at 5%.

Table 8A.3 Regression Analysis (All Male vs. All Female)

	Foreclosures	Evictions	Actions in rem	Evictions and actions in rem		All cases	
	Time from beginning of case until						
	Auction	Eviction	Dispossession	Probability of extension	Total extended time	Total case duration	Probability case is still ongoing
	A	B	C	D	E	F	G
Estimation method	OLS	OLS	OLS	Probit	Tobit	OLS	Probit
Woman	95.7 (52.2)*	23.5 (42.1)	8.4 (54.9)	0.19 (0.10)*	12.69 (8.65)*	49.8* (30.9)	0.00 (0.25)
Woman* (promissory purchase agreement)							0.06 (0.82)
Woman* (purchase agreement)							
Woman* (foreclosure)							0.01 (0.29)
Woman* (action in rem)							-0.15 (0.00)
Household income	-0.0 (0.1)	-0.0 (0.1)	0.2 (0.2)	-0.00 (0.00)	-0.02 (0.02)	0.0 (0.1)	-0.00 (0.00)***
House value	-0.6 (0.3)*	-0.3 (0.3)	-0.6 (2.2)	0.00 (0.00)	-0.04 (0.16)	-0.4 (0.2)	0.00 (0.00)
Debt (2nd quartile)	121.0 (76.0)						
Debt (3rd quartile)	-24.7 (53.3)						

(continued)

Table 8A.3 Regression Analysis (All Male vs. All Female) *(continued)*

	Foreclosures	Evictions	Actions in rem	Evictions and actions in rem		All cases	
	Time from beginning of case until						
	Auction	Eviction	Dispossession	Probability of extension	Total extended time	Total case duration	Probability case is still ongoing
	A	B	C	D	E	F	G
Debt (4th quartile)	263.3 (66.5)***						
Woman judge	−158.3 (57.9)***	17.5 (51.3)	10.2 (101.6)	0.11 (0.17)	6.62 (14.14)	−72.9 (40.2)*	0.10 (0.15)
Private defense	264.0 (86.1)***	111.5 (38.3)***	240.2 (153.2)	0.26 (0.11)**	22.34 (9.34)**	112.6 (37.3)***	0.39 (0.17)**
Type of court (de Paz)	349.6 (92.9)***	49.2 (34.2)	−55.9 (55.5)	−0.10 (0.18)	20.11 (12.57)	−177.4 (33.5)***	−0.67 (0.17)***
Control for type of case included							
Constant	539.1 (61.6)***	215.7 (101.2)**	268.2 (163.1)	−0.50 (0.23)**	−69.78 (19.89)***	532.2 (55.3)***	−5.76 (0.00)
Observations	136	172	59	503	503	366	945
R-squared	0.30	0.06	0.12	0.332	0.13	0.13	
Mean dependent variable	595.1	305.7	377.5		13.9	425.3	0.134

Source: Authors' compilation.
Note: OLS = Ordinary least squares. Cluster standard errors in parentheses.
* Significant at 15%.
** Significant at 10%.
*** Significant at 5%.

Notes

1. The most common eviction proceeding is when a tenant stops paying the rent due, and the landlord initiates the eviction process. In 2002 there were about 3,000 such cases. Although we acknowledge that it would have been interesting to have these cases in our database, they were not included for two reasons: (a) we were unable to collect a database of more than 5,000 cases, and (b) we preferred to focus on the other types of proceedings, which are more directly related to homeownership.

2. For instance, although the universe was defined with the cases that were initiated in 2002, we found files corresponding to cases that started before that date. These cases were dropped from the final database. We also found cases that started after 2002. These cases were included in the database since they were the continuation of judicial cases initiated in 2002; examples of such cases include actions in rem after a foreclosure mortgage.

3. The fieldwork was carried out between July and September 2006.

4. The clustering adjusts the standard errors for possible intragroup (neighborhood or zone) correlation.

5. We explored interactions of household income and house value with the gender dummy and found no differences worth reporting.

References

Curran, Debra. 1983. "Judicial Discretion and Defendant's Sex." *Criminology* 21 (1): 41–58.

Gandelman, Nestor. 2008. "Gender Differentials in the Housing Markets in Latin America." Research Network Working Paper R-547, Inter-American Development Bank, Washington, DC.

Ladd, Helen. 1998. "Evidence on Discrimination in Mortgage Lending." *Journal of Economic Perspectives* 12 (2): 41–62.

Manning, Kenneth, Bruce Carroll, and Robert Carp. 2004. "Does Age Matter? Judicial Decision Making in Age Discrimination Cases." *Social Science Quarterly* 85 (1): 1–18.

Mustard, David. 2001. "Racial, Ethnic, and Gender Disparities in Sentencing: Evidence from the U.S. Federal Courts." *Journal of Law and Economics* 44 (1): 285–314.

Peresie, Jennifer. 2005. "Female Judges Matter: Gender and Collegial Decision Making in Federal Appellate Courts." *Yale Law Journal* 114 (7): 1759–90.

Schanzenbach, Max. 2005. "Racial and Sex Disparities in Prison Sentences: The Effect of District-Level Judicial Demographics." *Journal of Legal Studies* 34 (1): 57–92.

Simon, Rita. 1975. *Women and Crime.* Lexington, MA: Lexington Books.

Steffensmeier, Darrell. 1980. "Assessing the Impact of the Women's Movement on Sex-Based Differences in the Handling of Adult Criminal Defendants." *Crime and Delinquency* 26 (3): 344–57.

Index

Boxes, figures, notes, and tables are indicated by b, f, n, and t following page numbers.

A

Altonji, J., 3
altruism
  as basis for pro-social
    behavior, 45
  dictator game for analysis
    of, 46
  experimental research findings
    on social preference
    effects, 46
Anderson, C. L., 5
Angrist, J., 124–26
Argentina, adolescent peer
    ranking in
  academic performance and, 102,
    105, 109, 113, 120–21t,
    123, 124, 127
  developmental significance of
    peer relationships, 98
  effects of individual
    characteristics on
    popularity, 109–19, 110t,
    111t, 112t, 116t, 118t
  evidence of discrimination in,
    126–27
  gender mix of schools and,
    116–19
  individual characteristics
    correlated with, 102–8,
    103–4t, 106–7t

measures of individual
    popularity, 100, 108–9
  perceived beauty correlated with
    popularity, 109, 110t,
    113, 114, 115t, 119,
    120–21t, 127
  questionnaires to assess, 127–31
  race/ethnicity and, 102, 105,
    108, 111, 113, 127
  research findings, 8, 126–27
  research goals, 7–8, 97
  research methodology, 97–99,
    100–101, 108, 109
  sample population for research
    on, 98, 102, 105
  social network formation and
    effects, 122–26
  socioeconomic status and
    parental education, 102,
    105–8, 109–11, 113, 127
  sociometric popularity, 132n.8
  student ranking of physical
    appearance, 100, 101
audit studies, 5, 6, 137–38
Ayres, I., 5

B

Balibar, E., 231
Becker, G., 4–5

www.ingramcontent.com/pod-product-compliance
Lightning Source LLC
Chambersburg PA
CBHW022348280326
41935CB00007B/115